CONCEPTUAL FRAMEWORKS
FOR BIBLIOGRAPHIC
EDUCATION

Conceptual Frameworks for Bibliographic Education
Theory into Practice

Edited by Mary Reichel
and Mary Ann Ramey

Libraries Unlimited, Inc.
Littleton, Colorado
1987

LIBRARIES UNLIMITED, INC.
P.O. Box 263
Littleton, Colorado 80160-0263

Library of Congress Cataloging-in-Publication Data

Conceptual frameworks for bibliographic education.

    Includes bibliographies and index.
    1. College students--Library orientation.
2. Bibliography--Methodology--Study and teaching.
3. Libraries, University and college--Use studies.
I. Reichel, Mary. II. Ramey, Mary Ann.
Z675.U5C726   1987   025.5'677   87-22587
ISBN 0-87287-552-0

Libraries Unlimited books are bound with Type II nonwoven material that meets
and exceeds National Association of State Textbook Administrators' Type II
nonwoven material specifications Class A through E.

To the Reference Department,
    Pullen Library, Georgia State University
                                    M.A.R.

To my mother, Dorothy Lahl Reichel, and
    my husband, Rao Aluri
                                    M.L.R.

CONTENTS

Part 3
HUMANITIES

Part 4
SCIENCES

Part 5
AUTOMATED SYSTEMS

ACKNOWLEDGMENTS

We are grateful to Ralph Russell and Carolyn Robison for creating an atmosphere at Pullen Library, Georgia State University, that is conducive to professional and personal growth. We thank the staff in Georgia State University's Reference Department and in the University of Arizona's Main Library Office and Photocopy Department for all their assistance. We thank Carolyn A. Kirkendall at Eastern Michigan University for her advice on this project and Richard H. Barbe at Georgia State University for his willingness to allow individuals to explore their expertise and for his reading of the proposal. We are grateful to Rao Aluri for his helpful comments on the manuscript. We appreciate the intelligence, ideas, imagination, and cooperation of the contributors without whom this book would not exist.

INTRODUCTION

In his 1984 book, *Mastering the Techniques of Teaching*, Joseph Lowman developed a two-dimensional model of college teaching. The first dimension is "intellectual excitement," while the second is "interpersonal rapport."[1] Intellectual excitement has two components: what is being presented and the way it is presented. According to Lowman, "outstanding instructors select and organize intellectually challenging content *and* present it in an involving and memorable way."[2] The interpersonal dimension deals with the teacher's interpersonal interaction with the students, "with his or her skill at communicating with students in ways that increase motivation, enjoyment, and independent learning."[3]

The primary focus of each chapter in this book is the intellectual domain, how to present interesting and challenging material. The chapters are model presentations, not to be used verbatim but rather as guides for organizing bibliographic instruction sessions that are appropriate to the individual library, the librarian presenting the material, and the students and their library needs. Each chapter also provides information on the interpersonal dimension, on how to get students involved in the learning process.

This introduction provides ideas on how to make the content of bibliographic instruction challenging, discusses briefly the theoretical basis for the idea of conceptual frameworks, and provides an overview of the sixteen chapters in the book.

Content

One of the key elements that makes a successful teacher is the ability to present ideas simply. Lowman states that "to be able to present material clearly, instructors must approach and organize their subject matter as if they too [like their students] know little about it."[4] Lowman is certainly not the only author on college teaching to emphasize the importance of simplicity.[5]

Simplification may seem contradictory to the idea of conceptual frameworks where the most important generalizations are presented in order to make the material intellectually challenging, but organizing principles in fact help the teacher to simplify materials by focusing on what is most important and to subsume less important material under the generalizations. Also Lowman emphasized the importance of stimulating students' thinking on a subject: "Excellent teaching captivates and stimulates students' imagination with exciting ideas and rational discourse."[6] It is hoped that conceptual frameworks will help to provide exciting ideas which will stimulate students' imagination.

Another important point made by Lowman, as well as in much of the teaching and bibliographic instruction literature, is that only three or four major points from a fifty-minute session will be remembered. With the use of conceptual frameworks, it is hoped that those three or four points will be major ones, ones from which students can generalize.

Theoretical Basis for Conceptual Frameworks

The theoretical basis for the use of conceptual frameworks in bibliographic instruction comes from a number of sources as described by Pamela Kobelski and Mary Reichel,[7] but the two most important nonlibrary sources are David P. Ausubel and Jerome S. Bruner.[8] There is a large body of literature on advance organizers written by educational psychologists, the purpose of which is to test experimentally if advance organizers improve learning and the transfer of learning. The purpose of this book, however, is to try to provide insights into how material related to information searching can be organized to be intellectually challenging and to bring out fundamental principles.

Conceptual frameworks in relation to bibliographic instruction is derived in large part from Bruner's theory of instruction, which has four major features.[9] Bruner stated that a theory of instruction should be concerned with the structure of the body of knowledge, which should help the learner understand the information presented and should be dependent on the subject and the status of the learner. A theory of instruction also should deal with the sequence in which information is presented. In addition, a theory of instruction should specify what the individual needs in order to be motivated to learn and should include information on rewards and punishments. It is Bruner's insights into the need for a structure and his concern about the sequence of material that lay the groundwork for the idea of conceptual frameworks applied to bibliographic instruction.

Ausubel emphasized meaningful learning over rote learning. In Ausubel's 1968 book, he gave this definition of meaningful learning:

> Meaningful learning takes place if the learning task can be related in nonarbitrary substantive (non-verbatim) fashion to what the learner already knows, and if the learner adopts a corresponding learning set to do so.[10]

With meaningful learning, students should be able to apply what they have learned, to transfer it to new situations, and to generalize from it. All of these characteristics are exactly what we want students to achieve from learning about information searching.

In development of advance organizers or conceptual frameworks for bibliographic instruction, chapters in this book should serve as guides to what has worked for various subjects and levels of students. Richard Mayer, in his excellent 1979 review article on advance organizers, stated "further research is needed to determine the best analogies, images, examples, etc., that serve as effective advance organizers for individual subject matters and learners."[11] He continued to develop the following questions which help to determine if advance organizers are effective:

> (1) Does the organizer allow one to generate all or some of the logical relationships in the to-be-learned material?... (2) Does the organizer provide a means of relating unfamiliar material to familiar existing knowledge?... (3) Is the organizer learnable, i.e., is it easy for the particular learner to acquire and use it? (4) Would the learner fail to normally use an organizing assimilative set for this material, e.g., due to stress or inexperience?[12]

These questions can be kept in mind while reading chapters of this book. How effective are the conceptual frameworks presented? Do they match one or more of these criteria?

The Chapters

In the general section, Gemma DeVinney provides a model presentation to be given to freshman students as an introduction to library research. She uses systematic literature searching as the framework and includes information on selecting a topic. This chapter should be particularly helpful to library school students, new librarians, and librarians presenting introductory bibliographic instruction for the first time. Deborah Fink also presents information in a way suitable to an introduction to library research. The framework used is the political dimension of information, and Fink is able to bring in many fundamental principles of librarianship, such as a discussion of censorship, in ways appropriate to an undergraduate audience. Many ideas discussed by Fink are seen again in other chapters; for instance, she discusses the continuing theme of teaching procedures versus concepts. She also discusses the political nature of reference sources which is the dominant theme of Charles A. D'Aniello's chapter and an important idea in Ellen Broidy's chapter.

In the chapters dealing with teaching literature searching in the social sciences, Mary Ann Ramey and Mary Reichel use publication sequence as the framework for a discussion of the literature in the field of education. This model presentation is appropriate for graduate students and includes some ideas on involvement of the students in the classroom presentation. Ramey's chapter on library sources for marketing information gives a model presentation for an area heavily dependent on library resources and other sources of information. Ramey uses a conceptual framework from marketing research itself which she emphasizes has the advantage of being familiar to the students. Throughout her chapter, she interweaves information on evaluating the sources found and used and presents entirely new ways of looking at very familiar sources.

Lyn Thaxton explores the current validity of the publication sequence model in psychology. By questioning psychology graduate students and faculty,

Thaxton provides insights on how the William D. Garvey and Belver C. Griffith model fits into the present world of scholarly communication. Thaxton provides an excellent review of the literature on bibliographic instruction for psychology students from library and psychological literature.

Sandra K. Ready's chapter has a large section on question analysis to serve as a model for teaching students how to analyze their research projects. She then applies Michael Keresztesi's model on the development of a discipline to sociology. Ellen Broidy modifies the development of a discipline model for sources in women's studies. She also takes Keresztesi's model and makes it more suitable for a discipline that includes both scholarly and popular sources. Broidy discusses the importance of both types of sources as Louise W. Greenfield does later in her chapter on wildlife management. Like other chapters in the book, Broidy discusses the politics of information and sources as cultural artifacts. Broidy provides useful insights on students' participation in this kind of bibliographic instruction presentation.

In the humanities, Edward H. Teague provides a model presentation for students in design disciplines which he correctly points out is an area neglected by the bibliographic instruction literature. Teague uses a conceptual framework from design and brings in many concepts which illuminate the way fine artists use library resources. He interweaves library resources very nicely with the conceptual framework approach. He also discusses how he and his colleagues follow up on the general presentations to provide individual help to students. D'Aniello provides a fascinating approach on reference sources as sociocultural artifacts. For many different types of reference sources, he discusses how they reflect society's values at the time of publication. He suggests assignments appropriate for advanced undergraduates and graduate students in history. Maureen Pastine provides a model presentation on reference sources in American literature using primary/secondary sources as a conceptual framework. She emphasizes the importance of guides to the literature, as well as access tools to secondary sources.

In the sciences, Pamela Kobelski uses index structure to provide a framework for a course on literature searching for chemistry majors. She provides insights into the importance of literature searching for chemists in academic and industrial settings. She brings new perspectives to the phrase "this will be useful for lifelong learning." Kobelski includes information on appropriate assignments. One of the types of index structures discussed is controlled vocabulary, which fits in nicely with Wygant's chapter on medical resources. Alice C. Wygant uses *MeSH* as a conceptual framework for teaching about medical resources. She offers an excellent explanation of *MeSH* and ties it to the indexes and other resources for which it serves as a base. Greenfield uses publication sequence to organize information sources useful to wildlife management students. She provides an example of research that has gone through the publication sequence, as well as examples of popular and scholarly works on a similar subject. Her use of specific examples serves as a model for all.

In the section on automated systems, Joan K. Lippincott emphasizes concepts including Boolean searching, the idea of a database, and set searching. She is interested in an information literacy program as opposed to a library skills program. Betsy Baker and Beth Sandore discuss a conceptual approach to teaching the online catalog. A thorough literature review reveals the debate in this area over teaching procedures and concepts — an old debate applied to a new type of tool. The idea of a database as a conceptual framework allows Baker and Sandore to introduce many concepts that should already be familiar to students.

The chapters in this book cover a wide range of subjects that are intended only as examples of the possible subjects covered by bibliographic instruction librarians. It is hoped that some of the ideas presented about specific fields might be useful in related areas. The chapters deal with audiences ranging from freshmen to graduate students.

Conclusion

The discussion of Lowman's teaching model, the theoretical basis for conceptual frameworks, and the chapters in this book should make it clear that there is great flexibility in using conceptual frameworks for bibliographic instruction. Although some conceptual frameworks seem to be very useful and suitable to a wide range of topics, such as systematic literature searching and publication sequence, there are also new frameworks introduced in this book coming from different disciplines and from librarianship.

When using these chapters as a basis for presentations, it is suggested that individual teaching librarians modify the chapters as much as they like. It is not the idea of the editors that a librarian could read one of these chapters at noon and give a presentation at 2:00 p.m. the same day. Rather, the chapters should serve as a way of looking at the resources in various fields and as a way of presenting those resources in a manner consistent with the most important ideas.

Mary Reichel

Notes

[1] Joseph Lowman, *Mastering the Techniques of Teaching* (San Francisco, Calif.: Jossey-Bass, 1984), 11-12.

[2] Ibid., x.

[3] Ibid., 15-16.

[4] Ibid., 11.

[5] Many authorities call for simplification in teaching. Two of these are Jerome S. Bruner, *Toward a Theory of Instruction* (Cambridge, Mass.: The Belknap Press of Harvard University Press, 1966) and Kenneth E. Eble, *Professors as Teachers* (San Francisco, Calif.: Jossey-Bass, 1972).

[6] Lowman, x.

[7] Pamela Kobelski and Mary Reichel, "Conceptual Frameworks for Bibliographic Instruction," *The Journal of Academic Librarianship* 7 (May 1981): 73-77.

[8]David P. Ausubel, *Educational Psychology: A Cognitive View* (New York: Holt, Rinehart and Winston, 1968); Jerome S. Bruner, *The Process of Education* (New York: Random House, 1963).

[9]Bruner, *Toward*, 40.

[10]Ausubel, 24.

[11]Richard E. Mayer, "Can Advance Organizers Influence Meaningful Learning?" *Review of Educational Research* 49 (Summer 1979): 382.

[12]Ibid.

CONTRIBUTORS

Betsy Baker
Bibliographic Instruction Librarian
Northwestern University

Ellen Broidy
Coordinator of Library Education
  Services
University Library
University of California at Irvine

Charles A. D'Aniello
Acting Assistant Director of
  Collection Development
Lockwood Memorial Library
State University of New York at
  Buffalo

Gemma DeVinney
Ph.D. Candidate
State University of New York at
  Buffalo and formerly Visiting
  Assistant Professor
School of Information and Library
  Studies
State University of New York at
  Buffalo

Deborah Fink
Instructional Services Librarian
University of Colorado Libraries

Louise W. Greenfield
Library Instruction Librarian
University Library
University of Arizona

Pamela G. Kobelski
Library Supervisor
Hoechst Celanese

Joan K. Lippincott
Head, Public Services
Albert R. Mann Library
Cornell University

Maureen Pastine
Director of Libraries
Washington State University

Mary Ann Ramey
Reference Librarian and Biblio-
  graphic Instructor Coordinator
Pullen Library
Georgia State University

Sandra K. Ready
Assistant Dean
Memorial Library
Mankato State University

Mary Reichel
Assistant University Librarian for
  Central Services
University Library
University of Arizona

Beth Sandore
Assistant Automated Systems
  Librarian
University of Illinois Library

Edward H. Teague
Head, Architecture and Fine Arts
  Library
University of Florida

Lyn Thaxton
Social Sciences Bibliographer
Pullen Library
Georgia State University

Alice C. Wygant
Bibliographic Instruction Librarian
Moody Medical Library
University of Texas Medical Branch

Part 1
GENERAL

CHAPTER 1

CONCEPTUAL FRAMEWORKS FOR BIBLIOGRAPHIC INSTRUCTION*

Pamela Kobelski and Mary Reichel

Conceptual frameworks are general principles drawn from a field of study and used to organize the content of an instructional presentation. They are the principles which are used to structure classes, courses, and textbooks. Conceptual frameworks may be explicitly discussed as part of a presentation or used implicitly to provide a meaningful sequence for the information covered.

Patricia Knapp was one of the first to recognize the importance of using conceptual frameworks, which she referred to as theoretical frameworks, in bibliographic instruction. As part of the Monteith College Library Program, the view of the library as a "system of ways" was used as a framework for library assignments.[1] Knapp felt that the development of this framework was one of the major accomplishments of the program.[2] The literature contains other discussions of the need for including general principles in bibliographic instruction presentations, for example, Frick and Smalley, as well as discussions of individual frameworks.[3] Kirk has provided an excellent explanation of search strategy as a conceptual framework, and MacGregor and McInnis have demonstrated the use of citation patterns as a method for teaching students bibliographic structure.[4]

Conceptual frameworks are crucial for teaching students bibliographic information in a meaningful and generalizable way. A discussion of cognitive learning theory which outlines the importance of conceptual frameworks is followed in this article by an explanation of seven such frameworks based on principles drawn from the literature of librarianship and from the authors' experience.

*Reprinted with permission from *The Journal of Academic Librarianship*, vol. 7 (May 1981): 73-77.

Cognitive Learning Theory

Many librarians have recognized, as Wiggins did, that "teaching skills in the use of the library falls into the definition of concept learning."[5] However, most of the attention to educational theory in the bibliographic instruction field has been to behavioral objectives. Cognitive learning theories can also offer some valuable insights for planning bibliographic instruction.

Jerome Bruner's works stress the importance of general principles in the learning process. The following summary of his ideas appears in *The Process of Education*.

> Teaching specific topics or skills without making clear their context in the broader fundamental structure of a field of knowledge is uneconomical in several deep senses. In the first place, such teaching makes it exceedingly difficult for the student to generalize from what he has learned to what he will encounter later. In the second place, learning that has fallen short of a grasp of general principles has little regard in terms of intellectual excitement. The best way to create interest in a subject is to render it worth knowing, which means to make the knowledge gained usable in one's thinking beyond the situation in which the learning has occurred. Third, knowledge one has acquired without sufficient structure to tie it together is knowledge that is likely to be forgotten. An unconnected set of facts has a pitiably short half-life memory. Organizing facts in terms of principles and ideas from which they may be inferred is the only known way of reducing the quick rate of loss of human memory.[6]

Students' inability to generalize from, become interested in or remember material presented without conceptual frameworks also can be understood from the theories of cognitive learning presented by David P. Ausubel.[7] Briefly, the learning process can be broken into three separate steps, acquisition, assimilation, and consolidation. Acquisition is simply the learner's becoming aware of or receiving new ideas, information or concepts. Assimilation involves students' relating new material to what they already know—their existing cognitive structures. Consolidation occurs when previously learned material is reorganized with new material. The cognitive structures formed in this integration process allow students to retain and recall the new information.

Learning is highly dependent on the cognitive structures available to the student. As Leith noted, "the existing patterns of mental structures possessed by students will powerfully influence what is learned. There is a strong tendency for well-established patterns to squeeze incongruent material into retrievable form."[8] Without appropriate cognitive structures, students cannot consolidate material in a meaningful form.

The use of conceptual frameworks allows the teacher to build a cognitive structure that will improve student learning. A recent review of the research indicated that such structures were most valuable (1) when the material to be learned was potentially meaningful, but appeared unorganized or unfamiliar and (2) when the learner lacked a context for the material or had no related knowledge or abilities.[9]

There is a great deal of similarity between these two conditions and the conditions encountered in most forms of bibliographic instruction. The context of such instruction is certainly potentially meaningful for students. In fact, the emphasis on course-related instruction is an attempt to make the material more meaningful by tying library instruction to course assignments. At the same time, the material is for the most part unfamiliar to students and too often seemingly unorganized. Students lack a context, since they have little knowledge of library patterns and bibliographic structure. Explicit conceptual frameworks will help make library instruction more meaningful and provide an organized context for its assimilation and consolidation.

Conceptual Frameworks
for Bibliographic Instruction

Planning bibliographic instruction presentations or classes involves identifying material to be covered, as well as choosing appropriate conceptual frameworks. Among the factors influencing the choice of material and of conceptual frameworks are student level, subject knowledge, and previous library instruction.[10] In the following discussion, suggestions are made on each framework's usefulness in terms of both material which can be covered and audience level.

These frameworks are presented separately, but they are not mutually exclusive. Some are very closely related to each other; for instance, there is much similarity between systematic literature searching and type of reference tool. Others complement one another. With systematic literature searching, sources are introduced in reverse of the publication sequence. More than one framework can easily be used to organize a course on bibliographic methods or even a single one-hour presentation. The list of frameworks discussed here is not exhaustive. These examples will hopefully stimulate thought about other frameworks.

TYPE OF REFERENCE TOOLS

Guides to reference sources, such as Malinowsky, and library workbooks, such as Dudley, frequently are organized by type of reference tool, because reference tools can be meaningfully grouped together by their format and the type of information that they provide.[11] Almanacs, handbooks, bibliographies, encyclopedias, etc. are studied as classes of material. Every item in a class, always with exceptions, will serve similar purposes and have a somewhat similar organization. This framework can be applied in a number of ways including an approach in which individual classes are simply described to an analysis of the type of information available in each class. McInnis has used types of reference tools as a theoretical method of studying the literature of a discipline.[12]

Many limitations can be found in trying to apply this framework to bibliographic instruction. Ideas, concepts, and general information about publications that are not reference tools are difficult to include. A discussion of the nature of periodicals or government documents cannot be combined with a discussion of a large number of indexes and bibliographies. Another problem is that more specific sources are often included in sessions than were originally planned just to expand and clarify a particular class of tool. The number of titles covered can become confusing.

The type of reference tool framework is the one most commonly used in library school reference and bibliography courses. The not uncommon criticism of bibliographic instruction, that it resembles library school, may well have its basis in the use of this framework.[13]

While this framework has proven to be a useful instructional organizer for reference classes in library school, emphasis on reference tools makes it limiting for other forms of instruction. Few librarians wish to cover only reference tools in their presentations. The introduction of other ideas, concepts, and forms of publications necessitates the use of additional conceptual frameworks.

SYSTEMATIC LITERATURE SEARCHING

Systematic literature searching, one of the most commonly used organizational principles for library instruction, is based on the idea that there are logical ways to gather information using library resources.[14] The framework involves a step-by-step process by which one can progress from having little or no background in a subject to having a great deal of information. A detailed explanation of a systematic search strategy is found in Kirk, and the theoretical background for this framework is given in Freides.[15]

Systematic literature searching can be used for presentations covering library resources generally or those in a specific subject area. A systematic literature search generally uses reference sources to seek introductory and background material, books, periodicals, government documents, and pamphlets. However, other types of sources can be part of this framework since the emphasis is on analyzing the kind of information needed. As Daniel Gore states in *Bibliography for Beginners*, it is necessary to develop a search strategy, but in order to develop a strategy, students must know about the types and purposes of various kinds of resources.[16] This framework combines an analytic approach with explanation of the major purposes of types of resources and the access tools which lead to them.

A section on introductory reference sources is placed into context by explaining that general and subject encyclopedias, dictionaries, biographical sources, and current awareness sources all provide background information which will be helpful in choosing or narrowing topics and beginning to understand a subject.[17] A section on periodicals should emphasize that they contain more current information than do books and may provide information not found in books. Periodical indexes and abstracts are introduced as the most efficient way of locating articles pertaining to specific subjects.

Systematic literature searching has a number of advantages as a conceptual framework. Emphasis is on understanding the types of resources and their basic purposes in such a way that students can develop their own searches according to their level of knowledge about a subject and according to the nature of the subject. Access tools, such as card catalogs and bibliographies, are put into perspective as vehicles leading to the needed information, and not as sources to be understood for some unknown, mystical reason. This framework can be used for sophisticated audiences as well as beginning college students. For instance, it is easy to include dissertations and their access tools for doctoral students. In short, it is a highly satisfactory framework for explaining types of library resources, their purposes, and how to decide which types to use.

As an organizational framework, systematic literature searching, like many of the other frameworks presented here, is not as satisfactory in explaining some classes of reference sources, such as directories. Other frameworks should be used if the decision is made to include a variety of reference works, although in most cases it is unnecessary to include all types of reference sources once students understand that there is a logical way to approach library research.

FORM OF PUBLICATION

Librarians have long recognized that various forms of literature, books, journals, documents, newspapers, and audiovisual material include different types of information intended for varying audiences. Libraries organize and handle these forms of publication in a variety of ways. The nature of these differences can provide a conceptual framework for covering many types of access tools. Understanding the way these forms of publication are designed makes both access tools and library organization comprehensible to users.

Classes can be organized around this framework by dividing material to be covered into groupings based on the form of publication. Obvious groupings include monographs, periodicals, and documents. Other groupings can be made around such publications as newspapers, audiovisual material, technical reports, and patents. Within each form of publication, its nature and access tools are discussed.

Since this framework organizes around form of publication, any tool or information bearing on that form can be logically included. A session on periodicals can cover the problems of title changes and lack of standardized abbreviations, which are often very vexing to students, yet cannot be easily included in other frameworks. Such common reference tools as *Ulrich's* and the *Union List of Serials* fit well into this sort of session as would an extended discussion of indexes and abstracts. Likewise, a discussion of the Superintendent of Documents Classification scheme and changing agency titles fits into sessions on documents.

This framework with its emphasis on the form in which information is published is very effective for bibliographic instruction. It shows students that library methods are rational attempts to solve problems created by the form that information takes and not just arbitrary rules. It can be used for an entire group of instructional sessions or in conjunction with other frameworks. Using this organizer early in an instruction program gives students the background to locate specialized materials used in succeeding class sessions.

PRIMARY/SECONDARY SOURCES

The principle behind this framework is that original research is reported in some types of sources and that in other types, i.e., secondary sources, this original work is explained, put into context, or restructured. Primary sources in the sciences and social sciences are those which report original research, for example, journal articles, conference papers, and technical reports. In the humanities, primary sources are those which reflect the original creative work, such as a treatise in philosophy, a painting in art, or a poem in literature. In a field such as history, primary works include those which were written as close to an event as possible, for instance, correspondence or personal diaries. Secondary sources rearrange, explain, or restructure primary sources. In the sciences and social sciences, indexes and books are examples of secondary sources. In literature, bibliographies and periodical articles, which are literary criticism, are secondary sources.

Students can be introduced either to the broad spectrum of primary sources or just to those in a single discipline. As a conceptual framework, the emphasis on primary knowledge and sources allows students to comprehend the excitement of generating and discovering original ideas, the importance of primary sources for shaping later knowledge, and the necessity for critically evaluating these sources. This framework lends itself well to the introduction of appropriate specific examples, such as the importance of Machiavelli's *The Prince* in shaping later political philosophy.

Primary/secondary sources as a conceptual framework provides an excellent means for distinguishing between the literature of the humanities and of the social sciences and sciences. It also can be extended to help explain the types of reference sources important in a field. For instance, one reason that periodical indexes are numerous and essential in the sciences is that they provide access to reports of original research. Descriptive bibliographies in literature are important for the same reason. This framework is more appropriately used with a fairly sophisticated audience and one which is already familiar with the basic types and purposes of library resources. The strong emphasis on original works makes it ideal for students who must use primary sources for their own research. Combining this framework with systematic literature searching or form of publication would make an excellent outline for a course.

PUBLICATION SEQUENCE

Related to the primary/secondary framework, this framework is based on the observed sequence in which a new idea or set of data appears in published works. While there are innumerable exceptions, each field or subdiscipline has a set order in which information appears first in primary works, then secondary sources, and finally reference tools. In any case, the emphasis in this framework is on the sequential flow from one type of publication to another, not on the primary or secondary nature of the publication. A theoretical analysis of publication sequence appears in Garvey and Griffith.[18]

Basically, a research idea is followed from the beginning. Various published reports of the work, conference proceedings, journal articles, and review articles, and the sources which pick up on those reports, such as current awareness sources, indexes and abstracts, are covered in the sequence in which information would appear.

Sequence of publication is an excellent framework for studying the structure of periodical indexes and abstracts but does not allow extensive coverage of reference books. It traces the literature searching process backwards, from idea through publication and indexing rather than from subject query to information. It allows a student to place sources covered in a time continuum, which can be of considerable value. As with primary/secondary sources, this framework may be most helpful for specialized or discipline-oriented audiences.

CITATION PATTERNS

The importance of citations is based on the fundamental premise that scholarly work is built upon previous research and studies.[19] The footnotes or references present in a given work are presumed to be linked by their subject content. These references can be used as a beginning bibliography of previous work on a subject. By using the various citation indexes from the Institute for Scientific Information, concepts can also be traced forward in time. Articles and books citing key articles form a bibliography of current work on a subject.

Using citation patterns is not new in bibliographic instruction.[20] As a framework, it can provide the basis of useful insights into the nature of research and access sources. Students start with a specific article, chapter, or work and trace the references given. Those references lead in turn to others. By carefully choosing examples and discussing the type of publications located as references, a broad framework for understanding scholarly publication can be developed.

The use of footnotes and references to find information is very specific in nature. Access tools, such as indexes, abstracts, and bibliographies, are not as specific. They cover more material, but their listings may be less pertinent than the bibliography of an article. In short, an author has reviewed a reference for quality and relevance while an indexer strives for inclusiveness.

A more sophisticated approach dealing with citations is that of "bibliographic mapping," which is the technique of describing a discipline or concept through various citations to key works.[21] This mapping technique gives students an understanding of the complexity of the research structure within a discipline or subdiscipline.

One of the greatest advantages of using citation patterns as a conceptual framework is that this method corresponds to the way many scholars and researchers gather information. Another advantage is that students often have a book or article which excites their imagination. A natural extension of this interest is following citations. A disadvantage of this method is the heavy reliance on books and journal literature. Many types of material, such as pamphlets or even government documents, are less likely to be cited. Generally, reference tools are not part of citation networks. If reference tools are going to be explained, it is necessary to do so with another framework.

INDEX STRUCTURE

This framework is based on a number of the basic assumptions on which indexes are built. The idea that the subject of a work can be briefly described or represented is the basis for all subject indexing. Each of the various forms of indexing, such as key-word or citation indexing, is based on an individual set of assumptions about the "best" way to describe subject content. For example, key-word title indexing is based on the idea that the words in the title of an article best describe the subject content of that article. Using index structure as a framework allows these assumptions to be identified and discussed.

Materials to be covered are grouped according to the indexing principles used in their structure. For example, indexes using standardized subject headings can be grouped together, as can indexes based on keywords or citations. As each new tool or group of tools is introduced to the student, the principles of its form of indexing are explained. Making comparisons to indexes covered previously allows students to get the kind of rudimentary feel for indexing theory that should help them understand some of the causes of the problems and deficiencies associated with the materials being covered. The items chosen as index headings highlight those concepts important in individual disciplines. The use of chemical compound names as primary index headings in chemistry clearly indicates the focus of that discipline.

This framework is most useful when discussing access tools such as indexes, abstracts, or bibliographies. The card catalog and, by extension, library call number classification can also be easily included in this framework. However, many types of reference sources do not fit well into this framework. Other forms of publications besides books and journals can be covered, but only through their indexing tools. While obviously designed for sophisticated audiences, this framework can be modified for beginning students.

Conclusion

Teaching forces one to rethink basic ideas, to eliminate or explain jargon, and to organize material in a way which is meaningful for the audience. The renewed emphasis on library instruction in the last decade or so has encouraged many librarians to study their resources and to understand them and their purposes far more clearly than in the past. The primary purpose of using conceptual frameworks is to use the fundamental principles of librarianship and bibliographic organization in a manner which clarifies and simplifies the material and yet intrigues students.

One of the problems often faced by librarians giving bibliographic instruction presentations is a preconceived boredom on the part of the students. This common reaction can, in part, be traced to the ineffective use or lack of use of conceptual frameworks. For too long we have taught students how to use the card catalog and periodical indexes without teaching them the relationship of these tools to library organization and structure. The proper use of conceptual frameworks can give students a real reason for learning about libraries and their resources.

Notes

[1]Patricia B. Knapp. *The Monteith College Library Experiment* (Metuchen, N.J.: Scarecrow, 1966).

[2]Patricia B. Knapp, "The Meaning of the Monteith Program for Library Education," *Journal of Education for Librarianship* 6 (Fall 1965): 117-27.

[3]Elizabeth Frick, "Information Structure and Bibliographic Instruction," *Journal of Academic Librarianship* 1 (September 1975): 12-14.

[4]Topsey N. Smalley, "Bibliographic Instruction: Questioning Some Assumptions," *Journal of Academic Librarianship* 3 (November 1977): 280-83; Thomas G. Kirk, "Problems in Library Instruction in Four Year Colleges," *Educating the Library User*, ed. John Lubans (New York: R. R. Bowker, 1974); John MacGregor and Raymond G. McInnis, "Integrating Classroom Instruction and Library Research," *Journal of Higher Education* 48 (January/February 1977): 17-38.

[5]Marvin E. Wiggins, "A Scientific Model for the Development of Library Use Instructional Programs," in *A Challenge for Academic Libraries*, ed. Sul H. Lee (Ann Arbor, Mich.: Pierian Press, 1972).

[6]Jerome S. Bruner, *The Process of Education* (New York: Random House, 1963), 31.

[7]David P. Ausubel, *Educational Psychology: A Cognitive View* (New York: Holt, Rinehart and Winston, 1968).

[8]G. O. M. Leith, "Implications of Cognitive Psychology for the Improvement of Teaching and Learning in Universities," *Educational Review* 31 (June 1979): 149-59.

[9]Richard E. Mayer, "Twenty Years of Research on Advance Organizers: Assimilation Theory Is Still the Best Predictor of Results," *Instructional Science* 8 (1979): 133-67.

[10]Sara Lou Whilden, "Plimpton Prepares: How to Win the Library Instruction Game," *Drexel Library Quarterly* 8 (July 1972): 223-29.

[11]H. Robert Malinowsky, Richard A. Gray, and Dorothy A. Gray, *Science and Engineering Literature* (Littleton, Colo.: Libraries Unlimited, 1976); Miriam Dudley, *Library Instruction Workbook* (Los Angeles, Calif.: University of California Library, 1978).

[12]Raymond G. McInnis, *New Perspectives for Reference Service in Academic Libraries* (Westport, Conn.: Greenwood Press, 1978).

[13]Hannelore B. Rader, "Formal Courses in Bibliography" in *Educating the Library User*.

[14]M. B. Stevenson, *User Education Programmes: A Study of Their Development, Organization, Methods, and Assessment* (Boston Spa, England: British Library, Research Reports, 1977).

[15]Kirk, "Problems in Library Instruction"; Thelma Freides, *Literature and Bibliography of the Social Sciences* (Los Angeles, Calif.: Melville, 1973), 123-30, 259-66.

[16]Daniel Gore, *Bibliography for Beginners* (New York: Prentice-Hall, 1973), 125-28.

[17]Marda Woodbury, *Guide to Sources of Educational Information* (Washington, D.C.: Information Resources, 1976), 4-9.

[18]William D. Garvey and Belver C. Griffith, "Scientific Communication: Its Role in the Conduct of Research and Creation of Knowledge," *American Psychologist* 26 (April 1971): 349-62; "Communication and Information Processing within Scientific Disciplines: Empirical Findings for Psychology," in *Communication: The Essence of Science*, William D. Garvey (New York: Pergamon, 1979), 127-47.

[19]Eugene Garfield, *Citation Indexing—Its Theory and Application in Science, Technology and Humanities* (New York: Wiley, 1979).

[20]Frick, "Information Structure and Bibliographic Instruction."

[21]MacGregor and McInnis, "Integrating Classroom Instruction and Library Research."

CHAPTER 2

SYSTEMATIC LITERATURE SEARCHING AS A CONCEPTUAL FRAMEWORK FOR COURSE RELATED BIBLIOGRAPHIC INSTRUCTION FOR COLLEGE FRESHMEN

Gemma DeVinney

For the past twenty years many bibliographic instruction librarians have been extolling the benefits of organizing their instructional material around conceptual frameworks.[1] For the most part, this concern with conceptually structuring library presentations and other types of bibliographic education to foster meaningful learning (i.e., transferable to new situations) has been a negative reaction to the all too common "type of tools" instructional approach, which emphasizes teaching the major categories of reference books and instructs in the technical manipulations of individual sources. For example, periodical indexes are presented during a course related presentation as an important reference tool category for students working on a course assignment requiring library use. The *Readers' Guide to Periodical Literature* (*RGPL*) is mentioned as a prominent example of this type of source. Students are then taught how to decipher a *RGPL* citation, that the *RGPL* has author and subject entries, that the *RGPL* is available online in addition to hard copy, etc. As Sharon J. Rogers observes, this approach is problematic because "there is little indication that they [students] will learn *patterns* which will be of use when they face another library information problem" (author's emphasis).[2]

Systematic Literature Searching as a Conceptual Framework

Systematic literature searching has been put forth as one useful conceptual framework for structuring user education.[3] The basic premise of the literature searching strategy is that there is a logical and systematic way of finding out what is available in a library on a particular subject. Systematic literature searching is generally presented as a strategy which involves: reading overviews of a topic (e.g., general and subject encyclopedias), using the library catalog to identify books on a topic, using indexes and abstracts to identify periodical articles, and consulting supplementary material to provide additional documentation on a topic (e.g., pamphlet material, statistics, government documents, etc.).[4] Central to the idea of systematic literature searching is that its emphasis on taking a step-by-step approach, starting with general summaries and leading to more detailed specialized analyses as are found in journals, is an efficient and effective method of learning about a topic of which one has little previous knowledge.

Consequently, one finds systematic literature searching (as described above or with minor variations) as the organizing principle for a variety of library instruction methods including slide-tape presentations, workbooks, term paper consultation forms, and course related classroom presentations.[5] Also, systematic literature searching has been put forth as an appropriate model for identifying library material in subject areas ranging from history to forestry to geography to biology.[6] Students undertaking cross-disciplinary work such as locating biographical material or finding information on public affairs concerns have been encouraged to use literature searching strategy as well.[7]

It would be unfair to give the impression that there is consensus in the world of bibliographic instruction (BI) on the value of systematic literature searching as an organizing principle. A central idea in the current BI literature is the notion that worthwhile library instruction teaches students to engage in critical thinking and problem solving. The premise is that students should be taught by librarians not only how to track down information but also how to critically evaluate the ideas presented in the various books and articles the student has located. As bibliographic instructor Mona McCormick writes, "Let's be sure that students don't get the idea—especially from us—that *finding* information is the important thing, not what they *do* with information."[8]

Indeed any librarian who considers himself or herself an educator working within the "heart" of the university will find it difficult to disagree with critical thinking advocates who view the "library as a functional organ of communication" where, for example, "students in the 1980s can enter a dialogue with Plato, Machiavelli, and Gandhi on the relationship of the individual to the state."[9] And, one must observe that attempts to combine "the *processes* of gathering information with the *uses* of that information"[10] are applaudable in their emphasis on teaching students to learn how to learn. Yet, even Harold W. Tuckett and Carla J. Stoffle, who are clearly proponents of critical thinking-centered instruction, such as Cerise Oberman's guided design technique which involves small group work in information gathering problem solving, concede that "this approach does not allow as much material to be covered in a single presentation, since the format of small group work and the students active role in class activities are time-consuming."[11]

Certainly it is all well and good for bibliographic instruction to foster the development of critical thinkers who, according to McCormick:

- identify main issues,
- recognize underlying assumptions,
- evaluate evidence

- evaluate authorities, people, publications

- recognize bias, emotional appeals, relevant facts, propaganda, generalities, language problems

- question whether facts support conclusions,

- question the adequacy of the data,

- see relationships among ideas,

- know their own attitudes and blind spots,

- suspend judgment until the search is ended.[12]

And it is understandable why Tuckett and Stoffle identify the British Schools Council nine essential questions for completing academic work as typifying what self-reliant, critical thinking, problem solving library users need to consider:

- What do I need to know? (formulate and analyze need)

- Where could I go? (identify and appraise likely sources)

- How do I get the information? (trace and locate individual resources)

- Which resources shall I use? (examine, select and reject individual resources)

- How shall I use the resources? (interrogate resources)

- What shall I make record of? (record and store information)

- Have I got the information I need? (interpret, analyze, synthesize, evaluate)

- How should I present it? (present, communicate)

- What have I achieved? (evaluate)[13]

However, it is this author's contention that oftentimes bibliographic instruction librarians find themselves in teaching situations where it is reasonable and pedagogically sound to address only the first three of the above questions. In particular, this is the case for those librarians who do course related, one-shot presentations. Although it is preferable to have two or more sessions with the same class so that information retrieval *and* evaluation can be addressed, it is a fact of life that, for the most part, bibliographic instruction librarians teach "at the pleasure" of the professorial faculty. Class time is a precious commodity and, even if a professor is willing to "give up" several class sessions to bibliographic instruction, often library staffing resources are so limited that it is unthinkable for the librarian to spend more than one session with the same group of students.

Systematic Literature
Searching and College Freshmen

One-shot sessions are a standard bibliographic instruction practice for freshmen composition and other introductory classes which require the traditional term paper and, in this author's opinion, systematic literature searching is a highly satisfactory conceptual framework for organizing such presentations. As Constance Mellon has observed, based on William G. Perry's stages of ethical and intellectual development, library instruction for beginning college students should "... be simple, straightforward and easily understood."[14]

Freshman college students have little patience for subtleties and detail. They want to know clear-cut, effective, and efficient ways of proceeding in a library when it is time to gather information on an area of inquiry. Often such students are encouraged by their professors to explore controversial topics on which they are expected to develop a thoughtful opinion. Typically college freshmen have not considered the problematic "gray areas" that surround the issues of life in the 1980s: What is the best way to combat international terrorism? Should heroin be given to terminally ill cancer patients to combat pain? What are reasonable goals for space exploration? (And so on.)

The intellectual process that freshmen are expected to go through in completing a term paper is one that takes a student from only the vaguest notion of what a topic is all about to the formation of a cogent and well-expressed opinion based on facts. The beauty of presenting bibliographic instruction organized around systematic literature searching (general overview ⟶ books ⟶ articles ⟶ supporting data) is that the framework is readily grasped by beginning college students and it mirrors the process involved in going from having a general notion of a subject to having a specific, informed perspective on it.

The librarian who organizes a one-shot presentation around the conceptual framework of systematic literature searching must keep two important goals in mind:

1. The course-related session should specifically aim to reduce what Mellon has termed "library anxiety" in the target audience by being a "warmth seminar" which helps users "... see the library as a great place with fascinating information and *warm*, friendly people available to help them."[15]

2. The audience must realize that although literature searching strategy is a well-organized, systematic way of finding out what a library has on a subject, false starts and dead ends are common experiences in undertaking library research, and one must often modify one's strategy. Naturally, students need to be alerted to the fact that librarians are available as expert consultants in the literature searching process. In other words, students who are the beneficiaries of the instructional presentation should not walk away feeling they can, or need, to know all of the ins and outs of successful library use because librarians with specialized training are available to help facilitate their educational experience.[16]

Model Presentation

What follows is a description of a one-hour presentation based on searching strategy as a conceptual framework that this author has successfully used with students in freshman composition classes, educational opportunity program classes for disadvantaged students, and foreign student orientation classes.

The librarian gives a brief welcome to the library and introduces the concept of systematic literature searching. The material is then presented in search strategy order: topic selection, reading encyclopedic overviews, identifying books, identifying periodical articles, and identifying additional material.

TOPIC SELECTION

The librarian addresses the concept of "topic blankout" in the belief that not having any notion of what subject to investigate contributes significantly to a student's library anxiety.[17] In essence, the librarian paints a humorously bleak picture of a student who wanders around campus in a daze talking to herself, talking to fire hydrants, indeed talking to anyone or anything *except* the course instructor or reference librarian about her inability to select a suitable, readily researchable topic to write on. The course instructor is depicted as ultimately suffering from "this-is-the-fiftieth-paper-this-semester-on-the-pros-and-cons-of abortion" blues. And the reference librarian is portrayed as sitting, surrounded by wonderful resources gathering dust, which could cure any "topic blankout" sufferer.

The librarian then presents approporiate topic-generating material including: *Congressional Digest*, *Editorials on File*, *Editorial Research Reports*, the *Journal of Social Issues*, the *Social Issue Resource Series*, and *Vital Speeches of the Day*. No attempt is made to teach the students how to retrieve or use these sources. Rather, a very brief description of what each source is and how browsing through it can help generate term paper topics is presented. The librarian takes care to introduce high interest examples of topics found within the pages of these sources such as personnel drug testing, sexual harassment on the job, the fundamentalist Christian right's fight against heavy metal music, dispensing birth control in high schools, children as court witnesses, artificial intelligence, the sanctuary movement, teenage suicide, etc.

The students are encouraged to consult with reference librarians and their course instructors to determine how to narrow and focus their selected topic. They are told that picking a topic that is too broad, such as "juvenile delinquency," will result in hours of floundering about with too much material to effectively assimilate. On the other hand, selecting a topic that is too narrow, such as setting out to gather library resources on street gangs in a particular neighborhood in Chicago, will lead to serious frustration over the dearth of appropriate library material. Here the librarian emphasizes that when the students become graduate students they may well go into a Chicago high crime area as researchers, to gather firsthand data which they will ultimately analyze and publish as library material for future information gatherers, just as many of their professors have done on a wide variety of subjects.[18] (While most college freshman will not go on to become scholars who contribute to the world of knowledge as found in published materials, it is highly motivating for them to realize that if they are so inclined this is a possibility, and the library assignment at hand is a step in the educational process leading to such subject expertise.)

READING ENCYCLOPEDIC OVERVIEWS ON THE SELECTED TOPIC

At this juncture it is suggested that, in addition to consulting with their instructors and their campus reference librarians for advice on focusing the subject under consideration, the students are well-advised to read encyclopedic overviews which will give them an adequate understanding of the scope and range of their topic. They are reminded that the sources they used to initially think of their topic may well provide just such an overview of the subject's parameters. In addition, the students are encouraged to consult encyclopedias for an introduction to their topic. The librarian acknowledges being aware that they have used general encyclopedias such as the *Americana*, the *Britannica*, *Collier's*, *Compton's*, etc., in the past and goes on to introduce the concept of subject encyclopedias. He or she shows them the *McGraw-Hill Encyclopedia of Science and Technology* (with "radioactive fallout" as an example of a topic that is given overview treatment in its pages), the *Encyclopedia of Bioethics* ("ethical issues in organ donation"), the *Encyclopedia of World Art* ("the psychology of art"), and even the *Encyclopedia of Occultism and Parapsychology* ("out-of-the-body travel").

The librarian suggests that in reading such encyclopedic material the students will occasionally come across unfamiliar terminology. He or she emphasizes that fortunately reference librarians can provide them with subject dictionaries such as the *Dictionary of Drug Abuse Terms and Terminology*, *The American Political Dictionary*, and the *Dictionary of Behavioral Science* from the arsenal of library sources designed to make students' lives easier.

At this point the librarian emphasizes that it is not the students' responsibility to be aware of specific topic selection tools, subject encyclopedias, subject dictionaries, or indeed any other type of reference material. That is the job of the reference librarian. The librarian points out that it is the students' tuition dollars which pay the reference librarians' salaries and enable the librarians to keep up with the great diversity of reference tools being published. Accordingly, it only makes sense for students, as smart educational consumers, to call upon reference librarian expertise when embarking on library research.

IDENTIFYING BOOKS ON THE TOPIC

The librarian now takes the opportunity to point out that most encyclopedic overviews contain brief bibliographies of sources on the subject of interest. While cautioning the students never to rely solely on such bibliographies to identify material, as they are often incomplete and dated, the librarian suggests that they may want to determine whether the library owns any of the listed books.

This naturally leads to a brief consideration of the library's catalog. With the knowledge that the students have been hearing about card catalogs since elementary school, the librarian emphasizes what the students are unlikely to know. For example, college may be the first time the students have encountered a divided catalog, a catalog with sections closed as a result of AACR2 implementation, a union catalog of various campus libraries' holding in a multi-library system, a COM catalog, or an online catalog.

The one-hour session is not the time to delve into the various features of the library's catalog. The librarian briefly mentions key features of the catalog but does not go into detail concerning filing rules, arrangement and punctuation of information on the individual cards or records, or even how to read call numbers. Attractive, clearly written, to-the-point handouts go a long way at this point. The students are reassured that long after they have tossed out these handouts the same informational material will be available at the actual catalog. And of course, the students are reminded that reference librarians are available for assistance.

During this portion of the presentation the librarian, depending on local circumstances (i.e., not having an online catalog), introduces the concept of controlled vocabulary. The basic idea is to have the students think about the fact that (1) while most books cover many discrete subjects it is currently only feasible to have a few subject headings assigned to them, (2) that the subject headings which are assigned are often not in the terminology the user has in mind when approaching the card catalog (e.g., "Ice Age" is under the "Glacial Epoch," "gun control" is under "firearms — law and legislation"), and (3) the user cannot always count on cross-references. The source of the controlled vocabulary is presented as the only truly authoritative tool to consult when trying to determine the most useful headings to search under. Most often this will be the *Library of Congress Subject Headings (LCSH)*. The extra benefits of the *LCSH*, such as its listings of what not to look under, its broader headings, its narrower headings, and its heading subdivisions are demonstrated. The "moving-pictures" entry in the *LCSH* provides a particularly effective example of these features. Many librarians emphasize that using the *LCSH* prior to taking a subject approach in the card catalog provides an opportunity for further subject refinement. For example, "see also" references in the "moving-pictures" example include: "Homosexuality in motion pictures," "Love in motion pictures," "Minority women in motion pictures," "Racism in motion pictures," "Sensationalism in motion pictures," "Supernatural in moving-pictures," and "Violence in motion pictures."

IDENTIFYING PERIODICAL ARTICLES ON THE TOPIC

At this point the librarian contrasts the type of material generally found in books with that found in periodical articles. Many of the students will be aware that for the most part periodical articles provide more up-to-date information on a topic than books. (To make this point crystal clear an example can be used such as contrasting book accounts of the Titanic's sinking with the scientific findings of the recent submarine exploration of the wreckage which has appeared in the periodical literature.) The students may not, however, be cognizant of (1) the benefit of exposing themselves to a variety of perspectives and theories on a topic (the point is made that there is more value in reading fifty ten-page periodical articles on a topic than two 250-page books) and (2) the difference between popular periodicals and scholarly journals. The students are reminded that one of the end results of their being college educated people is that they will, as a matter of course, probe all types of subject matter more critically and with a more sophisticated understanding than those who limit themselves to reading, say, the local newspaper, *Readers' Digest, Good Housekeeping*, etc., and that this transition is unlikely to take place unless they begin to read specialized work written by experts in a field.

The students are then urged to conserve their precious time by resisting the urge to identify periodical articles on their topics by merely browsing through the periodical section of the library and leafing through likely magazines and journals. The librarian emphasizes that this hit or miss (mostly miss) approach is a sure way to end up spending countless wasted hours on gathering material of limited usefulness.

The key point here, of course, is that there are numerous access tools which efficiently lead to identifying articles on a topic. The students are reminded that they have probably used a key access tool in high school, namely, *Readers' Guide to Periodical Literature (RGPL)*. Some students' eyes may glaze over at the mention of the drab olive green set, others may appear somewhat embarrassed because they have never used it. The librarian using an appropriate audiovisual aid quickly goes over the key elements of a *RGPL* citation and "reminds" students that *RGPL* is itself published periodically, that librarians are available to help students determine which years to search, and that the *RGPL* does not index scholarly journals.

The students are then told that fortunately it is no more difficult to identify scholarly material on a topic than it is to use *RGPL* because the publisher of the *RGPL*, the H. W. Wilson Company, publishes the *Social Sciences Index* and the *Humanities Index*. These indexes are described as being as easy to use as the *RGPL* because they have the same arrangement and format. The basic distinguishing characteristic is that the *Social Sciences Index* and the *Humanities Index* give access to the scholarly literature within their subject parameters.

The librarian then introduces the concept of being able to consult not only a wide range of indexes such as the various other H. W. Wilson indexes, *PAIS*, and the *Magazine Index*, etc., but also abstracting tools such as *Psychological Abstracts, Sociological Abstracts*, and *America: History and Life*. The major advantage of using abstracts—that the actual abstract summary helps inform retrieval decisions—is explained. The students are invited to consult with reference librarians for one-on-one instruction on how to use these sources since they do not have the standard dictionary arrangement of the *RGPL*.

It is a good idea here to review a bit by contrasting an interesting topic in psychology (e.g., dating behavior, birth order research, dream research, etc.) by presenting an article in *Psychology Today* with its *RGPL* citation and then the same research as reported in a scholarly journal and both its *Social Sciences Index* citation and its *Psychological Abstracts* citation and abstract. Then a customized online database printout on the topic is presented. The librarian hands out a pamphlet describing online policy and pricing structure and invites students to consult with reference librarians for assistance in assessing whether a manual search of the printed indexes and abstracts or an online search is more appropriate for a given information gathering task.

Retrieval of periodicals is mentioned at this point. The various periodical formats (bound, unbound, and microfilm) are briefly described and the students are referred to the handouts and point-of-use instruction available to assist in using the library's periodical locating tool. And, of course, students are invited to consult librarians for assistance in determining retrieval information.

The librarian then reiterates that it is not up to students to be aware of the wide variety of indexes and abstracts available for researching a topic. Reference librarians can be expected to suggest index and abstract titles, to suggest index vocabulary, to advise on the feasibility of an online search, and to assist in obtaining periodical retrieval information.

IDENTIFYING ADDITIONAL MATERIALS ON THE TOPIC

The librarian now suggests that the students will want to consider identifying additional material on the topic, after reading and evaluating the material gathered in the previous steps, either to fill in information gaps, or to garner further documentation to support their own perspective on the subject.

The librarian offers the services of the reference department staff in helping students locate pamphlet material (the librarian shows examples of pamphlets from the library's vertical files), newspaper articles (the librarian briefly mentions the *New York Times Index* and *NewsBank*), government documents (sample documents are shown), and statistical material (*Statistical Abstract of the United States* is mentioned). Finally, book-length bibliographies are discussed and the students are told that these marvelous sources for citations are most useful when they have sufficient lead time to utilize the Interlibrary Loan Department to request material from other libraries.

The one-hour presentation ends with the librarian reviewing the steps in systematic literature searching and giving a final, upbeat invitation for all to consult with her and her colleagues in the future.

Conclusion

The model presentation just described does not pretend to foster self-sufficiency in the college library. Rather the end result of such a presentation should be that the students will be less apprehensive about starting a literature search, they will have a notion that they should make use of an effective and efficient literature searching strategy, they will feel comfortable in using librarians as searching consultants, and they will ask informed and to-the-point questions when approaching the reference desk.

Obviously this model presentation can be modified in various ways. Some librarians will prefer to follow one topic through the literature searching steps. Other librarians will prefer to skip encyclopedic overviews for some classes.[19] Many will choose to introduce book-length bibliographies early on in the search strategy.

Whatever the variations, systematic literature searching provides freshmen with a conceptual framework which can be readily used to complete library research for an assigned term project, and it can be used as a foundation for future, more sophisticated, bibliographic instruction in the upcoming semesters. Systematic literature searching as a conceptual framework is a beginning, not an end, and it is a beginning which can lead to a lifetime of effective and efficient library use.

Notes

[1]Pamela Kobelski and Mary Reichel, "Conceptual Frameworks for Bibliographic Instruction," *The Journal of Academic Librarianship* 7 (May 1981): 73.

[2]Sharon J. Rogers, "Research Strategies: Bibliographic Instruction for Undergraduates," *Library Trends* 29 (Summer 1980): 71.

[3]Kobelski and Reichel, in "Conceptual Frameworks," identify six conceptual frameworks in addition to systematic literature searching: (1) type of reference tool, (2) form of publication, (3) primary/secondary sources, (4) publication sequence, (5) citation patterns, and (6) index structure.

[4]See, for example, Daniel Gore's *Bibliography for Beginners*, 2nd ed. (Englewood Cliffs, N.J.: Prentice-Hall, 1973).

[5]Patricia A. Berge and Judith Pryor, "Applying Educational Theory to Workbook Instruction," in *Theories of Bibliographic Education*, ed. Cerise Oberman and Katina Strauch (New York: R. R. Bowker, 1982), 91-110; Gillian Debreczeny, "Coping with Numbers: Undergraduates and Individualized Term Paper Consultations," *Research Strategies* 3 (Fall 1985): 156-63; James Hart, "Al 'Scarface' Capone: A Search Strategy," in *Teaching Library Use Competence*, ed. Carolyn A. Kirkendall (Ann Arbor, Mich.: Pierian Press, 1983), 109-23; Jeanne V. Schramm and Frances H. Stewart, "The Search for Chief Joseph," *West Virginia Libraries* 32 (Summer 1979): 17-22.

[6]James Brewer, *The Literature of Geography*, 2nd ed. (Hamden, Conn.: Linnet Books, 1978); Elizabeth Frick, *Library Research Guide to History: Illustrated Search Strategy and Sources* (Ann Arbor, Mich.: Pierian Press, 1980); Thomas G. Kirk, "Problems in Library Instruction in Four-Year Colleges" in *Educating the Library User*, ed. John Lubans, Jr. (New York: R. R. Bowker, 1974), 83-103; Jacquelyn M. Morris and Elizabeth A. Elkins, *Library Searching: Resources and Strategies* (New York: Jeffrey Norton, 1978).

[7]Inez Larson Alfors and Mary Hong Loe, " 'Foremothers and Forefathers': One Way to Preserve and Enhance the Library Research Paper," *Research Strategies* 3 (Winter 1985): 4-16; Sarah Barbara Watstein and Stan Nash, "Researching 'Hot' Topics in the Social Sciences," *Research Strategies* 1 (Spring 1983): 77-82.

[8]Mona McCormick, "Critical Thinking and Library Instruction," *RQ* 22 (Summer 1983): 339.

[9]Jon Lindgren, "The Idea of Evidence in Bibliographic Inquiry," in *Theories of Bibliographic Education*, 41; Joan M. Bechtel, "Conversation, a New Paradigm for Librarianship?" *College and Research Libraries* 47 (May 1986): 222-23.

[10]Lindgren, "Idea of Evidence," 30.

[11]Harold W. Tuckett and Carla J. Stoffle, "Learning Theory and the Self-Reliant Library user," *RQ* 24 (Fall 1984): 63.

[12]McCormick, "Critical Thinking," 340.

[13]Tuckett and Stoffle, "Learning Theory," 59.

[14]Constance A. Mellon, "Information Problem-Solving: A Developmental Approach to Library Instruction," in *Theories of Bibliographic Education*, 79-80.

[15]Constance A. Mellon, "Library Anxiety: A Grounded Theory and Its Development," *College and Research Libraries* 47 (March 1986): 164-65.

[16]Constance McCarthy, "Library Instruction: Observations from the Reference Desk," *RQ* 22 (Fall 1982): 36-41.

[17]For further discussion of "topic blankout" see Roger D. Cherry and Gemma DeVinney's "Using Library Reference Materials to Help Students Generate Writing Topics," *The English Record* 35 (4th quarter 1984): 17-19.

[18]For further discussion of the difference between information gathering (library skills) and research, see Stephen K. Stoan's "Research and Library Skills: An Analysis and Interpretation," *College and Research Libraries* 45 (March 1984): 99-109.

[19]See, for example, Watstein and Nash's "Researching 'Hot' Topics," 79.

CHAPTER 3

INFORMATION, TECHNOLOGY, AND LIBRARY RESEARCH

Deborah Fink

The Information Society as a "Hook" for Library Lectures

Technology and information are the primary elements of change in today's society. Popular futurist authors have dramatized the effects and significance of the information revolution. In *The Third Wave*, Alvin Toffler foresees "nothing less than a complete transformation at least as revolutionary in our day as industrial civilization was 300 years ago. Furthermore, what is happening is not just a technological revolution but the coming of a whole new civilization in the fullest sense of that term."[1] And he claims that, "For Third Wave civilization, the most basic raw material of all—and one that can never be exhausted—is information...."[2] John Naisbett, in *Megatrends*, states: "Change is occurring so rapidly that there is no time to react; instead we must anticipate the future."[3] And, "The information society is an economic reality, not an intellectual abstraction."[4]

Escalating advances in electronic technology have brought about a major transition in society and created general interest in the role and value of information. Teaching librarians can capitalize on this interest and bring about a transition in bibliographic instruction. Moving beyond the mundane view of library use instruction as merely procedural explanations of search strategies and reference sources, teaching librarians can impart an appreciation of information and library resources in a broad social context.

The concept of the "Information Society" offers just such a context. The concept is developed in the best-selling *Megatrends* and reiterated in both popular and scholarly media. Although Naisbett's methodology for determining "megatrends" has been questioned, and his penchant for reduction to aphorisms can be annoying, his data and projections are fascinating. A few, well-chosen facts from his chapter entitled "Industrial Society—Information Society" can be used to convey the relevance of this transition to students, wage earners, and citizens. From there, it is easy to expand upon the role of the library in the information structure. This is a simplistic but effective approach for suggesting the existence of a sociology of information.

Establishing a social context for bibliographic instruction serves several purposes. There is the potential for catching the interest of the student: this library presentation is not just another tour and explanation of the *Readers' Guide to Periodical Literature* (*RGPL*). Library research will be viewed as a useful social skill, not just a necessary evil to pass a course. The library itself is seen in a new light and engenders a new respect. And bibliographic instruction is elevated from a basic skills level to the academic mainstream.

Despite such compelling incentives, the constraints of the standard fifty-minute guest lecture inhibit the extent to which a librarian may feel free to enhance the "absolutely necessary" content of a library presentation. Nevertheless, in only five to ten minutes it is possible to "hook" a class with references to the information society.

A hook is an attention catching and motivating introduction to an instructional session. According to David Peele, "The librarian should try to bait his opening in such a way that he might be able to attract — hook — his audience."[5] Teaching librarians can create a hook, which will place library use in a broad social context, by asking a class questions such as: How many of you have heard the term "information society?" What does it mean or what do you think it means? What does this development say about the value or power of information? How do you use information in your everyday lives? Why are you here in the library today?

Because such questions are unexpected at the beginning of a library session, and because they shed new light on the library and its materials as key components in an emerging, dynamic society, students are in fact "hooked" and their interest is likely to carry through the session and perhaps into their research as they recognize the general usefulness of library proficiency.

Information Processing as a Conceptual Framework for Intensive Bibliographic Instruction

When opportunities for intensive bibliographic instruction are available (e.g., multiple course integrated sessions, workshops, credit courses), it is possible to develop the social context as a "conceptual framework" for the instruction.[6]

Elizabeth Frick suggests "the structure of information" as a framework for bibliographic instruction. She maintains that "bibliographic instruction can help the student recognize that by understanding who generates information, who publishes it, who disseminates and classifies it, how, and for whom, he will develop a more subtle grasp of the value and limitations of that information."[7]

Frick's suggestions are the basis of the paradigm for "information processing"[8] (see figure 3.1) that is, the many operations which cycle information from communication to dissemination to acquisition and organization to access to assimilation to communication.

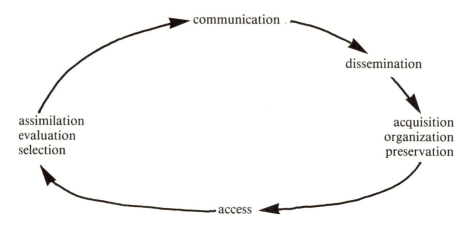

Fig. 3.1. Information processing.

The paradigm outlines the functions of authors, publishers, librarians, researchers, and writers and provides a conceptual framework for organizing and presenting a variety of procedures and issues relevant to this time of transition. It can be used to overview the cycle of information processing, to provide context for any of the stages, and to explore the political dimensions of information. It can also be used to "anticipate the future," as John Naisbett calls for, by demonstrating the current applications of emerging technologies and suggesting the potential applications which will dramatically alter information processing in the new society.

The stages in the flow of information are explicit in the model, but the politics of information and the role of technology are implicit. Also implicit are those items outside the cycle, such as government documents, ephemera, and fugitive materials.

For multiple, course integrated library sessions and workshops, the figure suggests introductory material which sets a substantive tone for the instruction because it focuses on information itself, not just access to it. For credit courses the figure suggests a series of discussions about information processing which provide a context for the units on library sources.

The Politics of Information

The politics of information is a broad category of provocative discussion topics. Politics can be defined simply as "promoting a particular interest" and includes: censorship and selection, which hinder the flow of information; propaganda, which is a distorting device of the author and/or disseminator; and bias, which is the researcher's conscious or unconscious selection and distortion. With an active awareness of these concepts, students can be encouraged to approach topic formulation, research, and writing more critically.

Following through the cycle of information processing, it is easy to discover a variety of approaches to the politics of information. Beginning with the communication of information, no author is completely objective, but some harbor a stronger bias than others, whether conscious or not. Even the disciplines with which authors identify themselves influence the perception and communication of information, as each discipline has its own "world view," manifested in the methodology, vocabulary, and literature of the field.

Propaganda is deliberate distortion, which may be created by the author, as well as by the disseminator through selective or out-of-context publication. Even the decisions of whether to disseminate and how are political choices. The author may limit distribution to colleagues for immediate feedback or seek commercial publication for tenure or other purposes. A publisher will generally accept an item only if it appears to have market value and is consistent with the publisher's public image.

Selection for acquisition is, of course, a politically charged process. Bookstores select those items which will bring a profit; organizations generally select those items which support their point of view; and, as institutions, libraries select those items which are congruent with their collection development policies. Institutions, however, do not select materials, individuals do. Within the parameters of the policies, individual librarians make choices based on their own interests and the perceived interests and needs of their constituencies.

The organization of library materials is less obviously a politically charged activity, but cataloging and classification tools are fraught with controversy: the *Library of Congress Subject Headings* has been labeled sexist, racist, and Anglo-Saxon. Even preservation efforts have political overtones, as decisions are made about what will be preserved, how, and where.

Access to information is the point of connection between the author and the researcher. This may occur without any intervening steps, but it is most likely to take place where published information has been collected and made available. Access is facilitated by organizational systems and reference sources and services, which make it possible for researchers to identify and locate sources of information. But bibliographic tools are not without politics, both in terms of the items selected for inclusion and their organization. As Frick asserts, "reference structures both open and close certain information channels, [for example] ... the rigidity of certain periodical indexes in regard to subject headings perpetuates certain views of the discipline."[9]

The processing of information by the researcher is prey to political perceptions from the outset. According to Charles K. West, "The way a problem is stated or conceptualized may exert some influence on the solution and on the pertinent information which is gathered."[10] He also notes that, as research continues, there are "potential distortive effects which emerge from preconceptions about previously gathered information; from prior knowledge; from emotional bias; from group norms; from particular items of information, and restrictions as to the sources of information."[11]

The entire cycle may thus be traced to overview the full spectrum of political issues. Another approach would be to focus on one or more particular issues for discussion as a way of demonstrating how the flow of information can be impeded; for example, the difficulties of accessing underground publications, such as the literature of radical special interest groups. Banned books and the Freedom of Information Act are also timely topics.

Possibilities for guest speakers for multiple sessions or credit courses using this approach include local librarians who have an interest in such subjects or who have been directly involved in a censorship case. The state library association may be able to suggest such individuals. Faculty in departments such as journalism or communication may also have expertise in the area. Representatives of concerned organizations, such as the American Civil Liberties Union or the National Organization of Women, could also be called.

The Impact of Computer Technology

The cycle of information processing can also be traced to highlight the impact of new technologies and to clarify the current relationship between conventional and electronic modes of access and manipulation. It is particularly important that researchers are enabled to make appropriate choices and effectively integrate modes during this time of transition.

Word processing certainly makes it easier for writers to prepare their work for submission to a publishing agency, and electronic networks are already enabling writers to communicate without an intermediary publisher, thus eliminating a significant portion of the information processing cycle. Such developments threaten to create an information elite and have implications for copyright and preservation.

The publishing industry is incorporating computer technologies to enhance standard functions such as typesetting. At the same time, computer capabilities are giving rise to entirely new aspects of publishing, such as online information retrieval services, computer disks, electronic journals, electronic document delivery, and electronic bulletin boards and mail systems.

Libraries are using computer technologies to perform routine functions, to expand storage potential, to take advantage of networking possibilities, to deliver messages and documents, and to provide new forms of access, notably the online catalog. Librarian intermediaries provide researchers with computer based access to the online equivalents of printed indexes and other reference sources. In some cases, end-user services are available in libraries.

It is important to clarify relationships between printed and electronic sources. Library users must know, obviously, what holdings are reflected in an online versus a card catalog, and when to use each and both. It is equally important that potential users of commercial databases understand to what extent a given field is covered online, and what sources may be available only in printed form or only online. There are also aspects of manual searching which may make that approach a worthwhile preliminary step or adjunct to an online search. Users of computerized access are known to become so enthralled with the technique that they will exclude other useful sources. The future may provide electronic access to all information, but in this time of transition, information seekers must effectively integrate all available modes of information access.

Traditional methods of organizing research and writing, such as index cards and outlining, become outmoded for those with access to a personal computer and the growing selection of software for conceptualizing, organizing, writing, editing, and formatting. Teaching librarians may or may not teach the mechanics of word processing, spreadsheets, or other programs, but appropriate applications of such techniques to the research process must be incorporated into bibliographic instruction.

Case Study: UCB Bibliography 301:
Methods of Library Research

Bibliography 301 has been offered on the University of Colorado at Boulder since the 1960s for two credit hours. Two sections are taught by librarians both fall and spring, and generally ten to twenty students enroll in each section. A course manual has been sold to students since 1981, which includes textual material closely reflecting lectures, lists and descriptions of reference sources, and various exercises and assignments. See the course outline in figure 3.2 on page 30.

COURSE DESCRIPTION

The course has evolved over the years into a fairly traditional search strategy/reference source course. The course description, taken from the manual, follows:

> Bibliography 301: Methods of Library Research will focus on the formulation of search strategy, including the selection and evaluation of reference tools and information sources, the selection of relevant information from such sources, and techniques for recording and organizing that information. The selection and evaluation of reference and information sources requires a knowledge of the various types of sources and an understanding of the functions and values of particular sources. The selection of relevant information for a research project requires the formulation of a thesis statement and/or preliminary outline as criteria for selection. The recording and organizing of information requires the use of bibliography and note cards and the formulation of a final outline or other organizational structure.
>
> The Bib 301 course outline has been structured as a broad, general search strategy, i.e., the course is organized by types of reference sources presented in the order that they are likely to be used when doing a research project in the social sciences or humanities. In class we will look at representative examples from each category of reference sources and learn their functions, values, and limitations. You will choose a topic and identify its scope as well as write an outline for a research paper on that topic. Although you will *not* actually write a paper for this class, you will complete six "hands-on" exercises designed to enable you to use and evaluate specific reference and information sources and help you develop a pathfinder or study guide for your topic. We will study documentation and notetaking, and you will compile, in conjunction with the exercises, bibliography cards to be incorporated into your pathfinder. This pathfinder will serve as the organizational framework for what you learn about approaching your topic and as a model for future search strategies.

1. information society

2. the course, tour of Reference Department

3. research

4. information and sources of information (the disciplines)

5. disciplines panel

6. problem formulation

7. the politics of information

8. guest speaker on the politics of information

9. search strategy and organizational techniques

10. encyclopedias

11. encyclopedia lab

12. dictionaries

13. guidebooks

14. tour of Special Collections

15. classification, call numbers

16. card catalog

17. LCSH

18. Public Access Catalog

19. bibliographies

20. tour of Audiovisual Department

21. periodical indexes

22. Computer Based Reference Service

23. end user searching (BRS After Dark)

24. periodicals lab

25. newspapers and other sources

26. tour of government publications

27. tour of Western Historical Collections

Fig. 3.2. Bibliography 301 course outline.

In the fall of 1985, the course was enlivened with the application of the information processing paradigm. The paradigm suggested new or expanded class sessions and provided a stimulating context for discussing the research process and types of reference sources. It was introduced on the first day of class, following a brief discussion of the "information age." The model was illustrated on the chalkboard as students had not yet purchased their manuals. The impacts of "politics" and technology on the cycle were touched upon. The following class session was spent overviewing the course and touring the reference department.

During the third class period, students were asked open-ended questions about research. Research was defined both as a means to an end—the location of specific, finite information—and as a form of inquiry—the seeking of understanding to increase knowledge. The research process was compared to the scientific method.

THE DISCIPLINES

The fourth unit, on information and sources of information, explored the nature of the disciplines and their impact on developing and accessing information. Most students did not have a clear idea of what a discipline or field is. However, the concept was easy to explain by referring to the structure of the university, with academic departments representing the various fields and introductory courses in each department presenting the structure, vocabulary, methodology, and key contributors of the field. The disciplines serve as a way of organizing knowledge and providing a perspective on a particular subset of knowledge.

Practitioners of a discipline communicate with each other and develop their field through their literature. In order to explore the literature of a discipline, it is necessary to know both what is available (i.e., the information sources) and how to access them (i.e., the reference sources). Further, as Frick recognizes, "To learn discrimination in the use of material, the student needs to understand the structure of the literature in order to control its access."[12]

Information needs were analyzed in terms of popular versus scholarly, point of view versus objective, primary versus secondary, current versus retrospective, and concise versus in-depth, although these categories are generally descriptive and not necessarily exclusive. Clarifying the type of information that is sought makes it easier to determine which reference sources will provide access to that information.

A "disciplines panel" was arranged for the fifth class session to dramatize variations among methodologies and source materials as well as the impact of the disciplines on the organization of knowledge and the researcher's access to information. A librarian or faculty representative of each of the three major discipline areas (sciences, social sciences, humanities) discussed approaches to, sources for, and attitudes towards research in his/her area. Through these presentations, it was apparent to the students that scientists rely on colleagues and current journals for information, while humanists look to primary materials and a wider time span of sources, and social scientists tend to be very eclectic. In addition, the business librarian discussed sources of information available beyond the library, such as companies and associations.

POLITICAL ISSUES

The political theme was expanded in the seventh session after a recap of the paradigm. Lists of banned books were circulated to open a discussion of censorship. The pervasive problem of selective dissemination was illustrated by pointing out the poor representation of alternative media in most libraries.[13] Bias was also considered in terms of the distorting influences upon both the individual and science itself.

A guest speaker addressed the social politics of publishing and accessing "nonmainstream" materials. She presented the broader issues, including ramifications of the first amendment and government policies. She also cited feminist writings as a specific example.

ORGANIZATIONAL TECHNIQUES

These new sessions set a tone of critical inquiry within social and individual contexts, which was brought to bear on the subsequent, preexisting units. For example, the use of a search strategy and other organizational techniques were presented as potential controls for individual distortion. A search strategy encouraged a systematic approach and the consideration of all possible types of information and access sources.

The search strategy models included in the course manual also emphasized the importance of vocabulary control. Throughout the course, focus was placed on the slippery, shifting, and inconsistent qualities of controlled vocabularies and indexing languages and how that affects perceptions and access.

Students were required to use a particular format on index cards for recording the bibliographic data on materials consulted, as well as the source of each citation and other information. Brief evaluative annotations were required to promote critical thinking through summarizing and assessing materials. Careful documentation of a search also encouraged a systematic approach and revealed much about the structure of the literature of the discipline.

However, it was pointed out that the index card convention is rapidly becoming obsolete. As personal and portable computers and telecommunication systems become more widespread, researchers will be relieved from manually accessing, recording, or formatting bibliographic data. The vision of a "scholar's work station," complete with hardware and software for all steps in the research process, was particularly appealing to students.

REFERENCE SOURCES

When the types and uses of encyclopedias were discussed, their generally accepted "authority" was questioned. Student evaluations of general and subject encyclopedias (in both small group discussions in class and individual take-home essays) included consideration of authorship, publisher, revision mechanisms, organization, documentation, and treatment of controversial subjects. The function and availability of subject encyclopedias within disciplines was also discussed.

Coverage of subject dictionaries and bibliographic guides tied in directly to understanding the disciplines. The specialization of fields is reflected in their vocabularies and the availability of a specialized dictionary is an indication of the maturity of a field. Where up-to-date guidebooks are available, the task of overviewing the literature of a discipline is simplified.

The vagaries of classification and call numbers were a revelation to students and provoked unexpected interest. The guest speaker on the politics of information had already pointed to problems related to the classification of women and feminism in the Library of Congress classification scheme. Examples of sexism, racism, a western orientation, and controversial subject headings abound in the *Library of Congress Subject Headings.*

Although the confusion of headings under Woman and Women in *LCSH* has been cleaned up, and Feminism has been added (although Women's Liberation Movement was deleted), Man is still used anthropologically and theologically instead of humans or humankind. The more popularly accepted term Chicano was not selected in favor of Mexican American. The range, depth, and variety of terms for Christian concepts far exceed the coverage of other religions. The negatively connoted Underdeveloped areas has been changed to Developing countries, but Third World is also commonly used and perhaps even less value laden. Such examples emphasize the impact of a controlled vocabulary on conceptualizing and accessing a subject.

Resistance to change and the problems of superimposition contribute to a card catalog which is inconsistent and illogical at best. Students were rather surprised to hear such a venerable source thus critiqued, but a realization of the complexities of the tool also engendered a new respect for the responsibilities of librarianship itself. Students no longer had any doubt that even the organization of information and the access provided to it could affect the research process.

The various uses of electronic technologies in libraries were considered as a prelude to coverage of the online catalog. Internal and national changes brought about by OCLC (Online Computer Library Center) in cataloging, interlibrary loan, and verification were described. Computer based developments in networking, transmission of information and documents, and in-house databases were also mentioned. Students then familiarized themselves with the online catalog and compared it to the card catalog.

Discussing types of periodicals, students referred to the guest presentation on the politics of information to explore the issue of access to "nonmainstream" or alternative publications. By this time, some of them were anticipating problems of coverage in standard printed indexes as well as the limitations of indexing language and structure. Students were alert to what periodical titles might be included or excluded by a particular subject index. They knew that coverage by an index affects the dissemination of titles and that a researcher's perception of the field is also affected by index coverage. The difficulties in locating cross-disciplinary, cutting-edge, or controversial materials were quickly perceived.

Advances in electronic publishing were introduced. Computer capabilities have spawned new types of sources, such as citation indexes and electronic journals, along with new forms of access. The development and techniques of database searching were covered as well as end-user services.

Each student in the class was given twenty minutes to conduct a search on BRS After Dark (a service which otherwise has a minimal fee). This generated considerable enthusiasm for computerized access and also led into a discussion of fees for information and the dangers of creating an "information elite."

Other units, particularly on newspapers and government publications, included relevant openings for referring to these themes. Development of such lectures is ongoing. It is clear that many of these sessions only scratched the surface and that additional possibilities exist. Continuous updating is required.

Citizenship in the Information Society

A goal of all of this discussion of the politics of information and the effects of technology is to convey a sense of what it means to be a citizen in the "information age." Information is both a form of power and a basic necessity to function in society. The value of research skills extends beyond the demands of academia to competencies already required of nearly half the work force and to everyday decision making.

Developing technologies have made information the primary resource in a changing society, but libraries remain key processors of information. Teaching librarians have the opportunity to explore the implications of this transition with their students and to stimulate new interest in libraries and research.

Notes

[1]Alvin Toffler, *The Third Wave* (New York: Bantam, 1980), 349.

[2]Ibid., 351.

[3]John Naisbett, *Megatrends: Ten New Directions Transforming Our Lives* (New York: Warner Books, 1982), 18.

[4]Ibid., 19.

[5]David Peele, "The Hook Principle," *RQ* 13 (Winter 1973): 135.

[6]Pamela Kobelski and Mary Reichel, "Conceptual Frameworks for Bibliographic Instruction," *The Journal of Academic Librarianship* 7 (March 1981): 73.

[7]Elizabeth Frick, "Information Structure and Bibliographic Instruction," *The Journal of Academic Librarianship* 1 (September 1975): 14. These concepts are further developed in Elizabeth Frick's "Teaching Information Structure: Turning Dependent Researchers into Self-Teachers," in *Theories of Bibliographic Education: Designs for Teaching*, ed. Cerise Oberman and Katina Strauch (New York: R. R. Bowker, 1982), 193-209.

[8]The paradigm was originally published in Deborah Fink's "Concepts for Bibliographic Instruction in This Time of Transition," in *Energies for Transition: Proceedings of the Fourth National Conference of the Association of College and Research Libraries* (Baltimore, Md., April 9-12, 1986), ed. Danuta A. Nitecki (Chicago: Association of College and Research Libraries, 1986), 49-51.

[9]Frick, "Information Structure," 14.

[10]Charles K. West, *The Social and Psychological Distortion of Information* (Chicago: Nelson-Hall, 1981), 78.

[11]Ibid., 80-81.

[12]Frick, "Teaching Information Structure," 198.

[13]An analysis of this situation is offered in the introduction to *Field Guide to Alternative Media: A Directory to Reference and Selection Tools Useful in Accessing Small and Alternative Press Publications and Independently Produced Media*, ed. and comp. Patricia J. Case (Chicago: Task Force on Alternatives in Print/Social Responsibilities Round Table/ American Library Association, 1984).

Part 2
SOCIAL SCIENCES

CHAPTER 4

LITERATURE SEARCHING IN EDUCATION
A Sample Approach

Mary Ann Ramey and Mary Reichel

Introduction

This chapter provides an approach to thinking about and teaching the process of literature searching in the field of education based on the concept of publication sequence. Presentations using this approach have been given to master's and doctoral-level students in a variety of subfields of education.

Literature searching is that part of research which involves identifying resources—books, periodical articles, conference papers, research reports, and government documents—which are relevant to the topic under investigation. Such resources may provide data or discussion which supports the researcher's own hypotheses, or they may contain findings in disagreement with the researcher's own work, in which case they will need to be taken into account or addressed. In any case, it is crucial to the research process to know the literature relevant to one's own research.

Usually graduate students already understand the importance of a literature search. Yet often they do not know how to gain access to all the types of resources available. In fact, sometimes they need information about what types of resources are available. Consequently, the librarian can give the student not only instruction in how to access and use resources but also a sense of the totality of relevant resources and a structure that provides the student with reassurance that he or she is not unknowingly excluding resources from a literature search.

Publication Sequence

In dealing with the literature of education, publication sequence is a useful framework for the librarian to employ in giving students both an overview of the totality of the literature and an explanation of access to the literature. Publication sequence is based on the chronological order of the formats in which a research idea appears in the literature.

The particular scheme shown in figure 4.1 is derived from the work of William D. Garvey and Belver C. Griffith.[1] While their study dealt with the literature of psychology, it provides a useful model for understanding the literature of the social sciences in general as well as education, which employs many of the techniques of social science research.

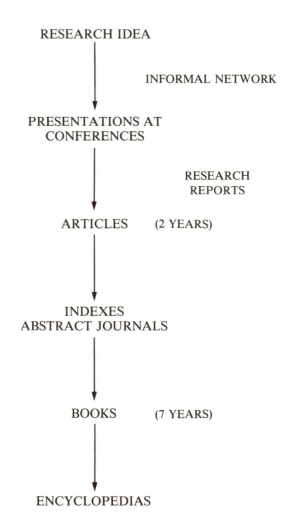

Fig. 4.1. Publication sequence. Adapted from William D. Garvey and Belver C. Griffith, "Scientific Communication: Its Role in the Conduct of Research and Creation of Knowledge," *American Psychologist* 26 (April 1971): 349-62.

The steps on the chart provide a general understanding of the concept of publication sequence. The use of the chart and a brief explanation of it are a good way to give students an introductory overview of the librarian's presentation.

The starting point of the publication sequence is a research idea. Many graduate students in a bibliographic instruction class will be grappling when they attend the class with their own research ideas for theses or dissertations. At this point there is no written report of the research generally available. While the research project is going on and perhaps for some time afterward, information about the project is not in the formal bibliographic network. In other words, it is not recorded in readily available print forms and can not be accessed through bibliographic tools. However, this certainly does not mean that information about the project is unknown to other researchers in the field. Information about the research may be transmitted through conversation, over the telephone, or through private correspondence. It is part of an informal network where resources are people rather than publications, and access is through experts in the area, through other researchers working on similar projects, and through dissertation advisors.

Often the first appearance of the report of a research project is as a paper or presentation at a professional conference. This stage marks the research idea's entry into the formal bibliographic network and possible access through the usual literature search techniques. The next step often is the appearance of a journal article based on the research. Garvey and Griffith found that it took, on the average, two years for the research project to be reported in the journal literature. In the field of education, an earlier or collateral report may also appear as part of a collection of research reports. The next step in the publication sequence is reference to the article or research report in periodical indexes and abstract journals. Considerably later the research idea may be reported in book form. It can take as long as seven years for a research idea to appear, often synthesized with other material, in a book in the field. The final stage in the publication sequence of the research idea represents yet further synthesis and appearance in a subject encyclopedia or similar tertiary source.

Graduate students occasionally ask whether this publication sequence truly is accurate for all or even most research ideas. It is worth emphasizing that the sequence is a model and not a law for the dissemination of a research idea. It is, however, a model which lends itself particularly well to explaining the literature of education.

Not every research idea, however, will follow the same pattern. Research ideas which move all the way through the publication sequence tend to be the most important ones. Reports of research may drop out early in the sequence because they are too narrow to be of general interest or because they do not make a significant impact on the field. In addition, often researchers write books and journal articles based on the same research at the same time, in which cases book material may be nearly as current as journal material. Similarly, experts will be called upon to write articles for subject encyclopedias, and they may include their latest findings, as well as synthesizing earlier work.

Informal Network

Having given this overview, the instructional librarian proceeds to use the framework of publication sequence as a guide in discussing the literature in greater detail, using some of the most important resources as examples. It can be worthwhile talking with the students about what they already know about the informal network. Have they attended conferences or meetings in their field and learned how much information is exchanged outside the formal presentations? Do they know the research going on in their own department in the university? Do they subscribe to or look at certain journals regularly to keep up with the news of their own field? If so, which journals do they find most informative? Have these journals indicated where to tune in to the informal network, who is getting grant or contract money, or which institutions are centers for particular types of research?

This discussion of the informal network early in the class helps the students to begin to participate actively in the class. Occasionally they may share points of information of which the librarian is unaware. Early participation by students in the class also tends to put them more at ease to ask questions and become active participants in the class rather than to remain passive listeners of a lecture.

Conference Presentations

With the first step in the formal bibliographic network—presentations at conferences—the librarian shifts back into the mode of providing information which is generally new to the students rather than talking with them about their own experience. This is also the beginning of the librarian's furnishing information about bibliographic tools. The librarian talks about access to conference proceedings through such tools as the *Index to Social Sciences and Humanities Proceedings*. This source indexes papers given at various conferences in such fields as education and educational research, special education, and educational psychology. It includes subject and author access to the listings.

The librarian can use this early stage of the publication sequence to begin to talk about characteristics and problems of access tools. For one thing, it is important to notice the scope of the index. In this case, for example, only published proceedings are included in the index, but of course many conferences never publish proceedings. For example, the *Research Conference on Teacher and Student Perceptions: Implications for Learning* held at the University of Pittsburgh in October 1979 was indexed in the 1983 volume of *Social Sciences and Humanities Proceedings*. This conference was listed after the papers had been published as a book in 1983.[2] It is important to note that there will always be some lag between publication and indexing or other access to that publication. For example, here the 1979 conference papers were not published until 1983, four years after their presentation, and it was even somewhat later that indexing was available for them.

The *Index to Social Sciences and Humanities Proceedings* also provides an opportunity for the librarian to begin talking about some of the types of indexing the students may encounter. It is worth pointing out the variety of indexes—author/editor, sponsor, meeting location, subject, and corporate indexing both geographically arranged and arranged by organization. There is also an opportunity for the librarian to point out some advantages and problems of the keyword indexing which the students will see later in the Permuterm Subject Index of the *Social Sciences Citation Index.*

Journal Articles and Indexes

The next step in the publication sequence is the appearance of a journal article based on the research project. Once again this is a point where the students may want to talk about some of the journals they are familiar with and which ones they may know to be the most important publications in their field. Many of them may already regularly scan some of these journals.

Following this discussion, the librarian talks about major types of journals and periodicals. There are periodicals that are primarily sources of news, periodicals that carry articles which are not necessarily based on research but which deal with important contemporary issues, and journals which publish largely or exclusively research findings. The librarian provides examples such as the *Chronicle of Higher Education* as a news source with its listings of contracts and grants, calendars, and extensive classified job listings. *Phi Delta Kappan* or *Change* might serve as examples of periodicals with articles on contemporary issues, while the *Journal of Educational Research,* is an example of a journal which publishes research.

As the students talk about scanning the important journals in a field, the librarian can point out that scanning is common behavior for most professionals and scholars in their fields. *Current Contents: Social and Behavioral Sciences* has taken such behavior and systematized it in education and the social sciences. This index lists tables of contents with some rudimentary keyword indexing to allow the user of the index to identify the most recent journal articles on a topic. Unlike most reference sources, *Current Contents* is published with almost no time lag. Students conducting a literature search may find it useful to make sure they are not missing very recent articles on their topic.

For access to most of the journal literature, however, the researcher will use the sources which are the next step in the publication sequence—periodical indexes and abstracts. Education researchers are fortunate to have a major indexing and abstracting source for journal literature in the *Current Index to Journals in Education* (*CIJE*) produced by ERIC, the Educational Resources Information Center. While many education graduate students will have used or at least heard of the *CIJE*, they may not have looked at it carefully. Also, they are often unaware of the *Thesaurus of ERIC Descriptors.*

It is possible for the librarian to compare the *CIJE* with the *Education Index* which is familiar to many education graduate students. The librarian can also talk about differences in the features of indexes and abstracts and generalize about other abstracting sources that the student may find useful. *Psychological Abstracts* or *Sociological Abstracts* may help some of the students in their research and are comparable to the *CIJE* because they are sources that deal with a large body of literature and to some extent in the way they are set up. The students also can be introduced at this point to the small, more limited and focused abstracting sources such as *Educational Administration Abstracts, Child Development*

Abstracts, *Sage Family Studies Abstracts*, or *Linguistics and Language Behavior Abstracts: LLBA*. Choice of which abstracts to mention to the students is largely dependent on the judgment of the librarian and may be geared to the interests of the particular class. In any case, the librarian can suggest to the students that they can generalize from the existence of these abstracts to others.

At this point in the presentation it may be a good time to talk about some of the help that reference librarians and other library staff can provide. The reference librarians can, for example, help students identify and locate some of the more specialized abstracts. If the student finds a citation of a journal article not owned by the library, the interlibrary loan service may be of help.

This is also a good point to talk about the availability of computerized literature searching and the library's policies about it. The librarian can offer pointers about when a computer search is advisable. The advantages of computer literature searching include the speed with which it can be accomplished and the specificity of material which can be retrieved. Topics can be combined when searching online in ways which are impossible with most print sources. It should be explained, however, that a student usually will not want a computer search for every paper he or she may write, largely because of the expense of such a search.

Research Reports

Research reports are sometimes a collateral method for dissemination of information about research. The librarian may explain that occasionally research reports may actually precede publication in journals. Education has a large and unusually well-indexed collection of such research reports gathered by ERIC which cover all areas within education. The librarian can explain the usefulness and limitations of these documents to the students. The students are often aware that not all of the literature of education is in journal articles, but also appears in such forms as reports of grant projects, papers given at conferences, bibliographies, and reports of teaching projects. The access tool for this collection is *Resources in Education*, which is a companion to *CIJE*. Both use the ERIC thesaurus and are arranged in similar manner.

Citation Indexes

The final type of indexing, one which is often new to graduate students, is citation indexing with specific reference to the *Social Sciences Citation Index* (*SSCI*). While much of what the librarian has said in the presentation has emphasized what literature is published and what sources can be used to gain access to the literature, it seems realistic to provide explanation of how this source is used. This explanation is necessary because the students are often seeing citation indexing for the first time and because it is by no means self-explanatory. In fact, it is not even easy for the librarian to find a clear way to explain the *SSCI*. Some kind of handout or audiovisual aid is especially useful at this point.

For example, the librarian can introduce citation indexing by saying, "This is the *Social Sciences Citation Index*. It is probably the most complicated reference source which is used heavily by researchers in education, and it is based on a different type of indexing. We have all found a book or journal article that interested us and then tracked down the sources which were footnoted or cited by the author of the book or article. We do this because we assume there is a relationship between the work we have read and the earlier scholarship it was based on.

"The *Social Sciences Citation Index* allows the reader to go the other way — to go forward in time and identify materials which cited an earlier publication. For example, I had read Lewis B. Mayhew's 1973 book, *The Carnegie Commission on Higher Education*, and wanted to find what authors had used Mayhew's work. In the citation section of the *Social Sciences Citation Index*, I looked up Mayhew and this specific work and found others who had cited him and who were also working on the Carnegie Commission on Higher Education. It may be that the later authors are agreeing or disagreeing with the work that has been cited. They may be applying the earlier research or replicating it — or, sometimes unfortunately, simply demonstrating that they have done their own literature searches and know the important works in their field."

The librarian then explains how to proceed from the Citation Index to the Source Index and can also explain other uses for the Source Index, the Corporate Index, and especially the Permuterm Subject Index. The latter is especially important and relates to the keyword indexing the students have already learned about in the *Index to Social Sciences and Humanities Proceedings* and contrasts with the indexing with a standardized vocabulary as in the ERIC sources. The keyword system is especially useful when trying to find new terms or phrases which do not yet have appropriate index terms. The system also allows for searching for two or more concepts because of the way it is set up. This feature is invaluable when trying to combine topics.

Books and Encyclopedias

The next step in the publication sequence is the appearance of the research in book form. The librarian has an opportunity at this point to talk about the particular library's catalog, about the *Library of Congress Subject Headings*, and about published bibliographies.

The final stage in the publication sequence is synthesis of the research into subject encyclopedias, handbooks, or other tertiary sources. Some of the important current encyclopedias in education are *The Encyclopedia of Educational Research, The International Encyclopedia of Higher Education, The International Encyclopedia of Psychiatry, Psychology, Psychoanalysis, and Neurology,* and *Encyclopedia of Psychology*. It may be of interest to the students that such sources can be used to get an overview of an unfamiliar area or to review major aspects of a topic. This is a starting place to learn about unfamiliar topics. The subject encyclopedia gives the student an overview before he or she proceeds to more specific sources.

Other Resources

Subject encyclopedias are at the end of the publication sequence, but they are not always at the end of what the instructional librarian would like to tell the students. Since publication sequence focuses on a model for the progress of dissemination of information about research, it has some obvious limitations. There are other types of information and sources that a graduate education student may find it useful to know about which are not included in the publication sequence. The librarian can explicitly say this to the student and finish the class by stepping out of the publication sequence outline. It is worthwhile to point out that students writing class papers (as opposed to theses or dissertations) generally start at this end of the sequence, trying to get an overview of a topic before looking for more specific studies.

For example, dissertations are important sources because they are full reports of research with methodology very carefully explained. They also have extensive bibliographies because of the necessity for doctoral students to do complete literature searches. At times dissertations may fall into the publication sequence. For example, a journal article or book based on the same research as a dissertation may appear after the acceptance of the dissertation. There are abstracts and indexes for dissertations. The two most important are *Dissertation Abstracts International* and its companion index, *Comprehensive Dissertation Index*.

An awareness of government documents can also be important to the graduate student. There are documents at every government level; the most active publisher by far is the federal government. Federal documents are often excellent sources of statistical information. Documents of interest to education students would include material published by the Departments of Education and Labor, and Congressional publications. As the students would suspect by now after seeing other types of indexes, there are indexes for government documents. Two of the most important titles are the *Monthly Catalog of United States Government Publications* and the *CIS (Congressional Information Service) Index*. It may be particularly important to talk at least briefly about government documents since they usually are kept in special areas of libraries and are not included in library catalogs. In addition, they are a class of publication which is often new to the students and which may not immediately occur to them as a type of information source.

Other types of resources not in the publication sequence which the librarian might choose to discuss include directories, biographical sources, archival material, audiovisual resources, sources of statistics, and sources on tests. The choices depend on the professional judgment of the librarian and the particular needs of the group of students.

Conclusion

Publication sequence serves both the librarian and the students as a useful framework to introduce graduate students to the literature of education. It provides the librarian an opportunity not only to talk about what resources are available and how to use them, but also to tell about their interrelationships. It also gives the librarian considerable professional discretion and flexibility to illustrate the steps of the publication sequence with a variety of sources. He or she may choose to describe and explain many sources or few depending on depth of discussion and the interests, needs, and background of the particular groups of graduate students. Publication sequence is also adaptable for various lengths of classes or for a series of classes.

For the students, it provides insight into the scholarly structure of communication in their chosen field. If the students are doctoral students, they will be particularly interested in this since they may be considering where their own dissertations and later publications will fit into this structure. Even for students not planning to pursue scholarly publication, however, the emphasis on the ideas and communication channels of their own field and the way in which an understanding of this communication system increases their power as researchers is an interesting, highly motivating approach to instruction.

Notes

[1]William D. Garvey and Belver C. Griffith, "Scientific Communication: Its Role in the Conduct of Research and Creation of Knowledge," *American Psychologist* 26 (April 1971): 349-62; "Communication and Information Processing within Scientific Disciplines: Empirical Findings for Psychology," in *Communication: The Essence of Science*, William D. Garvey (New York: Pergamon Press, 1979), 127-47.

[2]J. M. Levine and M. C. Wang, *Teacher and Student Perceptions: Implications for Learning* (Hillsdale, N.J.: Lawrence Erlbaum Associates Publications, 1983).

CHAPTER 5

ADAPTATION OF MARKET RESEARCH CONCEPTS FOR BIBLIOGRAPHIC INSTRUCTION

Mary Ann Ramey

Introduction

Marketing research is a preeminently practical type of research. Often working with severe limitations as to time and budget, the market researcher needs to reach definite conclusions in his or her research as quickly and cost-effectively as possible. For students of marketing research, it is never too early to begin to develop knowledge, skills, and expertise which will aid in solving research problems efficiently and in a way that directly relates to making wise marketing decisions. More than other business students, those going into marketing careers can expect to apply directly research skills learned in college to work situations.

Consequently, the academic librarian providing instruction for a marketing research class does well to emphasize the practical nature of library research in this field, to relate strategies for finding information to concepts familiar to marketing students, and to begin to sensitize students to the importance of understanding the potential of sources that can meet particular types of informational problems and needs as well as the costs and limitations of those sources.

One way to integrate the librarian's instruction with the rest of the marketing research course is to apply concepts and conceptual models from marketing research to bibliographic instruction. This chapter gives a flavor for some of the ways a librarian may want to begin talking about finding, examining, and evaluating publications and information in libraries in terms of such marketing research concepts as "data fit" and "data accuracy." It also outlines the use of a model of a marketing system as a conceptual framework for a bibliographic instruction class or series of classes for undergraduate marketing research students.

The theory behind the use of conceptual frameworks to organize library instruction involves helping students to assimilate material more readily by providing them with an overview to which they can connect new information. A framework may be taught by the librarian along with bibliographic techniques and tools, or it may be a framework that is already familiar to the student. An example of the first method—initial presentation to the student of an organizing framework by the librarian—is the use of publication sequence. Most students will be unfamiliar with this model before coming to the library instruction session. Publication sequence teaches the student something about the communication structure of the discipline. In such a case, the framework and the more detailed bibliographic material are both new to the students.

On the other hand, in some situations the librarian may choose to use a conceptual framework that the students already know. For example, a presentation on legal publications based on the three branches of American government uses a conceptual framework already known to most college students—the government's division into executive, legislative, and judicial branches. This already familiar framework has the advantage of giving the student less unfamiliar material to absorb—a major advantage if the instructional librarian is confined to a one- or two-hour presentation. It also may be reinforcing to the students since they discover that the already familiar material will be useful to them in the new, perhaps strange setting of the library, and that the new bibliographic information is useful to learn more about already familiar concepts.

A variation of this use of an already familiar conceptual framework involves using the model of a marketing system and other concepts already introduced to marketing research students. The model of a marketing system shows the informational problems that marketing professionals confront in making marketing decisions and easily lends itself to learning about some of the patterns of publication useful to meet these problems. The use of such a model illustrates to the students the way that library research can help to solve practical problems in a marketing context.

This orientation to solving categories of informational problems through understanding patterns of publications is surely something that the librarian should convey to students. It is not only important that the librarian provide the students with concepts to think about libraries and library research in marketing, but also show where libraries and the information they can provide fit into a broader research structure. The marketing research course attempts mainly to teach students methodology for doing primary market research, but it also teaches when it is not necessary to go to the time and expense of doing such research. The cost-effectiveness of a method of gathering information is important to a businessperson. Whether sending someone to a public or university library, using a corporate library, paying for a computerized literature search, buying a very expensive market research report, or conducting primary research, the marketing professional must be sensitive to what types of information are available, from what sources, and at what expense. The librarian can talk to the students about the desirability of beginning to think in these terms now while they are in school and of beginning to develop knowledge and expertise that will serve them later in the business world.

This idea relates closely to the message that with a conceptual framework it is possible to generalize from the specific examples that the librarian presents to other materials if the student understands the framework within which those materials exist. This kind of generalization has been suggested as a desirable goal for library instruction in other areas.[1] For example, if students have been introduced to *Psychological Abstracts* and understand the purpose it serves for research in psychology, they may be able to deduce that sociology would have a similar source and so locate on their own, or with the help of a reference librarian, *Sociological Abstracts.*

This is a particularly important goal for library instruction for marketing students because marketing researchers, whether students or professionals, may wind up doing research on widely differing topics. For example, in a recent marketing class that I taught, students were working on projects on comparing publicity from the Atlanta Zoo to that from the Los Angeles Zoo, on the feasibility of opening a discount appliance store in North Carolina, and on new product lines for a medium-sized commercial bakery. Marketing professionals may find themselves dealing with topics ranging from information about a major firm to learning about sociological trends among the immigrant populations who arrived in the United States in the 1970s and 1980s to technological advances in the fiber optic industry. The librarian can make explicit to the students the challenge that such diverse information needs entail and consequently the importance of their becoming familiar not just with specific sources mentioned in the presentation, but with the types and structure of publications in not just one, but a number of areas.

The use of a conceptual framework to organize a presentation to marketing students is also helpful to the librarian because there are so many publications either specifically directed to an audience of marketing professionals or potentially useful to them. It would be impossible—let alone pedagogically effective—to try to include more than a small number of such resources in a presentation. The librarian can tell the students that they are fortunate to be working in an area where so many publications are directed to them. On the other hand, continuing with the theme that the students should not just learn about sources of information, but also actively evaluate the information and sources, the students should be made aware that many of these sources are very expensive. The librarian may choose to include description of a few sources which are not in the academic library because of expense. In a business situation, even a very expensive source may be well worth buying if it satisfies the needs of a particular project. As future marketing professionals or even those who will work with such professionals in an allied field such as management, the students need to learn something about how to select materials or at least how to learn about their availability. The message to the students is the importance of development of knowledge, expertise, and selectivity in relation to published information. They are already learning about the importance of knowledge, expertise, and selectivity in doing primary marketing research so these ideas dovetail to reinforce each other.

While the librarian may make the point that there is a great deal of information published for a marketing audience, at the same time the librarian can indicate that marketing researchers often would like to have information that simply is not available in libraries, or sometimes anywhere else. An obvious example is the desirability of having as much information as possible about a company's competitors. Much of this information, however, is proprietary so that there is often no legitimate way to discover the information. As an example, the librarian can explain that even if the government collects and publishes statistical information about businesses, if the publication would reveal proprietary information, it will be suppressed in government documents.[2]

Secondly, the information that a student wants for a particular project may, in fact, not have been collected so that the student is forced to use less than optimal data for his or her purposes or to make the decision to do primary research (i.e., to collect his or her own data). These decisions relate to concepts presented in marketing research textbooks of which the librarian can make effective use in bibliographic instruction. These concepts are those of "data fit" and "data accuracy." They can be introduced in relation to components of the marketing system model, which will be explained below.

Data Fit

Considered by marketing theorists to be one of the major problems with using "secondary data sources," the concept of data fit involves the appropriateness of the already published data to the needs of the particular user.[3] For the students it may help them to realize the integration of library instruction by using a concept in the library instruction already introduced in the marketing research course. This approach tends to lend credibility to the value of what the librarian is saying. The library seminar, thus, is perceived not as something that is tacked on to the marketing research course or something that takes the student away from the main thrust of the marketing research course.

In relation to published statistical data, the students have already been sensitized by their textbook to look for units of measurement, definition of classes, and publication currency. The librarian can point to the importance of evaluating not only statistical sources, but other sources using such criteria. The librarian can emphasize that the students should not always be content with the first sources they find. In the case of a source where the data fit of the source to their information needs is not close enough, this may be a signal that they need to continue the process of research to find other sources that may better meet their needs.

Since the concept of data fit is introduced in relation to statistical information, the librarian may begin to employ the concept in evaluating a statistical source. For example, in discussing the *Statistical Abstract of the United States*, the librarian can explain that data in the tables are usually for the country as a whole, for a region, or for a state. The student, on the other hand, may need data for a county or a city. Furthermore, statistics in the *Statistical Abstract* lag by two or three years while the students may want the most recent information available, in which case the information is not a good fit to the students' needs. In some cases this might indicate the need to conduct primary research. In the case of the *Statistical Abstract*, however, the lack of fit instead probably signals the necessity to pursue the library search further. The librarian can point out that every table in the *Statistical Abstract* is footnoted with a source and that many of these can be found in the library's government documents collection or elsewhere in the library. The source publication often will provide a closer data fit. If a table in the *Statistical Abstract* has data by state, the source publication may well have data by county or city. If a *Statistical Abstract* table has data by year, the source publication may well include data by month. Finally, the source publication or a related publication may provide an update to the information in the *Statistical Abstract* to give the student more current information. Furthermore, the librarian can explain that a close examination of the *Statistical Abstract* itself can often lead to these source publications by looking carefully at information in footnotes, introductory sections, or conclusions. The librarian can emphasize that just as the students are learning to look critically at data and to analyze the data to make marketing decisions, so they can use similar skills in critically examining and analyzing the sources of such data.

The librarian can also extend the use of this concept from statistical sources to other publications the students may use. Thelma Freides has analyzed library research in the social sciences as a search for data and for "literature," or discussion.[4] While the concept of data fit starts from a consideration of sources of data, it can also be expanded to apply to sources of discussion. Students often first come across books or articles that provide information (i.e., data) or theory (i.e., literature) not quite on the topics which they wish to research. If the article does not provide exactly the information that the student needs, the comparison is obvious to a statistical source with a problematic data fit. If the source provides discussion or theory that is not quite what the student wants, the analogy to problems with data fit may be less obvious, but the decisions the student may make at this point are similar. Does he or she use the materials, deciding that they are close enough? Does it make sense to continue the search? Or should the researcher go through a process similar to primary market research and formulate his or her own theories? As with the decisions about statistical data, each of these courses of action is progressively more expensive at least in terms of time. If the student decides to use the article despite an imperfect fit with what he or she wants to prove or demonstrate, the search stops at that point, but he or she runs the risk of constructing an inaccurate, weak, or unconvincing argument. At the other extreme, if the researcher decides to conduct his or her own research or construct his or her own theory, the amount of time involved may be formidable.

The researcher, therefore, may decide to continue the search for information, research, or discussion closer to what he or she needs. The librarian can suggest that, as with a statistical source like the *Statistical Abstract*, the article that the student has in hand may bear close analysis to find research or ideas that provide the basis for getting to articles with a better "fit" with the student's needs.

If the librarian is dealing with research articles, it is possible to expand upon the way in which research is usually based on earlier ideas and research. Consequently, the student may find material with a closer fit through the obvious procedure of examination of footnotes and bibliography. Not only does this teach the students methods of broadening a literature search, it suggests to them the way in which research is conducted in the sciences and social sciences and, by extension, in business. Such research is done as teamwork with current research building on earlier research.

This point also gives an opportunity for a natural transition to discussion of the *Social Sciences Citation Index* (*SSCI*), which indexes some of the more scholarly or academic marketing journals. If the literature the student finds initially does not have a close enough fit to his or her needs, it may be that later articles based on the article he or she has found will have developed the ideas in a manner more useful to his or her particular needs. The librarian may, however, choose not to include tools to access the more academic resources of marketing, such as the *SSCI*. The choice of whether to include academic resources may depend on consultation with the marketing teaching faculty about what is appropriate for students at this level in the particular institution, on projects or papers the students may need to complete for this particular class, and on the librarian's professional judgment of what is necessary and useful for the students.

If the librarian chooses to emphasize instead business or trade magazines or other less scholarly publications, he or she can still use the approach of suggesting that internal clues in the first document may lead to information with a closer fit to the student's needs. To take a simple example, if the student is interested in the frozen baked goods market, he or she may identify articles through *Business Periodicals Index* using the index term, "baked goods, frozen." An article may deal in a general way with the market, but may also list particular company names such as Mrs. Smith's, Sara Lee, or Chef Pierre. The student can extend such research by following up on the individual company name in such sources as *Predicasts F & S Index*, the *Business Index*, or INFOTRAC. Such an example enables the librarian to introduce the students to several periodical indexes in business and to discuss their characteristics, but it also presents the key technique of examining the first source or sources identified in order to lead to other sources.

Data Accuracy

The discussion of data fit is designed to suggest to the students the importance of actively evaluating the sources they find. The concept of data accuracy is also important and has already been presented to the students by their teacher and textbook in relation to evaluation of the source of information, purpose of the publication, and evidence concerning quality.[5]

For example, the students are advised of the importance of the market researcher's using the "original source" rather than an "acquired source." In their textbook, Thomas C. Kinnear and James R. Taylor write about the importance of going to "original sources" that form the basis for the *Statistical Abstract* because their more detailed explanation of methodology and their more detailed data enable the researcher better to evaluate their accuracy. The librarian can extend this idea beyond the *Statistical Abstract* and other statistical sources to research articles and even articles in popular magazines and trade journals, emphasizing the importance of noting clues to how the information published was gathered and analyzed.

The same type of sensitivity to the purpose of the publication and evidence concerning quality can also be applied to both publications providing data elements and those that are mainly sources of discussion. Closely allied to the purpose of the publication are the identity and credentials of the author. For example, is the source the annual report of a company, in which the organization has considerable discretion about what to print, or is it a 10-K report, which has legally mandated requirements? In considering a writer of an article, is the author an independent researcher or journalist or is he or she the vice-president of the firm that is the subject of the article?

In relation to evidence concerning quality, the librarian can talk about the evaluation of quality using both external and internal evidence of the publication's quality. The publisher's good reputation, for example, can be a clue that sound methodology is likely to be used. The question sometimes arises from students as to how they are to know the reputation of the publisher. For the students, advice can come from teachers or librarians. For researchers in the business community, the company librarian or others active with research in the same firm or elsewhere in the community can sometimes provide advice. As market researchers do more and more research, they will also develop their own opinions about particular publishers.

Internal evidence is provided by the publications themselves in their discussion of methodology of information gathering and analysis. In the case of a statistical publication, methodology is often explained in introductory or footnote material. The same is true of the research article. Even in the more popular, journalistic article or book, the author often gives information about information gathering—who was interviewed and over what period of time.

The students can also be made aware that sometimes in marketing sources information about original sources may not be very specific. For example, the source of data in a table may simply be given as the organization which compiled it such as "SAMI" or "Arbitron" without information about how the data were collected. This lack of detailed information is likely to be related to the proprietary nature of information of commercial firms and groups dealing with business information. For them, the information they collect is a commodity and one not generally to be shared, or at least not shared in detail, with the general public except at a price. In such a case, the librarian can suggest that the student is thrown back on the reputation of the source of the information and probably also needs to take into account the lack of detail about how the information was collected and analyzed in evaluating the usefulness of the information for the student's particular purposes.

Library Primary
and Secondary Sources

These marketing concepts of data fit and data accuracy and the imperatives they create for the researcher to find information as near to the original source as possible enable the librarian to relate these concepts to the idea of primary and secondary literature. Note that it is important to distinguish this use of the terms from "primary data" and "secondary data" as those terms are used in marketing. In a marketing context, primary data is that which is collected, usually through surveys, specifically for the present study; secondary data is "published data which has been compiled for a purpose other than the present study."[6] Of course, both primary and secondary sources, as those terms are generally used in a library context, are secondary data under the marketing definition.

By presenting the concept of primary and secondary sources in the context of the needs of the students for the best possible data fit and accuracy and consequently for the original source, or at least for one not far removed from the original source, the librarian illustrates the usefulness of understanding the way in which information is published and particularly the way in which secondary sources depend upon and grow out of primary sources. It also illustrates characteristic differences between primary and secondary sources (e.g., that the former are more detailed). The students learn that often the primary source can be identified by careful examination of the secondary source. A secondary source like a business directory often describes the basis of its information in an introduction. Students may find more information by going to primary sources, such as a collection of 10-K reports, annual reports, and other financial statements.

The Marketing System

Many marketing research textbooks present a model for a marketing system or a marketing information system in an introductory or early chapter. The concept may be presented as a diagram as in Kinnear and Taylor's *Marketing Research: An Applied Approach* (see figure 5.1) or may be presented in the narrative.[7] In either case, the concept provides an effective framework to structure a bibliographic instruction session.

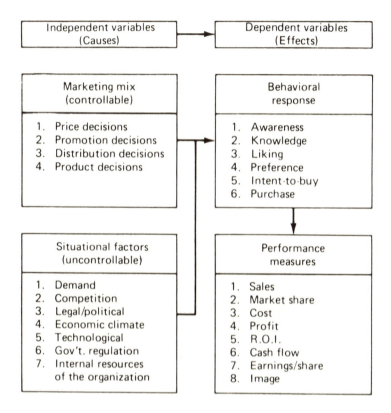

Fig. 5.1. Model of the marketing system. From Thomas C. Kinnear and James R. Taylor, *Marketing Research: An Applied Approach*, 2nd ed. (New York: McGraw-Hill, 1983), 6. Reprinted with permission of McGraw-Hill.

The use of such a framework has several advantages. First, the students will already be familiar with the concept from discussion in their class and therefore will be able to use the conceptual framework as a familiar structure to which they can relate new material about library resources and techniques. Secondly, the relationship of the librarian's class session to the model in the textbook will suggest the importance and integration of the information about library research with marketing the decision-making process and with the subject matter of the marketing research course. Attention to course textbooks might be commended to instructional librarians in many fields. It seems too rare for instructional librarians to be aware of the context of bibliographic instruction in relation to the rest of what students hear and learn in the course. Finally a marketing system is a model for a highly practical, real-world process. The integration of library research with the model, by showing the way in which library concepts, techniques, and resources can support this system and so aid in marketing decision making, emphasizes the practicality of the material that the librarian is teaching. This conceptual framework, therefore, reinforces the problem-solving nature of the information provided and discussed by the librarian.

The Kinnear/Taylor marketing system identifies factors from the perspective of a selling organization that lead to performance results assessed in terms of performance measures. This is the model we will use in detail as an example to structure a library class. Leading to the performance measures first are independent variables, both "marketing mix," the controllable decisions made by the marketing professionals, and the uncontrollable "situational factors," which come from the environment and about which the marketing professionals need to be all the more informed because of the factors' uncontrollable nature. Altogether the system presents a number of points where information is necessary and helpful in making decisions and in measuring the success of those decisions.

Using the Kinnear/Taylor Model
for Class Presentation

It is possible to structure a bibliographic instruction class or series of classes around the marketing system model of Kinnear/Taylor, particularly for students using their textbook. The instructional librarian starts by passing out materials including bibliographies, library handouts, and other printed material. Recommended are photocopies or easily visible transparencies of pages from sources that may be difficult for the students to visualize and understand without a page in front of them, such as *Predicasts F & S Index* or census tables. The students should also have available in a separate photocopy, in their textbook, or on a chart at the front of the class a diagram of the marketing system since this serves as an outline of the class and more importantly of the interrelation of the materials.

Bibliographic handouts can also aid in making the content of the class clearer and in facilitating a smooth presentation. The librarian can prepare an outline based on the marketing system with categories and/or titles and call numbers of sources under components of the system. This technique helps the students remember the types of sources that are useful for providing the information needed in relation to components of the model. It also makes the class move more efficiently since the librarian will not have to stop to clarify names and locations of sources.

Such a bibliographic outline might begin:

I. Situational factors

    A. Demand

        Census data (or names of specific census publications)

        County and City Data Book

        Statistical Abstract of the United States

        American Statistics Index

        etc.

    B. Competition

        Standard and Poor's Register

        Moody's manuals

        U.S. Industrial Outlook

        Standard and Poor's Industry Surveys

        etc.

The librarian should emphasize that the sources included are highly selective and illustrative rather than exhaustive. In fact, they will have been chosen depending on the librarian's professional judgment, on the holdings of the library, and perhaps on the students' particular research project for the class. This is a stage where the librarian can begin to talk with the students about the vast amount of information that is available and potentially useful for marketing researchers and about the need to be selective among these plentiful resources.

The librarian may also wish to provide a more conventional annotated bibliography of marketing resources for the students to use themselves outside of class. He or she should also be aware of bibliographies or commentary on sources included in the students' textbook. Such bibliographies and commentary are often in the chapters on secondary data sources.

The librarian continues from these preliminaries by asking which part of the marketing system can most obviously be helped by library resources. The students generally will identify situational factors. The librarian can then start with that area. Depending on the time available, most of the session may in fact deal with research on situational factors since this parallels the most common type of library research conducted by marketing professionals.

DEMAND

Since questions of demand are closely related to demographic data, a discussion of demand can serve as a prelude to talking about sources of statistical information. Putting statistical information first disposes of a difficult topic early. Also it is related to what the students have already been discussing since much of marketing research classes deals with the collection and analysis of statistics.

Since only a tiny percentage of statistical sources can be discussed specifically, different librarians using this approach may choose illustrative sources that are very different. Whatever the choice of specific sources, it probably is a good idea to tell the students that because statistical sources are many, varied, and complex, they are an area where librarians expect to give an especially great amount of help to library users. Another way of putting this is, "In library jargon, bibliographic control of statistical information is problematic, which is another way of saying that statistics can be tough to find."

A possible illustrative approach is to explain to the students the importance of statistical data coming from the federal government and then to explain three keys to finding such information. First, it is important to recognize patterns of recurring statistical publication. Census of population publications are a good example, including *General Population Characteristics*, *Detailed Population Characteristics*, and *General Social and Economic Characteristics* as well as tract and block statistics. Comparability of the statistics gathered is a particular advantage of using such recurrent statistical publications. The librarian can also indicate, without necessarily going into great detail, that many other recurrent statistical publications come from the federal government.

Another technique of identifying statistical sources is the use of statistical compendia not only for the information printed in them, but also for the original sources to which they may lead. The *Statistical Abstract* is a good example to illustrate this type of use of compendia. If the librarian chooses, much of what was discussed above about the use of internal clues to lead to original sources and on data fit might be incorporated at this point.

Finally, the librarian can talk about indexes to statistical publications. He or she may wish to begin with the *American Statistics Index* as particularly appropriate to a discussion of federal statistical publications. If the librarian decides not to go through the fairly lengthy explanation of the index and abstract volumes of the *American Statistics Index*, he or she can use other more quickly explained examples, such as *Statistics Sources* or *Datamap*.

In pointing out the problems with currency of census data, the librarian can also talk about some of the specialized marketing sources designed to supplement and update census statistics. Examples are the *Survey of Buying Power* and *Data Service* from *Sales and Marketing Management*, sources which use sampling methods to update demographic information as well as providing indexes of buying power and various market rankings. These can be related to the large number of publications to help meet a specialized marketing audience's needs for current figures to assess demand.

More specific advertising sources can be mentioned such as *Simmons Study of Media and Markets* or *M.R.I.*, both of which regularly give market share statistics for leading brands of various products and relate characteristics of consumers buying or using the products to their habits of reading and watching television. To make the usefulness of these publications more concrete, the librarian can explain that an advertiser or advertising agency can use them to find out how many women who are heavy consumers of Scotch watch *Dallas*. Note that many libraries do not have such sources in their collections because they are very expensive. The librarian may, on this basis, choose to omit mention of a publication if the students will not be able to use it immediately. However, there is also an argument for including such a source even if it is not in the library in order to introduce publications characteristic of marketing information which are designed to meet very specific needs, but are also very expensive. To understand the use of such information for marketing professionals in the business world, it is important that the students are aware of the existence of such publications.

The question sometimes arises at this point from the students of how they can learn about such specific marketing information publications. *Findex* can be presented as an example of an index designed to provide access to marketing research reports and similar publications. Again, the librarian can note that few of the publications indexed in *Findex* are in the library, but that at some point the indexing and descriptive annotations of *Findex* or a similar source may lead a marketing researcher to a publication that meets his or her organization's needs and therefore is well worth the purchase price.

COMPETITION

In using the conceptual framework of the marketing system, the librarian can use the component competition to help students approach the problem of researching news about an industry or specific competitor companies. In an academic setting such research is related to the frequently assigned class project of a market audit—a survey of history and trends of an industry.

It is possible to approach sources that may help with research in this area by pointing out the differences between those sources that provide a little information on many companies, usually with predictable format and frequency, and those sources which give a great deal of information on one or a few companies, often in a less regular way. Sources giving a big picture of an industry, but with little detail about any particular company, are business directories such as *Standard and Poor's Register of Corporations* or Dun and Bradstreet's *Million Dollar Directory*, and investors' sources such as the Moody's manuals or *Value Line*. Also in this category are such publications as Standard and Poor's *Industry Surveys* and the *U.S. Industrial Outlook*, which give narrative analysis of trends in various industries along with some statistics.

In relation to getting an overview of an industry, the librarian may also choose to talk about books at this point. While it probably makes sense to deemphasize books in a marketing research class because of their lack of importance to researchers in relation to periodical articles, the librarian may wish to talk a little about when books on industries can be helpful to marketing students. He or she can also discuss the library catalog, call numbers, and other necessary mechanics for access to books in the particular library.

Moving to sources of more detailed information on specific companies, the librarian can talk about characteristics of financial reports such as 10-K reports or annual reports. Depending on the emphasis of the class, the librarian may want to emphasize the different characteristics and purposes of these reports and explain what valuable sources of information they can be about a specific company. A simple example of such discussion is the freedom of companies in preparing annual reports in contrast to the legal requirements of the 10-K. On the other hand, the annual report may sometimes in its narrative give more of a feeling for what the company is like and where it is going.

Periodical literature is of course also helpful in learning about industries and particular companies. The librarian can explain the importance of the business press as it keeps its special audience informed of happenings in the business world. He or she can also talk about characteristics of indexes useful for answering particular types of research questions from periodical literature. For example, for the researcher looking for information on a particular company, especially a medium-sized or smaller company, *Predicasts F & S Index* is usually more effective than the *Business Periodicals Index* because of differences in their indexing practices.

The librarian may also want to talk about the use of developing technology in accessing periodical literature and the fact that computerized literature searching is becoming increasingly characteristic of the research conducted in corporate libraries or research departments, in market research firms, and in other business settings. The librarian may describe some of the databases available through DIALOG or BRS which are particularly useful to those in marketing such as ABI/INFORM, Industry Data Sources, PTS Marketing and Advertising Reference Service, and Adtrack. However, as with a number of other sources mentioned in the class, treatment should probably be brief since most students will not be able to afford searchers of these expensive files. If the library has INFOTRAC or another suitable CD-ROM product, the librarian can point out the potentials and limitations of such a source.

ENVIRONMENT

Depending on the time available and the emphasis of the class, the librarian may choose to talk individually about the legal/political, technological, and governmental regulatory aspects of situational factors from the model. Since it is quite possible to occupy all or most of a one-class presentation with the discussion described thus far, however, the librarian may instead group these as environmental factors. Information from the general news media, from researchers in the social sciences, and from governmental agencies is helpful to the marketing researcher in learning about the environment and its likely effect on marketing decisions.

The librarian can talk about parallels between sources already discussed and those that are available for general news and social sciences literature. Many students, for example, will already know about the *Readers' Guide to Periodical Literature*. While the librarian can explain that it is not the best source for looking for business articles, he or she can also talk about instances where the marketing researcher may want information from the general press and should use this index. Similarly, it is possible to compare the purpose and scope of the *Business Periodicals Index* to that of the *Social Sciences Index*. Discussion of access to government publications and the peculiar characteristics and problems of accessing them fit well at this stage in the presentation as well.

(A librarian may wish to confine a presentation largely to situational factors as a model emphasizing the way in which effective research in library resources affects whatever decisions may have been made in relation to marketing mix, the decision component of the model, and impacts of those decisions on the "behavioral response" and "performance measures.") Such a presentation probably covers much of the use marketing researchers are likely to make of secondary data sources in real-world situations. However, in a longer presentation or a series of presentations or where the emphasis of a particular class calls for such treatment, the librarian can go on to relate library resources to other components of the marketing system model.

MARKETING MIX

Marketing mix deals with the decisions made by the marketing professional. Books and articles containing theory or case studies on how to make such decisions may aid the decision-maker as may the types of books and periodical articles described earlier in the chapter under "Competition." If the librarian can give a series of presentations, he or she may choose to emphasize techniques to access more specific topics in relation to competition (e.g., trends in the natural food industry or emphasis on a particular brand and its competitors) and more general, theoretical topics at this point (e.g., methods for assessing consumer food preferences).

Because this component of the model provides a good place to emphasize an overview of the theories and concerns of marketing, it is also appropriate to talk about guides to the literature of marketing. The librarian may review the differing approaches and the usefulness of such guides as *Marketing Information: A Professional Reference Guide* and the *Information Sourcebook for Marketers and Strategic Planners*.

DEPENDENT VARIABLES

Finding information about the areas of behavioral response and performance measures presents an opportunity, as does marketing mix, to teach the students about library research sources and techniques that may give them useful sources of comparison with which to develop expectations of a marketing research project and assess its results.

Behavioral response may lead students to some of the same types of sources examined in relation to demand and to the environment. If the librarian chooses to emphasize this area, he or she may go into more depth talking about access to periodical literature in psychology and sociology, possibly discussing *Psychological Abstracts* and *Sociological Abstracts* as useful sources for information about consumer behavior. Here again, the librarian can discuss the wide variety of sources from a number of fields that may be relevant to marketing research.

As with behavioral response, the marketing researcher may want information with which to compare the performance measures of the results of his or her own project. Many of the sources, related to finding information on competition, such as investors' services and periodical literature, are also relevant to learning about such factors as sales, market share, costs, and image of firms. In addition, the librarian might wish to introduce sources for quantitative comparison of performance. Examples of such sources are Dun and Bradstreet's *Industry Norms and Key Business Ratios*, Robert Morris Associates' *Annual Statement Studies*, and Troy's *Almanac of Business and Industrial Financial Ratios*.

Conclusion

The use of a conceptual framework borrowed from marketing to structure bibliographic instruction for marketing research students offers the instructional librarian an opportunity to tap into interests and concerns that are already being developed with the students. It also provides considerable flexibility for discretion and individual choice about the detail of the presentation depending on the particular students' needs, the expertise of the librarian, and the library collection. Finally, it ties the bibliographic instruction not just to the limited forum of the particular course, but to real-world marketing decisions and to the potential careers of many of the students in the class. For all of these reasons, it provides an effective conceptual framework for the librarian working with marketing research students.

Notes

[1]Elizabeth Frick, "Information Structure and Bibliographic Instruction," *The Journal of Academic Librarianship* 1 (September 1975): 12.

[2]See, for example, the section "Data Withheld from Publication" in the introduction to each issue of *County Business Patterns*. ("In accordance with title 13, section 9, U.S. Code, data that may disclose the operations of individual employers are not published.") U.S., Department of Commerce, Bureau of the Census, *County Business Patterns*, 1946- .

[3]Thomas C. Kinnear and James R. Taylor, *Marketing Research: An Applied Approach*, 2nd ed. (New York: McGraw-Hill, 1983), 159.

[4]Thelma Freides, *Literature and Bibliography of the Social Sciences* (Los Angeles, Calif.: Melville Publishing, 1973), 2.

[5]Kinnear and Taylor, *Marketing Research*, 160.

[6]Ibid., 158.

[7]For other examples of marketing system models that might be adapted, see David J. Luck, et al.'s *Marketing Research*, 6th ed. (Englewood Cliffs, N.J.: Prentice-Hall, 1982), 22ff. and Donald S. Tull and Del I. Hawkins's *Marketing Research: Measurement and Methods*, 4th ed. (New York: Macmillan, 1987), 12ff.

CONCEPTUAL FRAMEWORKS FOR BIBLIOGRAPHIC INSTRUCTION IN PSYCHOLOGY

Lyn Thaxton

Introduction and Review of Literature Related to Bibliographic Instruction in Psychology

The major purpose of this chapter is to provide suggestions for innovative approaches to bibliographic instruction for psychology students, especially those in graduate or advanced undergraduate classes. In order to provide a context for these suggestions, the first part of the chapter presents a literature review of publications on particular strategies used for bibliographic instruction in this area, as well as theoretical articles on conceptual frameworks and communication patterns with relevance to psychology. The second section of the chapter reports the results of a research study in which faculty members representing a number of areas of psychology were interviewed about their perceptions of the process of the dissemination of information in their areas. In addition, this study included a survey of graduate students in psychology regarding their use of library resources and services. The final section of the chapter covers specific recommendations for the use of conceptual frameworks in bibliographic instruction for various sub-disciplines of psychology, with specific emphasis on developing programs in connection with teaching faculty.

William D. Garvey and Belver C. Griffith have pointed out patterns of communication and dissemination of information in psychology, which shares characteristics with both the physical and social sciences.[1] Nevertheless, published materials on library use and literature searching in psychology generally do not reflect the complexity and sophistication of the discipline. Most material is aimed at undergraduates with little library experience; basic tools and rudimentary literature searching skills are stressed. Several programmed texts have been developed to lead a student through the steps that he or she should follow in writing an undergraduate research paper in psychology. Howard Pikoff prepared a workbook that covers such topics as the reasons for concentrating on book or journal literature, basic sources of bibliographies, location of dissertations, and the development of computer literature searching strategy.[2] Programmed texts by Brad H. Manning and Donna M. Buntain, and Judy McArthur and Pat Kenney trace the steps that a student might follow in researching a term paper in the library.[3] The latter is especially useful in pointing out how a student can make critical, evaluative judgments through the use of such sources as book reviews, citation indexes, and biographical tools.

Bobbie J. Pollard and Pauline M. Rothstein developed instruction materials for nonlibrary teachers rather than students. The package is aimed at preparing students to find printed reference sources in industrial psychology. It consists of two sections which focus on different forms of literature and the procedure for locating materials in libraries. Like the instructional materials mentioned above, this package gives some attention to the research process but focuses more on the characteristics of specific sources (such as *Psychological Abstracts*) or types of sources (such as handbooks, dictionaries, and government documents). Also, the role of the librarian in the instructional process appears limited to the development of the programmed texts.[4]

Evidence exists that psychology faculty probably do not perceive librarians as active partners in bibliographic instruction. Several professors have written about ingenious methods for luring students into the library and introducing them to reference sources. Arnold D. LeUnes, a teacher of developmental psychology, created a "nonsense assignment" consisting of twenty-four questions that would require students to use such library resources as journals, biographical dictionaries, and directories. The students are asked to determine the names of U.S. presidents who were firstborn children and to find the names of two books on childhood schizophrenia, among other questions. According to LeUnes, this assignment leads to increased awareness of the breadth of developmental psychology. The issues of improved knowledge of library materials and of enhanced search strategies are not, however, addressed.[5]

James B. Mathews deplored the lack of depth of information and alternative hypotheses in laboratory reports from an introductory psychological research course. As an attempt to rectify this problem, he developed a quasi-experimental exercise in which the students were divided into teams for a "treasure hunt." The assignment required that students use such sources as *Psychological Abstracts*, the *Annual Review of Psychology*, and *Dissertation Abstracts*. The team members were assessed on accuracy and completeness as well as speed. Mathews reports that the assignment resulted in significant increases in the number of items listed and number of sources used in a bibliographic generation exercise.[6]

Louis E. Gardner emphasizes that the expectation of an extensive and creative literature search can be met only by developing research skills early in a course, ideally in a context that stimulates creativity and ingenuity. He introduces students to "the usual sources" in the first class period, then assigns each student a cliché or old saying such as, "opposites attract" or "like father, like son." The students are required to find empirical studies that support or refute these adages, write abstracts, and present the information in class. Evaluations indicated that most students completed the assignment and found it interesting, challenging, and enjoyable.[7]

Interestingly, neither LeUnes, Gardner, nor Mathews mentioned the involvement of librarians in library instruction or development of assignments. The students are apparently given (at best) a cursory introduction to specific sources and then let loose in the library. (Mathews did, however, indicate that his "treasure hunters" were "urged to follow full library decorum.") The difficulty with the exercises suggested by these professors lies in their lack of relationship to the process of information development and dissemination. The assignments might have resulted in lengthier bibliographies in student papers but not necessarily in a more sophisticated research process or better evaluation of empirical research.

To this end, Pam M. Baxter urges that librarians conduct in-class bibliographic instruction for psychology students and gives several reasons. First, librarians are oriented toward the presentation of pertinent reference sources as well as the idiosyncrasies of specific sources. Perhaps more important is the role that librarians can play in presenting paper topic definition as a logical process. Given the "information avalanche" in psychology, students need to be made aware that a thorough analysis of the literature on stress, as an example, cannot be encompassed in a fifteen-page paper. The librarian can teach the usefulness of such sources as subject encyclopedias, handbooks, and review articles in identifying a topic with manageable scope.[8]

The collaboration of librarian and psychology faculty member in bibliographic instruction will perhaps be most useful within the context of conceptual frameworks, an approach largely neglected in the literature cited above. Elizabeth Frick suggests that students who do bibliographic research must learn discrimination, judgment, and an understanding of bibliographic structure. In order for these skills to be attained, persons who teach bibliographic instruction should translate their information into the conceptual frameworks and habits of the user.[9] Pamela Kobelski and Mary Reichel indicate that this has generally not been done in the past, as library instruction has tended to focus on types of reference tools, the approach generally used in library school. While this approach may sometimes be necessary, it is seldom meaningful or interesting to students and should be supplemented by other frameworks. Of these, systematic literature searching is probably most common and is reflected in some of the programmed texts and articles discussed above. This viewpoint is based on the notion that there is a logical procedure for gathering information using library resources. This procedure begins with more general sources, such as encyclopedias, then proceeds to indexes, abstracts, and other access tools. This framework can be useful in both undergraduate and graduate classes.

Other conceptual frameworks may, however, be useful for bibliographic instruction in psychology, especially at a graduate level. Kobelski and Reichel discuss the value of the form of publication as a framework, especially in areas in which specific forms such as technical reports and government documents are useful but often overlooked. The framework of primary and secondary sources can also be extremely valuable. While the concept of the primary source is usually considered in humanities disciplines such as literature and history, it is pertinent to psychology as well. Here, primary source is viewed as an original report of research in a journal article, technical report, or conference paper. Secondary sources, such as review articles, will evaluate or restructure primary sources. This approach can be combined with the citation pattern framework to indicate how primary sources are the building blocks for both integrative reviews and additional primary sources.[10]

A particularly useful framework for bibliographic instruction in psychology is that of publication sequence. Garvey and Griffith have developed a communication model based on extensive study of the communication process in psychology.[11] According to this model (figure 6.1), psychologists usually spend twelve to eighteen months developing an idea and conducting research before the results can be presented informally at local colloquia. The researchers receive feedback at this level, then may rework their material and give presentations at state or regional meetings and/or the annual conference of the American Psychological Association. Authors may disseminate copies of their conference presentations and obtain additional feedback in this way. One author in ten produces and distributes technical reports, and many also disseminate preprints of articles accepted by journals. Thus, much information in psychology is available to scholars before it is published in journal form. This is especially important because of the relatively long time lag between submission of articles to psychology journals and their publication. Approximately one-fifth of articles published in primary psychology journals were previously rejected by one or more other journals. This fact may partially explain the finding that the average interval between submission of a manuscript and publication in the social sciences is ten months longer than in the physical sciences.

The information process continues with the inclusion of an article in *Psychological Abstracts* seven to eight months after publication. The few published articles of scholarly importance may then be included in the *Annual Review of Psychology*, *Psychological Bulletin*, or a similar reviewing source. If the work is of substantial, continuing scholarly importance, it may be referenced or summarized in a treatise, specialized text, or encyclopedia a decade or more after the original research was conducted.

James Olivetti suggests using a similar model, the "natural structure of the research literature in psychology," as an alternative to the search strategy method of bibliographic instruction.[12] This author uses the social psychologist Leon Festinger's theory of cognitive dissonance as an example. Festinger originally published his research in primary source journals and, almost simultaneously, in conference proceedings. Within two years a monograph was published, along with other journal articles elaborating and elucidating the theory. As the theory developed, "Cognitive Dissonance" was introduced as a subject heading in *Psychological Abstracts*. The theory was later communicated to the general public through the secondary source journal *Scientific American* and was finally reviewed in *Psychological Bulletin*.

Olivetti's model varies in some respects from that of Garvey and Griffith, a finding that suggests several questions that may have a bearing on bibliographic instruction formats. Since Garvey and Griffith's research was conducted in the 1960s and 1970s, it is possible that the publication sequence has changed over the years. Factors that may have influenced the change include the increased use of online computer databases and the publication of *Psychological Documents* (formerly *Catalog of Selected Documents in Psychology*), intended to "bridge the gap between formal journal publication and informal information exchange." Furthermore, Olivetti's example from social psychology leads to the question of whether various subareas of psychology disseminate information in different ways. It appears likely, for example, that humanistically oriented clinical psychologists and experimental psychologists view and use information quite differently. The latter may perhaps rely on "classic" works, such as those by

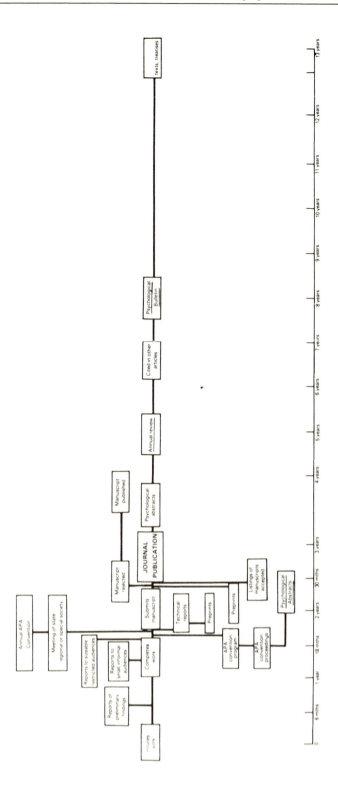

Fig. 6.1. The dissemination process from the time the research scientist initiates his work until his findings become integrated into the fund of scientific knowledge. (The abscissa gives the median time, after initiation of work, of each form of dissemination shown in the figure.) Reprinted with permission from William D. Garvey, *Communication: The Essence of Science* (New York: Pergamon Books Ltd., 1979), 134.

Abraham Maslow and Carl Rogers, while experimental psychologists focus on new and often unpublished work. A final question relates to the difference in information dissemination and use among established researchers and those new to the field, including graduate students. The study summarized below was designed to consider these questions.

Dissemination and Use of Information by Psychology Faculty and Graduate Students[13]

This study focused on the faculty and graduate students in the psychology department at Georgia State University. This department is unusual in the wide range of specializations represented. In addition, a number of faculty members have published extensively and have national and international reputations. The department has about thirty faculty members and approximately 170 graduate students, primarily in the clinical area, which offers programs in psychotherapy, general clinical, and clinical child/family psychology. Nonclinical graduate programs include community/organizational, cognitive, developmental/comparative, physiological, and social. The master of arts and doctor of philosophy degrees are offered. Admission is highly competitive, especially in the clinical area, in which only one applicant in ten is accepted.

The first aspect of the study involved in-depth, semistructured interviews with ten faculty members representing the areas of family psychology, behavior therapy, psychotherapy (two faculty members), organizational psychology (two faculty members including one whose primary appointment is in the management department), experimental psychology (two faculty members, one specializing in primate language learning and the other in brain research), social psychology, and clinical neuropsychology. The interviews concentrated on the faculty members' perception of the research process in their areas, especially as it related to the Garvey/Griffith model.

A second aspect of the study involved brief questionnaires completed by fifty-one graduate students in the areas of general clinical, psychotherapy, clinical child/family, community/organizational, and social psychology, as well as six students from the counseling program in the College of Education who were taking psychology courses. The questionnaire assessed the frequency of use of various sources selected to represent Garvey and Griffith's stages of dissemination of information. These sources are *Dissertation Abstracts*, *Index to Social Sciences and Humanities Proceedings*, *Psychological Documents*, *Social Sciences Citation Index*, *Psychological Bulletin*, and the *Annual Review of Psychology*. In addition, students were asked if they had scheduled online computer literature searches or had attended library orientation seminars developed especially for psychology graduate students.

Results of interviews with faculty members indicated that the Garvey/Griffith model is basically accurate but an oversimplification. Several researchers, including those in brain research, primate research, family psychology, and behavior therapy, stated that they did not communicate with an "invisible college" of colleagues but instead worked more or less alone in development of research ideas. It should be emphasized, however, that these faculty members all have distinguished publication records and are on the cutting edge of their disciplines. In a field in which many journal articles are read by very few persons, let alone cited, these professors are the elite. The organizational psychology faculty members also indicated little contact with colleagues but pointed out that a network presently developing in the region may make a difference. The psychotherapy faculty members, on the other hand, pointed to frequent communication with others in their area of interest, and the clinical neuropsychologist stated that this contact was crucial in a relatively new, constantly evolving area such as his. The social psychologist also pointed to constant interaction with colleagues at all stages of the research process.

The importance of conference presentation varied among subdisciplines. The organizational and neuropsychologists expressed the belief that conferences were more helpful for informal exchanges of information than for conference sessions. The faculty members in family and primate research (among the most senior persons interviewed) indicated that they seldom made conference presentations, considering them of little use. One person interviewed suggested that this form of dissemination was most useful for young faculty members just embarking on their careers.

Several faculty members stated that they tended to submit materials directly to journals without obtaining formal or informal feedback first. A surprising finding was that four faculty members often pulled their material together into book form rather than submitting it piecemeal to journals, a finding that seems to support Garvey and Griffith's encouragement of better integration of information in this discipline. One person pointed out, however, that the pragmatics of grant funding and the "publish or perish" mentality discourages this approach, at least for new faculty members.

Most persons interviewed agreed that the time lag in publication had not improved appreciably in the last fifteen years. It was suggested that the lag might be in part due to the refereeing process, in which referees who were not sufficiently knowledgeable about a topic were assigned articles to review. The faculty members also generally did not believe that the dissemination process had changed because of the presence of *Psychological Documents*. Only one faculty member indicated that he used this tool; most persons interviewed were not even aware of the index and its accompanying microfiche, both available in the library. Faculty members were, however, enthusiastic about computer literature searching, available free for faculty research projects (within limits) through the library's reference department. This process was especially useful for research in unfamiliar areas, the respondents stated.

The majority of faculty members, including clinicians, agreed that clinical psychologists who are not university faculty do not tend to be involved or interested in research. One faculty member pointed out that different value systems are involved, with clinicians stressing the importance of the provision of services rather than the identification and dissemination of information through the research process. One psychotherapist, however, pointed out the difference between experimental literature and the literature of ideas, with the latter being of interest to clinicians. The other psychotherapist indicated the importance of studying new therapeutic techniques. The organizational psychologists also emphasized the importance of staying abreast of published research with practical implications.

Comments by these faculty members indicated agreement with Garvey and Griffith's finding that most articles are read by very few persons and that most citations are to a few seminal works. The fact that "classic" studies are cited again and again does not necessarily imply stagnation, however; many significant theories are still pertinent and have not been disproven. One researcher stated the importance of reading classic studies so as not to "reinvent the wheel."

While faculty members were able to articulate their own research process, they tended to be vague about expectations for students in their classes. A typical comment was, "I expect students to be able to use the library well and efficiently." The importance of *Psychological Abstracts* and *Social Sciences Citation Index* was frequently mentioned, as were computer literature searching and interlibrary loans. The consensus, however, was that students generally do not understand research as a process and rely on a few journals in writing their papers.

The survey of graduate students by and large supported the faculty members' contentions. The students were asked if they used specific sources frequently, sometimes, or never. Only *Psychological Abstracts* was used frequently—as defined as at least twice a quarter—by the majority of the students. Sources from both the "innovative" and "integrative" ends of the spectrum (*Dissertation Abstracts* and *Psychological Bulletin*) were used sometimes by the majority, however. *Social Sciences Citation Index*, despite its acknowledged importance for both librarians and psychology faculty, was used sometimes by less than half of the students. Both *Psychological Documents* and *Index to Social Sciences and Humanities Proceedings* were used infrequently. Since these sources had not been widely "advertised" by reference librarians, this result was not surprising. Computer literature searching has become a popular service, according to the respondents. Approximately half had arranged for searches through the DIALOG system, despite the average cost of $25 per search.

A rather disappointing finding related to the attendance at library orientation seminars. Only a quarter of the respondents had attended these seminars, despite the fact that they had been widely publicized in the psychology department. Furthermore, there was little difference in use of sources between those who had attended seminars and those who did not. Those who had attended were slightly more likely to use sources sometimes or frequently and were much more likely to use computer literature searches. It is impossible to determine, however, whether these findings were due to the seminars or merely reflected the basic library orientation of students who elected to attend.

Because of the limited population in this study, any conclusions must be tentative. Nevertheless, it is probably safe to assume that the publication sequence in psychology is highly variable and may be influenced by a number of characteristics, including the nature of the discipline and the "applied" or "theoretical" orientation of the researcher, as well as his or her publication history. Thus, the publication sequence model of bibliographic instruction should be used with considerable discretion and may be supplemented with other models, as suggested below. The continuing reliance on classic studies was rather surprising and indicates that older monographic literature must be stressed. One of the most revealing findings was the lack of library sophistication on the part of a carefully selected and intelligent body of students. Obviously, these students, who are required to write many papers as well as theses and dissertations, are not receiving sufficient instruction to guide them in collecting and evaluating literature, despite one teacher's cavalier assertion that students are "expected to be able to find everything." Improvement of this condition will require the collaboration of teaching faculty and librarians in bibliographic instruction.

Librarian-Psychology Faculty Collaboration

The first step in developing a successful bibliographic instruction program in psychology is establishing a good rapport with the faculty members for whom classes may be taught. This statement may appear self-evident but is often neglected. Due in part to time constraints, contacts between psychology instructors and librarians may often be limited to brief telephone conversations in which classes are scheduled. Often, psychology classes may be offered essentially "packaged" presentations with a few references to psychology sources brought in. For the many classes for which faculty members do not choose to schedule bibliographic instruction or are not aware of this option, students are expected to fend for themselves with no orientation or what little instruction the teachers may provide.

Outreach is necessary to rectify this situation and is probably most feasible in libraries that have a subject specialist in psychology. This person will probably be functioning as a liaison with the psychology department and may stress the availability and importance of bibliographic instruction in faculty meetings or in conversations with individual faculty members. Given an expression of interest on the part of a faculty member, the librarian may arrange a meeting to discuss the specifics of bibliographic instruction sessions.

These meetings will call for all the interpersonal skills that accomplished reference librarians use in interviewing patrons. While there are certainly misanthropic exceptions, most professors are attracted to psychology because of their interest in the interpersonal dimension and fascination for individual differences. A librarian with good communication skills will be most likely to convince the teacher of the importance of one or more library instruction sessions, possibly team-taught with the faculty member.

The librarian's respect for individual differences may be reflected in knowledge of the faculty member's research interests. A computer literature search may provide this information. Many colleges and universities also publish a newsletter in which faculty publications, presentations, and grants are listed. Basic knowledge of a teacher's research orientation may lead to a discussion of his or her approach to gathering and dissemination of information. The Garvey/Griffith model may serve as a framework for this discussion and may reflect variations representative of the individual or his/her subdiscipline.

The faculty member may be surprised at the notion that his or her students' information collection process should in certain particulars reflect that of the faculty mentor. Especially at a graduate level, however, many students plan a career in research and/or teaching and will appreciate assignments that are relevant to experiences they will probably have later in their careers. The librarian may perform a valuable service to both faculty and students by relating classwork to a broader context. At any rate, the librarian should elicit very clear information from faculty members as to their expectations for student work. Assignments that require evaluation of literature will elicit a different bibliographic instruction approach from those that require only a descriptive summary of existing literature on a topic.

Once the librarian has a clear idea of the faculty member's expectations, possible conceptual frameworks for bibliographic instruction may be discussed. The frameworks presented by Kobelski and Reichel may form a basis for the discussion. For many classes, especially undergraduate and graduate classes in research methods, a combination of systematic literature searching with publication sequence may be most useful. It may be pointed out that research for a class paper often proceeds in the reverse order in the publication sequence model. Thus, the student, especially one who is not familiar with a field, may begin with more integrative sources such as handbooks and encyclopedias, then proceed to look for monographs and journal articles. An important point to be made, however, is that the stage in the process in which to begin will relate to whether a topic is established or new. A student who is doing research on systematic desensitization, a well-established behavioral technique, will proceed quite differently from a student who is writing about therapy with children of alcoholics, a recent area of clinical interest. The former will be able fairly easily to identify entire books, as well as book chapters and articles. The latter may find little through the usual information-access tools, including *Psychological Abstracts*. Instead, the student may need to look for dissertations, conference papers, and publications of professional organizations not always readily accessible through standard bibliographic methods.

The publication sequence framework will often need to be combined with form of publication, especially in areas such as experimental psychology in which technical reports and government documents are particularly useful. *Psychological Documents*, which covers reports too lengthy to publish in journals, is of great importance in this area. NTIS publications may also be mentioned. The publication sequence discussed in experimental areas will relate more to that of the physical than the social sciences and will probably include the discussion of sources such as *Index Medicus* and *Science Citation Index*.

The frameworks related to primary/secondary sources and citation patterns may be especially useful in areas in which classic works exist. Pioneers such as Freud, Wundt, and Skinner continue to be cited; however, students may need to be made aware, through the use of sources such as *Social Sciences Citation Index*, that the citation pattern will vary over time and will be relative to the orientation of the citing researcher. A specialist in object relations, which developed directly out of a Freudian perspective, will, for example, be much more likely to cite Freud favorably than will a feminist psychotherapist. Both clinical and social psychology are areas in which citation patterns may be profitably explored. J. M. Innes has pointed out that social psychology is a creative area with a high degree of innovation in which researchers tend to follow fashion. The author indicates the differences in citation patterns for the literature on cognitive dissonance, which is steady over time, and on the risky shift in group dynamics, a topic of briefly intensive but not strong continuing research interest.[14]

These examples may present an idea of ways in which conceptual frameworks may be integrated into bibliographic instruction in psychology. The finding that psychology students, even at a graduate level, do not use literature according to a systematic pattern is somewhat ironic in the discipline that spawned cognitive learning theory. The lack of a systematic approach is, however, probably due to lack of instruction more than to choice of information-gathering method on the part of students. Personal experience indicates that both students and faculty members are highly appreciative if a framework for library orientation is introduced. This response may offset the difficulties of developing such a program in conjunction with teaching faculty.

Notes

[1]William D. Garvey and Belver C. Griffith, "Communication and Information Processing within Scientific Disciplines: Empirical Findings for Psychology," in *Communication: The Essence of Science*, ed. William D. Garvey (New York: Pergamon Press, 1979), 127-47.

[2]Howard Pikoff, *Workbook for Library Research in Psychology* (Bethesda, Md.: Educational Resources Information Center, 1978). ED 151 025.

[3]Brad H. Manning and Donna M. Buntain, *A Module for Training Library Researchers* (Bethesda, Md.: Educational Resources Information Center, 1976). ED 145 849; Judy McArthur and Pat Kenney, *Researching a Paper in the Library. A Programmed Text: Psychology Version* (Bethesda, Md.: Educational Resources Information Center, 1983). ED 244 646.

[4]Bobbie J. Pollard and Pauline M. Rothstein, *Fundamentals of Research in Industrial Psychology. Teacher's Notes, Transparencies, Bibliography, Exercises* (Bethesda, Md.: Educational Resources Information Center, 1981). ED 229 021.

[5]Arnold D. LeUnes, "The Developmental Psychology Library Search: Can a Nonsense Assignment Make Sense?" *Teaching of Psychology* 4 (April 1977): 86.

[6]James B. Mathews, " 'Hunting' for Psychological Literature: A Methodology for the Introductory Research Course," *Teaching of Psychology* 5 (April 1978): 100-101.

[7]Louis E. Gardner, "A Relatively Painless Method of Introduction to the Psychological Literature Search," *Teaching of Psychology* 4 (April 1977): 89-91.

[8]Pam M. Baxter, "The Benefits of In-Class Bibliographic Instruction," *Teaching of Psychology* 13 (February 1986): 40-41.

[9]Elizabeth Frick, "Teaching Information Structure: Turning Dependent Researchers into Self-Teachers," in *Theories of Bibliographic Education: Designs for Teaching*, ed. Cerise Oberman and Katina Strauch (New York: R. R. Bowker, 1982), 193-208.

[10]Pamela Kobelski and Mary Reichel, "Conceptual Frameworks for Bibliographic Instruction," *The Journal of Academic Librarianship* 7 (May 1981): 73-77.

[11]Garvey and Griffith, "Communication," 132-43.

[12]L. James Olivetti, "Utilizing Natural Structure of the Research Literature in Psychology as a Model for Bibliographic Instruction," *Behavioral & Social Sciences Librarian* 1 (Fall 1979): 43-46.

[13]Lyn Thaxton, "Dissemination and Use of Information by Psychology Faculty and Graduate Students: Implications for BI," *Research Strategies* 3 (Summer 1985): 116-24.

[14]J. M. Innes, "Psychology and the Scientist: XLV. Collaboration and Productivity in Social Psychology," *Psychological Reports* 47 (December 1980): 1331-34.

CHAPTER 7

SEARCH STRATEGY IN THE RESEARCH PROCESS
Sociology

Sandra K. Ready

Most reference librarians will agree that nearly all students will launch a research project without having narrowed or defined their topics sufficiently. Most students enter the library knowing they need "some information"; some have decided they need "some books" or "some articles"; few have a concrete idea what specific material they need or how to go about finding it.

The first step an intervening librarian will take in this situation is to discuss the problem at hand with the student, obtaining needed background information in order to be better prepared to make referrals to specific information sources. This questioning process may seem time consuming and tedious to the student, but analysis of the problem is essential if the librarian is to effectively "do the job."

While it would be unreasonable and undesirable to attempt to eliminate this librarian intervention entirely, we can assist students to become more independent and better prepared for their library research by helping them to understand and apply the concept of problem analysis to their research topics before actually launching their projects.

The Question Analysis

One method of illustrating this activity can be found in *Learning the Library: Concepts and Methods for Effective Bibliographic Instruction* by Anne K. Beaubien, Sharon A. Hogan, and Mary W. George. Their method divides the intellectual activity of question analysis into eight steps.

1. Surveying the topic and clarifying unfamiliar terms.

2. Breaking the topic into its simple subtopics.

3. Determining appropriate formats of primary and secondary materials necessary to research the topic.

4. Estimating the quantity of material needed.

5. Specifying the quality of authority of material needed.

6. Budgeting the time available to do the research.

7. Listing the relevant disciplines concerned with the topic.

8. Indicating the categories or types of reference tools that will help to identify and locate the necessary materials.[1]

For clarification, further information about each step in the process should be included.

1. Surveying the topic and clarifying unfamiliar terms.

    Assuming the researcher is not familiar with the topic and the terminology it involves, this step necessitates using specialized dictionaries, encyclopedias, and handbooks for insight into the topic.

2. Breaking the topic into its simple subtopics.

    Background insights gained in step one lead the researcher to see the topic from various perspectives. Isolating and noting the subtopics allows for selection of appropriate approaches to the topic and, perhaps, selection of one on which to focus the research effort.

3. Determining appropriate formats of primary and secondary materials necessary to research the topic.

    Step three focuses on determining the physical materials which will provide the needed information. This is essentially predicting whether books, audiovisual materials, periodical articles, etc., will be the most useful sources for consultation. Also included in this step is prioritizing the formats so that the most useful sources will be consulted first and the least useful last, if at all.

4. Estimating the quantity of material needed.

    This step is basically making a "guesstimate" of the number of books, articles, etc., which will be needed to complete the research project. Are only a few articles for a brief paper needed, or is an extensive bibliography for a senior thesis being compiled? The quantity of materials goes hand in hand with the formats considered in step three since the quantity should be considered for each format.

5. Specifying the quality of authority of material needed.

    Quality of authority refers to the authority of the source material. Should the information come from scholarly journals, or will popular periodicals suffice? Is the author a recognized authority or a "crackpot"? Consideration of quality of authority has impact later on reference tool selection.

6. Budgeting the time available to do the research.

Since undergraduates tend to delay their research until the last possible minute, it is crucial that they understand the importance of allowing enough time for the information gathering process. Beginning early enables the researcher to take full advantage of interlibrary sharing systems when necessary. In addition, adequate preparation time will allow for appropriate revisions and eliminate the need for the inevitable all-night typing sessions.

7. Listing the relevant disciplines concerned with the topic.

This step may be challenging for most undergraduates, since they usually have difficulty examining a topic from any perspective other than the most obvious one. However, since nearly all topics are somewhat interdisciplinary, the various contributing fields should be considered and articulated. This consideration has a major impact on the final step in the question, tool selection, since without insight into topic related disciplines, appropriate research tools cannot be identified.

8. Indicating the categories or types of reference tools that will help to identify and locate the necessary materials.

The final step in the question analysis is the listing of specific tools to be used for identification of information resources. Consideration of quality of authority needed and contributing disciplines allows the researcher to make appropriate choices and to avoid wasting valuable time looking in unproductive sources.

The order of completion for the steps in the question analysis can be varied as needed based on the topic researched; and, with the exception of step one, the steps can be completed without ever entering the library. Completion of the process will lead the researcher to planning an effective search strategy with which to launch the research project.[2]

Planning the Search Strategy

Once the question analysis is completed, the next logical step in the research process is the development of the search strategy. A search strategy can be defined as a "conceptual framework for logically organizing use of the library."[3] A variety of methods may be used to illustrate this process for students. Flow charts and lists of specific steps can be found throughout the literature.[4] While no one method has been identified as "best," it is generally agreed that the articulation of the plan for library use allows for more efficient and effective use of time.

The choice of strategy is dependent on the disciplines related to the topic and the methods of communication used within those disciplines. Understanding the history of the specific discipline—how it grew from its beginnings to its current status—and the communication vehicles used at each stage of growth will enable the student researcher to identify appropriate information resources to "plug into" the strategy at each step.[5]

The importance of this activity is that it gives students an organized plan to follow. Combining the question analysis and the articulation of a specific search strategy will give researchers the self-confidence they are usually lacking at the start of a new project.

Growth of the Discipline: Sociology

According to Thelma Freides in *Literature and Bibliography of the Social Sciences*, "the aim of science is to account for what goes on—to explain.... Science does not consist ... of a collection of facts. Rather, science uses facts to suggest and support explanations."[6] Generally, "scholars are concerned with satisfying their own particular research needs"[7] while researchers are concerned with collection of facts and explanations to further support new theories. Beaubien, Hogan, and George assert that "if one understands the nature of a discipline, its age, and its stage of development, one can predict the ... bibliographic structure available in that field."[8] Knowledge of a discipline and its bibliographic structure enables one to construct an effective search strategy in that discipline.[9]

Beaubien, Hogan, and George use Michael Keresztesi's model for defining the growth of a discipline.[10] Essentially, the stages are defined as follows:

1. Pioneering

    —Single "great thinker" or small group with similar interests
    —Data/idea generation
    Source material: minutes, letters, pamphlets, articles
    Tools: indexes, bibliographies

2. Elaboration

    —More followers and contribution
    —New terminology
    —Founders recognized
    Source material: collections of essays, memoirs, journals
    Tools: journal reviews

3. Proliferation

    —Worldwide spread of interest
    —Undergraduate major
    —Conferences
    —Methodology established
    Source material: proceedings, annual reports, books
    Tools: guides, handbooks, encyclopedias

4. Establishment

    —Academic departments set up
    —Doctorates awarded
    —Specialized publishers
    Source material: dissertations, government publication
    Tools: special encyclopedias, bibliography of dissertations

Using this system we can analyze the growth of sociology, thus gaining insight into the source materials appropriate for research within the discipline.[11]

Stage 1:   Pioneering (early nineteenth century)

Stage 2:   Elaboration (late nineteenth-early twentieth century)

Stage 3:   Proliferation (1910-1940)

Stage 4:   Establishment (1941-)

Search Strategy for Sociology

Since sociology is a relatively young discipline, researchers should tend to rely heavily on current information. Library sources for this current material would include journal materials, annual reviews, and bibliographies. A strategy for following the most current to least current thought on a sociological topic could be shown using the following list.

Steps in sociological research:

1.   Define and clarify topic.

2.   Identify journal articles.

3.   Review current thought.

4.   Support hypothesis of current thought.

5.   Examine distillation of thought.

6.   Verify validity of sources.

In addition to being familiar with the logical steps to be taken in sociological research, students must also understand which types of referencing tools will be appropriate for use at each phase of their projects. To enhance the search strategy for sociology, types of reference tools should be added.

Step	Tools
1. Define and clarify topic.	Dictionaries, encyclopedias, handbooks
2. Identify journal articles.	Indexes, abstracts
3. Review current thought.	Annual reviews
4. Support hypothesis of current thought.	Bibliographies
5. Examine distillation of thought.	Card or online catalog
6. Verify validity of sources.	Citation indexing

Resources for Sociology

In addition to being familiar with the types of tools used at each phase of the search strategy, students of sociology also need some knowledge of specific sources which may be "plugged in" at each step. This knowledge will allow them to proceed independently through the process. The following are suggested titles which may be used as resources. However, since sociology can be divided into numerous subdisciplines, librarians should consult the American Library Association's *Guide to Reference Books* for information about specialized tools which may be more relevant to a specific subdiscipline.

DICTIONARIES

Gould, Julius, and William Kolb, eds. *A Dictionary of the Social Sciences*. New York: Free Press, 1964.
   Includes terms from political science, social anthropology, social psychology, and sociology. Terms whose meanings have been adequately described in standard dictionaries are omitted. Contains discussion of controversies or divergencies of meanings.

Theodorson, George A., and Achilles G. Theodorson. *A Modern Dictionary of Sociology*. New York: Crowell, 1969.
   Provides brief definitions for students, general readers, and professionals in related fields.

ENCYCLOPEDIAS

Encyclopedia of Sociology. Guilford, Conn.: Dushkin Publishing Group, 1974.
   Includes brief definitions or descriptions of sociological concepts.

Seligman, E. R. A., ed.-in-chief. *Encyclopedia of the Social Sciences*. New York: Macmillan, 1930-1935.
   The first comprehensive encyclopedia of the social sciences. Aims to cover all important topics of the era.

Sills, David L., ed. *International Encyclopedia of the Social Sciences*. New York: Free Press/Macmillan, 1968.
   Complements the *Encyclopedia of the Social Sciences*. Represents sociology of the 1960s.

HANDBOOKS

Bart, Pauline, and Linda Frankel. *The Student Sociologist's Handbook*. Morristown, N.J.: General Learning Press, 1976.
   Brief notes on the study of sociology.

Inge, M. Thomas, ed. *Handbook of American Popular Culture*. Westport, Conn.: Greenwood Press, 1978-1980.
Discussion of various aspects of past and present American culture.

Mohan, Raj P., and Don Martindale. *Handbook of Contemporary Developments in World Sociology*. Westport, Conn.: Greenwood Press, 1975.
Includes discussions of historical and intellectual background of the discipline.

INDEXES AND ABSTRACTS

Abstracts for Social Workers. Albany, N.Y.: National Association of Social Workers, 1965- .
Offers abstracts and articles in the field of social work and related areas. Superseded by *Social Work Research and Abstracts*.

Criminal Justice Periodical Index. Ann Arbor, Mich.: Indexing Services, University Microfilms, 1975- .
Indexes areas of police administration, corrections, juvenile delinquency, criminal law, and security.

Social Sciences Index. New York: H. W. Wilson, 1974- .
Author and subject index to journals in the fields of anthropology, area studies, economics, environmental science, geography, law and criminology, medical sciences, political science, psychology, and sociology. Covers over 250 journals. Supersedes *Social Sciences and Humanities Index*.

Sociological Abstracts. New York: Sociological Abstracts, 1952- .
Cosponsored by the American Sociological Association, Eastern Sociological Association, International Sociological Association, and Midwest Sociological Society. Indexes professional and scholarly journals on an international basis.

ANNUALS

Criminology Review Yearbook. Beverly Hills, Calif.: Sage Publications, 1979-
Discusses a wide variety of topics crossing all aspects of social science.

Sociological Methodology. San Francisco: Jossey-Bass, 1969- .
Cosponsored by the American Sociological Association. Gives current research theory and guidance on specific topics.

BIBLIOGRAPHIES

C.R.I.S. (Combined Retrospective Index Set to Journals in Sociology) 1895-1974. Washington, D.C.: Carrollton Press, 1978.
Some 137 subject categories with data and keyword indexes. Six volumes including one for author access.

International Bibliography of Sociology. Chicago: Aldine, 1952- .
A classified listing of books, pamphlets, periodical articles, and government publications indexed by author and subject.

CITATION INDEXES

Social Sciences Citation Index. Philadelphia, Pa.: Institute for Scientific Information, 1973- .
Indicates sources in which a known work by a given author has been cited. Subject searches may be conducted through the "Permuterm" index.

Presenting the Search Strategy

Librarians involved with bibliographic instruction are no doubt aware that there are a variety of modes available for presentation of information. Self-instructionals, point-of-use materials, and lectures have been used effectively. Of these, only the classroom lecture mode is appropriate for presentation of the question analysis/search strategy. Since this process is complex, it requires a clear explanation, both of the growth of the discipline and its application to the search strategy.

This conceptual framework lends itself well to one-hour single lectures and can be easily adapted to course related and course integrated instruction. It also serves as an excellent outline around which a course could be developed.

THE ONE-HOUR LECTURE

The one-hour lecture is more accurately called the "one-shot." The librarian has only one opportunity to meet with the group. The time available is typically fifty to sixty minutes, but may be longer or shorter, depending on the specific situation. Since the librarian has no opportunity for follow-up, the lecture must be carefully planned so that each minute of time is well used. In a one-shot lecture, it is possible to present the question analysis step by step and discuss how it relates to the search strategy. The strategy for sociological research can be explained and appropriate tools suggested for each phase of the strategy. However, since this is a tightly packed hour, little time is available for questions or discussion.

A one-shot lecture incorporating the question analysis and the search strategy for sociology might be organized using the following outline.

1. Introduction—fifteen minutes.

   Explain steps in question analysis and search strategy.

2. Growth of the discipline—fifteen minutes.

   Present overview of history of sociology.

3. Steps in sociological research — twenty minutes.

    Cite examples of specific tools to be used at each step in the search strategy.

COURSE RELATED INSTRUCTION

When the instruction is expanded beyond the single one-shot encounter, the librarian has the opportunity to present an exercise by which the students apply the theoretical concepts from the lecture to an actual research situation. Students are given a topic related to the course and then work individually or in groups, using suggested tools to identify appropriate source material which might be used for the hypothetical research project. This controlled experience encourages questions and interaction between students and librarian and allows clarification of difficult areas. (See figure 7.1 for a sample exercise.)

Topic: _____

Work through the steps in sociological research using the topic assigned above. Use the sources suggested at each step to prepare your answers.

Step	Suggested Sources
1. Define and clarify topic	*A Modern Dictionary of Sociology* *Encyclopedia of the Social Sciences*
2. Identify journal articles	*Social Sciences Index* *Sociological Abstracts* *Abstracts for Social Workers*
3. Review current thought	*Criminology Review Yearbook* *Sociological Methodology*
4. Support hypothesis of current thought	*C.R.I.S.* *International Bibliography of Sociology*
5. Examine distillation of thought	catalog
6. Verify validity of sources	*Social Sciences Citation Index*

Complete this exercise within one week. Be prepared to discuss your experience and ask questions.

Fig. 7.1. Sociological research assignment.

COURSE INTEGRATED INSTRUCTION
AND COURSES

In course integrated instruction and library research courses (often called "the literature of ..."), the librarian has the opportunity to work with the faculty member from the discipline to design specific exercises or assignments which apply the theoretical concepts from the question analysis/search strategy to real research topics. Ideally, these exercises would culminate in an assigned paper or project. Each exercise would lead the students through one step in the process. This expanded experience allows for more in-depth discussion of the growth of the discipline, communication systems common among practitioners, and specific source tools appropriate to the literature of the discipline. (See figure 7.2 for a sample assignment.)

Your assignment is to compile a 500-word, typed paper on a topic of your choice. The topic must be approved by your instructor (due one week from today). Upon approval of the topic, work through the steps in Sociological Research, listing *at least two* sources you will use at each step of the process (due three weeks from today). The term paper will be due one week prior to final exam week.

Topic approval due _____

Steps in Sociological Research due _____

Term paper due _____

Feel free to consult with the librarians for advice on sources for the project, footnote and bibliography format, or for other assistance you may need with the project.

Fig. 7.2. Term paper assignment.

Conclusion

Sociological research can be taught effectively using the question analysis/ search strategy approach. Explanation of the historical growth of the discipline combined with discussion of appropriate source tools will give students a logical, organized method of approaching their research assignments. This systematic method also can be applied to other disciplines and provides a workable conceptual framework for information retrieval in general.

Notes

[1]Anne K. Beaubien, Sharon A. Hogan, and Mary W. George, *Learning the Library: Concepts and Methods for Bibliographic Instruction* (New York: R. R. Bowker, 1982), 75.

[2]Ibid., 76-83.

[3]Thomas Kirk, "A Comparison of Two Methods of Library Instruction for Students in Introductory Biology," *College and Research Libraries* 32 (November 1971): 90.

[4]For specific illustration of search strategy techniques, see Jacquelyn M. Morris and Elizabeth A. Elkins's *Library Searching: Resources and Strategies* (New York: Jeffrey Norton, 1978), 8-9, and Virginia Frank and Elaine Trzebiatowski's "Designing Search Strategies: An Approach to Library Instruction," *Illinois Libraries* 63 (October 1981): 573-77.

[5]Beaubien, Hogan, and George, *Learning the Library*, 95-102.

[6]Thelma Freides, *Literature and Bibliography of the Social Sciences* (Los Angeles, Calif.: Melville Publishing, 1973), 5.

[7]Beaubien, Hogan, and George, *Learning the Library*, 95.

[8]Ibid.

[9]Ibid.

[10]Ibid., 97-107.

[11]Asa S. Knowles, ed., *The International Encyclopedia of Higher Education* (Washington, D.C.: Jossey-Bass, 1977), 3864-68.

CHAPTER 8

BIBLIOGRAPHIC INSTRUCTION IN WOMEN'S STUDIES
From the Grassroots to the Ivory Tower

Ellen Broidy

In order for a scientific or scholarly discipline to be productive, it must gain society's approval. This approval is symbolically granted when the discipline is embraced by the university. There is no bona fide scientific or scholarly discipline in the United States today outside the university.

Michael Keresztesi[1]

Scholarly institutions, most commonly colleges or universities, divide intellectual activity into comparatively neat units labeled "academic disciplines." As Michael Keresztesi and others have pointed out, the university not only provides an intellectual home, a base, for these well-defined academic and scholarly enterprises but, beyond that, the university dispenses approval of and legitimation to them. Moreover, the university tends to foster an atmosphere that encourages and rewards standardization of theories and methodologies that, in turn, help reinforce the neat categories.

This chapter explores one approach to research methods in a discipline only recently, and somewhat reluctantly, "embraced" by the academy—women's studies. Two salient features of women's studies make research in this field both challenging and uniquely rewarding. The first is that the legitimation and approval the university provides share the stage with legitimation coming from a completely different source—a grassroots political movement, women's liberation or the feminist movement. Taken together, these dual sources of legitimation pose positive challenges to established structures within the academy, but also create difficulties for the researcher attempting to fully "control" the literature of the discipline.

The second noteworthy feature is that women's studies, as an academic undertaking, is not "neat." It is, by design and necessity, highly interdisciplinary. As such, it requires creativity, vision, and a heightened degree of persistence and perseverance on the part of the researcher.

The interrelationship between the political and social movement and the academic discipline, coupled with the demands of interdisciplinary research, offers compelling arguments for the necessity of developing a conceptual framework to aid bibliographic education in women's studies. What follows is, in part, an outline of a presentation based on one such conceptual framework, the model of "development of a discipline" first articulated by Keresztesi. But this paper attempts to do more than fit (or force) women's studies into this existing framework. Woven in and out of the discussion of a possible classroom session is an examination of the role of library instruction within women's studies, calling attention both to the academic and political nature of the enterprise.

Development of a Discipline:
Initial Steps

Women's studies, viewed within a traditional academic context, presents a good example of a discipline moving through Keresztesi's four developmental stages: pioneering, in which the initial seeds of the discipline are planted, usually by an individual or small group of individuals stepping out of the academic mainstream; elaboration, marked by a slow but steady increase in activity and interest; proliferation, at which point the discipline can be said to be truly standing on its own, gathering both a scholarly and student following (advent of majors and programs); and finally, establishment, with all the trappings of a long-standing position in the academy (chairs, foundation funding, consultants, etc.).

As an introduction to library based research on women, Keresztesi's model helps students conceptualize growth and change that occur within academic disciplines. In a sense, the model anthropomorphizes the disciplines as it provides a "family tree" upon which to trace the maturation (or, in some cases, the aging or fossilization) process. It is a particularly useful illustrative device for women's studies, provided that the philosophy and content of the discipline drive the model rather than being forced to slavishly follow it for the sake of the classroom session.

The decision to use Keresztesi's model as an organizing principle for describing research methods in women's studies requires a commitment to flexibility both in terms of the model itself and how it is presented to a group of students. For example, although it is difficult, and ultimately undesirable, to ignore the imbalance in technical expertise between a professional librarian and a class of novice researchers, the library instruction session is more productive if the librarian adheres to some basic philosophical tenets of the women's movement. One tenet, the value of shared learning and shared experience, is particularly relevant. In as much as women's studies strives both to correct the historical record as well as to amplify the accumulating body of human knowledge, each participant in the living and learning experience is contributing his or her own life to the available store of data. Students as well as faculty and librarians are sharing perceptions and experiences, and thereby changing the information and data at hand. The class should be encouraged to take the traditional model of development of a discipline and examine it in terms of the discipline's relevance to women's daily lives and experience as well as in terms of traditional academic and library materials.

One cautionary note worth mentioning at the outset is that a library research session in women's studies should be as course integrated as time and faculty will permit. A research session, falling too close to the beginning of the term, may prove frustrating and ultimately scholastically counterproductive. In order for the development of a discipline model to be effective, students need some basic awareness of the subject matter. With respect to women's studies and the desire to have an exchange of ideas not simply a monologue, students settled into the course and with some background information (even rudimentary facts) are much more apt to contribute.

Another "danger" occasionally encountered in women's studies classes is the tendency to overemphasize the personal while neglecting the academic. One way to guard against these possible hazards is to schedule the bibliographic instruction session towards the middle of the term. The ideal time for the research class is right at the point at which students are expected to select a paper topic. The more ambitious students may already have experienced some of the difficulties inherent in researching information on women, while the entire class should have some basic feel for the subject matter.

One way to begin the library instruction session is to outline Keresztesi's stages and activities. Use the chalkboard or a large piece of paper to do this. The exercise is most productive when it is collective, with each student helping to outline the "picture" of the developing and evolving discipline. Borrowing a pedogogical strategy from elementary school, it is helpful to provide each student with a blank outline. In that way precious time is not lost while the class scurries to label stages and activities. Although the maintenance of the "public record" is a crucial element of the librarian's presentation, supplying the preformatted sheets to the class is one way to ensure that students both take notes that will be helpful to them later and contribute to the session.

Figure 8.1 represents the first of two slightly modified versions of Keresztesi's chart. The changes in this version are quite minor, designed mainly to remind the class of the dual foundations of the discipline by adding the term "activists" to the communication column, and to free the chart from some of the library based jargon of the original.

Stage	Activities	Communication between scholars, activists, other thinkers	Sources of information	Library research aids
Pioneering				
Elaboration				
Proliferation				
Establishment				

Fig. 8.1. Initial discipline development model.

Rather than asking the students to define each phase, or attempt to come up with the appropriate vocabulary for activities, communication patterns, sources, and research aids, start the session off by letting the students tell you what they do know rather than struggle to identify what they do not. The librarian's role here is gently to remind students of the information (facts) central to their study. For example, this chart might be used in an introductory women's studies class that emphasizes feminist theory. If the timing of the presentation is right, the students should have been exposed, through reading and discussion, to a number of seminal thinkers/theorists. The librarian starts the discussion off by defining the activities marking the primary stage of development (single great thinker or group of thinkers moving away from the mainstream). Definition in hand, the students should be able to come up with names of feminist theorists encountered in their reading or class discussions. In an effort to incorporate the grassroots, or less traditionally academic contributions, students might be encouraged to consider women whose ideas and work have influenced their own lives.

In some instances, a discussion of the pioneering stage may make up the entire content of the session. However, if the names suggested as representing pioneering great thinkers are as chronologically (or intellectually) diverse as Betty Friedan, Germaine Greer, Simone de Beauvoir, or Juliet Mitchell, the librarian has an opportunity to change the direction of the lecture. Rather than adhering to an orthodox presentation of the development of a discipline model, the class may instead jump to a rather more sophisticated examination of the need to analyze proposed topics in terms of time (chronology) and place (both geographic as well as hierarchial).

Should the choice be to remain within the boundaries of a fairly traditional discussion of discipline development covering all four stages, it is possible to look at women's studies solely as the product of academic discourse. Within each of the four stages, activities may be identified which mirror those undertaken by other disciplines. This rather conservative approach tends to serve a purpose quite distinct from imparting knowledge about the generation of information and its attendant bibliographic control. The conservative approach, or making the subject fit the model, works to legitimate women's studies within the structures and strictures of university-bound academic discourse. Communication and cooperation between the library and the instructor are crucial in women's studies; if tradition and orthodoxy drive the syllabus, the library session can accommodate that.

Expanding the Model

If, on the other hand, the instructor is inclined to travel beyond institutional boundaries and embrace the concept of the dual foundations of women's studies, the library instruction session may serve that end as well (probably better). As the librarian begins to guide the class through the four stages, from pioneering to establishment, further refinement of the allowable categories in the model will enrich the discussion. One useful approach to modifying the chart is to divide all the activities (communication method, finding aids) into "academic" and "grassroots" (or "movement," depending on the tenor of the times and the class). Examples of this division may be brought to light by creating a brief list of topics that fall under each. For academic women's studies, subjects such as women's history, feminist literary criticism, or feminist theory might be listed. Grassroots examples might include such topics as the women's peace movement, popular culture as mirrored in *Cosmopolitan* or Harlequin Romances, or national political action undertaken by groups like the National Women's Political Caucus.

Although in terms of research these distinctions often fail to hold up under close scrutiny, they are instructive in the initial stages of inquiry. The divisions help underscore how information is generated and transferred in different arenas. The divisions, artificial as they may seem, also highlight research as a dynamic process demanding creativity in identification of sources and flexibility in tapping those sources. In other words, expanding the allowable categories to include academic and grassroots invites a discussion of search strategy.

In conjunction with the separation of the categories into academic and grassroots, an additional augmentation to the chart might be the introduction of the concept of audience, or more precisely, intended audience, to the communication column. In this way sources of information such as newsletters, broadsides, or manifestos, particularly important in both the early days of women's studies as well as throughout the activist women's movement, can be introduced without stumbling over esoteric concepts such as ephemera. Mention of these types of material leads naturally into a discussion of "bibliographic control," by fostering an awareness of formats that are at once vital and hard to control. The class thus gains an awareness of some of the difficulties inherent in tracking this material and, at the same time, a recognition of its importance.

The new chart might look something like figure 8.2.

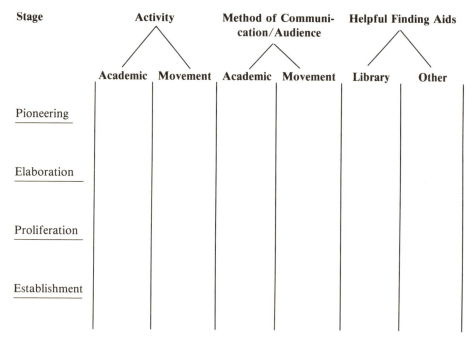

Fig. 8.2. Expanded discipline development model.

Information Sharing in the
Broadest Sense

Women's studies, even adorned in all the trappings of orthodox scholarship, remains a guerrilla endeavor in most academic settings. The new, almost experimental nature of the discipline allows both instructor and librarian to break out of established forms and to define and share information in its broadest sense. Development of a discipline permits this elasticity of definition and creates the space to share vital information. For example, in the standard model, an important feature of the proliferation stage is the appearance on the academic scene of departments, programs, and majors dedicated to the subject under consideration. In terms of women's studies, the library session is the ideal opportunity to introduce those sources, directories, catalogs, etc., that describe the various programs "proliferating" throughout academia. Some titles or sources to consider at this point are: *Everywoman's Guide to Colleges and Universities* (Feminist Press, 1982), *Who's Who and Where in Women's Studies* (Feminist Press, 1984), and the annual listing of women's studies programs in the United States that appears in *Women Studies Quarterly*. While this may seem totally unorthodox in a formal classroom setting, the librarian in a women's studies class is in an ideal position to help break down isolation amongst present and future women's studies scholars (another important developmental activity), and to facilitate communication of information, both academic and practical.

Librarians and faculty involved in women's studies must be cognizant of the fact that many students, even those at the graduate level, are approaching this material for the first time in a systematic manner. But unlike students "experimenting" with courses outside their major or enrolling in classes designed to fulfill a degree requirement, women's studies tends to attract students more personally involved with the subject, though not necessarily more knowledgeable about it. The instructor's role is to harness (and help sustain) that initial personal interest and enthusiasm by lighting the way through a maze of concepts, theories, and facts, many of which challenge accepted patterns and cultural norms. The librarian's task is to illuminate another kind of intellectual darkness. The library has long been viewed as a bastion of male learning, the veritable cornerstone of "men's studies" within the university. The librarian's job, whether in the classroom or at the reference desk, is to break down that perception and make information on women accessible, even in the most inhospitable environments.

Political Nature of Women's Studies
Bibliographic Instruction

Women's studies is a highly political undertaking. Librarians play neither a neutral nor apolitical role within the context of a women's studies class. In some respects, the librarian's position is the more obviously political as he or she challenges and encourages others to challenge the exclusion of women from the controllable written record. A major virtue of using discipline development as an organizing principle emerges when, as it draws attention to the dual foundations of women's studies (using the modified chart in figure 8.2), it reveals a tension between "acceptable" scholarship and popular culture generally absent from other academic disciplines. Librarians can play on that tension in several ways. In the first place, it illustrates the isolation many women's studies scholars feel when their work is deemed to be less worthwhile because the subject matter, women, is determined to be outside the pale of serious scholarship. On a level more immediate to the library/research enterprise, the librarian can use that tension to illustrate the many "shapes, sizes, and packages" of information in which scholars of women must search for useful and usable material.

A bibliographic instruction session on research in women's studies should accomplish several ends. The first is obvious: students assigned research papers or projects need the intellectual strategies and knowledge of specific sources to collect and analyze the necessary information and data. Another goal of equal importance, though less immediately apparent, is the flip side of the first. The first goal stresses finding information, while the second provides an object lesson in the difficulty of finding information. These difficulties can often be traced to historical patterns within institutionalized scholarship and within institutions such as libraries. An analysis of the reasons information is hard to locate may be as vital to the education/research process as a discussion of the sources to use to track that information.

Once the stage has been set for looking at library research on women as both a traditional academic endeavor and a scavenger hunt through a grassroots move-ment, the next step moves beyond the development model and tackles actual sources. The ensuing discussion of "primary" and "secondary" sources has a twist; it should be framed both to offer working definitions for each type of source, but also to investigate scholarly and institutional inclusion and exclusion. Why are some facts easier to come by than others? Are some more valid or more important? Do societal norms incorporate some and exclude others?

Introducing the Concepts of Primary and Secondary

In an effort to avoid library based (or biased) jargon, the introduction to the concepts of primary and secondary materials might be accomplished by asking students to consider their own experience with sources of information. The object here is to make the unfamiliar familiar, (to "demystify," another tenet of feminism) by suggesting that research concepts can be understood in terms of daily activities. In many ways, teaching research methods is no more than helping students assign some logical and systematic order to relatively ordinary actions or events. Examples that draw on the commonplace, such as reading the morning paper, watching the evening news, or consulting a textbook or journal article, help students reframe these activities in terms of the research concepts we seek to introduce. One or two examples, illustrative definitions if you will, such as the report of an event in the daily paper and the subsequent analysis of that event in a journal article, bring the idea of primary and secondary to life. With a bit of prompting, students can usually come up with dozens of other examples.

Primary sources ranging from diaries, manuscripts, and interviews to quilts, furniture, and photographs offer some idea of the variety of packages in which unique and valuable information may be found. Librarians, along with faculty and students, are often amazed at the range of information options that a group will suggest, and the sheer number actually available in, or traceable through, some type of standard library source. The list of secondary sources may not be as colorful, but should also serve to expand the definition of acceptable research material.

Researching "Academic" and "Popular" Topics

Once having arrived at workable definitions and illustrations of primary and secondary sources, the next step is to lead the class through a structured exercise using two topics, one academic, the other popular. The object here is twofold: to illustrate differences in how information is generated, transferred, and accessed in an academic setting and in the "real world," and to reinforce the use of primary and secondary sources in research.

As an example, the scholarly topic might be feminist literary criticism, a subject currently in vogue in a number of institutions. The popular subject might be women's presence in the antinuclear and peace movements. Both are reasonable research topics and each lends itself to an argumentative paper, the perennial undergraduate favorite. But more to the point of the conceptual lecture, each topic reveals the different strategies necessary for successful research. In addition, each topic illustrates as much about information hidden or distorted as it does about data easily identified or acquired.

The first topic, feminist literary criticism, illustrates the development of a discipline model particularly well. Not only is it "traceable" through its own historical development, but the genesis of the discipline, the merging of women's studies (literature) with critical theory, reveals a unique feature of the establishment phase, "twigging" (the merging of one discipline with another to form a unique discipline). An additional useful dimension to feminist literary criticism is that, although it is an undeniably academic undertaking, the "texts" used as the basis for analysis are often examples of popular culture (paperback romances or current cinema). As a topic for investigation, feminist literary criticism requires the researcher to look both at primary sources—the text itself (novel, poem, play, film)—and secondary sources—the critical analysis of the text. Without splitting hairs too finely, the librarian might also suggest that the critical work itself, particularly if it is the work of an established scholar, may also be considered a primary source. The chain is endless. In this subject, the student deals with material that is, by and large, accessible, controllable through standard bibliographic sources, and part of the written body of work traditionally found in a library (although many academic librarians may blanche at the thought of adding Harlequin Romances and *Vogue* to the collection).

The second example, women's involvement in the antinuclear and peace movements, might also be considered part of a newly emerging academic discipline—peace studies—but for the purposes of this exercise will be considered a grassroots rather than academic phenomenon. The documentary evidence or data on this topic, as well as many of the secondary sources, fall outside typical library collecting patterns and are therefore harder to characterize and capture. Pamphlets, interviews, and artifacts are essential sources of information only sporadically caught in the bibliographic net. Communication tends to be personal, among participants (women), focusing on topics considered marginal to academic discourse.

Such topics, falling as they do outside of traditional scholarly arenas, demand creativity on the part of both the student researcher and the librarian guiding the bibliographic inquiry. Librarians, almost by definition, are bound to the tools and sources of their trade—materials found in a library. The challenge comes in presenting the same generic sources as ways to satisfy the research demands of very different topics.

Analyzing Standard
Bibliographic Sources

The most difficult part of a bibliographic instruction session based loosely on the model of discipline development comes at the moment when tools rather than concepts take center stage. In a women's studies class this may result in an abrupt change from a lively interaction between librarian and student to the dry recitation of catalogs, bibliographies, and indexes. One option is to interweave specific titles throughout the discussion. This has the benefit of preventing the abrupt change of tone, but also detracts from the theoretical or conceptual content (and intent) of the discussion. Another option for enlivening that tedious yet necessary portion of the class is to present each source as a cultural artifact. This entails describing, along with the mechanics of how the source is used, the political dimensions of the material included in it and the material excluded from it. Moreover, each source should be examined in light of the dual foundations of women's studies, with concrete suggestions on how best to capture elusive and seemingly ignored information.

One essential source, the *Library of Congress Subject Headings* (*LCSH*), provides marvelous illustrations of the marginalization of women in the library research setting. Headings such as "women as astronauts" or "women as consumers," with their accompanying *see* and *see also* references, offer an excellent introduction to the world of controlled vocabularies as well as clear evidence of the separation of women from the intellectual (cultural, social, economic, etc.) mainstream. The library is revealed to be more than a passive storehouse of information in the form of books and journals. As a social institution it takes on new meaning as a gatekeeper of culture and learning. It soon becomes clear that libraries play a central role in the social and institutional construction of reality.

The preceding, somewhat negative portrait of the library becomes particularly germane when faced with students new to women's studies, who may be attracted to topics falling at the more popular end of the research spectrum. Standard library finding sources must be examined for their possible unorthodox uses. In describing a particular source, pay careful attention to indexing terms and to the list of journals covered. Librarians may need to reacquaint themselves with less frequently used finding aids and come to terms with the necessity of describing a citation index in language meaningful to an undergraduate. Given difficulties in language, and the sexism manifest in sources like the *LCSH*, a permuted subject index becomes one of the more flexible, and therefore necessary, access points.

Since a lengthy recitation of titles is (or should be) anathema to a "conceptual" lecture, the choice of sources described is crucial. A bibliographic instruction session that aims to provide a conceptual framework still must include some basic information about actual library use. The librarian's role as information intermediary is especially significant at this juncture as students tend to interpret the mention of a title, used as an example or illustration, as a firm endorsement of its value and its usefulness in all cases. Keeping such student inclinations in mind, it does not suffice simply to introduce the *Social Sciences Index* or INFOTRAC, while ignoring the *Alternative Press Index*.

Equally important is a critical analysis of the standard tools highlighted, particularly in terms of their indexing practices. Indexes tied to the *LCSH do not* reflect current trends in feminist scholarship, nor is it always apparent under what heading more popular information about women may be listed. Useful information is often masked by outdated terminology. Clearly, language is one area in which the development of a discipline model fails to hold true for women's studies. In more traditional disciplines, remedying the disjuncture between the language of the discipline and the language of bibliographic access occurs at a fairly early stage. Women's studies still lacks a universally agreed upon thesaurus, and controlled vocabularies such as the *LCSH* create more gaps than they fill.

The desire to be scholarly, in a rigid sense, occasionally blinds us to the usefulness of some of the most common sources in a reference department. Sources such as telephone books, organization directories, and faculty lists may provide access to the groups and individuals who are the best, and often the only, sources of information on subjects as diverse as battered women's shelters or feminist performance art. For the student selecting a topic falling outside the traditional academic realm, information about these everyday tools becomes crucial. At least a portion of the bibliographic instruction session should focus on identifying these sources and reminding students (and ourselves) of their potential value.

Conclusion

Ideally, when using development of a discipline as an organizing principle, each library finding source will correspond to a developmental stage in the model, an activity, and a form of communication. But the universe is rarely so neatly ordered. In the evolving world of women's studies, at the point when activities and stages seem to fit most closely, a new trend, theory, or movement emerges and the model is thrown off. The librarian's ultimate challenge in the instruction session is to acknowledge the difficulties inherent in embarking upon research and study in a dynamic (one might say explosive) field without appearing to be discouraging potential scholars away from the field. It is wise to remember, whatever the theoretical framework, that these are models or guidelines, not immutable rules or regulations, for either the structure of information or the presentation of a class.

Students in women's studies tend to present an interesting paradox. On the one hand they often exhibit a degree of enthusiasm and commitment rarely found in college classrooms (or anywhere else, for that matter). However, the down side of the paradox is that this enthusiasm frequently masks, for lack of a better term, profound ignorance about the subjects they select for papers and projects. A library instruction session in women's studies may well make the difference between success and failure in the research enterprise.

In the long term, information that the instruction librarian shares with women's studies students, particularly entry-level students, may help shape the future of women's studies as an academic discipline. On a more personal level, it may well alter the course of student's individual lives, whether or not they pursue women's studies throughout their academic career. Students have a well-developed sense that information about 51 percent of the population must be out there somewhere; finding or being introduced to ways to actually locate that information, in spite of social, cultural, and institutional barriers, gives them a new sense of power. Nowhere does the phrase "knowledge is power" ring more true than in a women's studies class. And nowhere is it so graphically illustrated than in a bibliographic instruction session in this dynamic, developing discipline.

Notes

[1]Michael Keresztesi, "The Science of Bibliography: Theoretical Implications for Bibliographic Instruction," in *Theories of Bibliographic Education: Designs for Teaching*, ed. Cerise Oberman and Katina Strauch (New York: R. R. Bowker, 1982), 8.

Part 3
HUMANITIES

CHAPTER 9

A PORTRAIT FOR THE LIBRARIAN
Bibliographic Education for Students in Design Disciplines

Edward H. Teague

Introduction

That the work of designers, whether they be artists, architects, or urban planners, has an impact upon almost every aspect of our lives underscores the importance of good design education. An integral component of that education — learning the skills essential to obtain information for design development — is an area which has received less attention than bibliographic education in other disciplines.[1]

Why the design student is the pariah of library instruction might be explained as follows. First, the population of design students, particularly majors in these disciplines, is relatively small. Also, the design product is not textual, not bibliographically oriented, and rarely requires documentation in the form of notes or bibliography. For some, the design student's inquiry seems vague, personal, and without context. Furthermore, design faculty rarely encourage library use. Many of these points obviously have some validity.

Another factor discouraging effective library instruction for design students is that library educators may be unfamiliar with the nature of design research. In *Learning the Library*, Anne K. Beaubien, Sharon A. Hogan, and Mary W. George rationalize their omission of the fine arts from their discussion of the humanities research process, making the observation that, "the fine or creative arts depend less on person-to-person communication than they do on talent, inspiration, perseverance, and opportunity — all fragile assets, the successful combination of which is notoriously unpredictable."[2] The creative arts, according to the authors, do not have the "complete communication structures and the corresponding sets of fact and finding tools" that can be found in other disciplines.[3]

If art is viewed as a mystical, inscrutable, and a largely unconscious undertaking, then some soundness might underlie the rationale that artistic endeavors are outside the boundaries of systematic bibliographic inquiry. However, art educators, psychologists, and artists have abandoned the romantic, and relatively recent, notion of art as "self-contained, mysteriously inspired from above, unrelated and unrelatable to what people do otherwise."[4]

This chapter is an initial attempt at exploring the many issues surrounding library use instruction for design students with the aim of making this instructional effort a viable enterprise. How designers resolve design problems and what information sources they use are explored. For the beginning librarian and the experienced librarian frustrated with other approaches, a library instruction model is developed within a conceptual context sympathetic to artists and designers and their problem-solving strategies.

Designers is defined here as those who make use of a graphic vocabulary to create works whose visual or spatial aspects are of primary significance. Designers include artists in all media, craftspeople, architects, landscape architects, interior designers, city planners, and those in related fields. In the academic setting, students majoring in design are preprofessionals in the sense that their creative products are of the same nature, if not the same quality, as their professional counterparts. This point is important because it suggests that the distinction between undergraduate and graduate bibliographic education for design students may be less obvious than in other disciplines.

"Products" of design students are varied. Works range from paintings, drawings, ceramics, and other artistic creations to architectural models and plans, if not building structures. The development of most design projects requires a substantial amount of information although much of it may be of a visual, rather than verbal, nature.

The Designer's Use of Information

The fact that visual data are not commonly perceived as research information may perpetuate a misconception that the visual arts are not library oriented. However, an analysis of how designers use information makes it clear that many aspects of data used in the design process can be found in the library setting.

The information used by design students can be organized into broad categories which cover requirements for technical expertise as well as needs for visually stimulating influences. Three basic categories are apparent: information about technique, information relevant to the specifications of a particular project, and information that serves to stimulate and motivate the designer. The three kinds of information can be labeled technical, contractive, and expansive data. Note that this information is not used sequentially, but interactively; that is, an expertise in technical aspects of a medium is not in many cases prerequisite to application but learned during the course of the creative act.

The term *technical data* refers to information which would lead to a comprehensive knowledge about a medium and its application. Architectural rendering, painting, sculpting, and printmaking are a few examples of the many types of media used by designers. *Technical data* implies a broader meaning than *technique*, which refers primarily to the skill used in employing a medium. The natural composition of a medium and other physical attributes are examples of technical data which are useful for developing good technique.

Technical information about paint, for example, includes such things as the composition of pigments, how well some pigments mix with others, and what pigments should be used cautiously because of potential health hazards. For painters, technical data also include the facts about assembling and preparing a canvas, the kinds of brushes and solvents to use, tips on framing pictures, and other kinds of information which are drawn upon to bring a work to completion. Design students who use many media for one object or project may require a wide range of technical information.

The term *contractive data* refers to information which defines the design parameters of a particular project regardless of whether this information is internally or externally imposed. Contractive data "contract" or put limits upon the scope of a design. In another sense, or in contractual terms, the data identify what is permissible and what is not in the creation of a design. For many design students, the faculty assignment is the primary contractive data apart from the limitations of their own intentions. Such assignments might be quite detailed and assume use of library resources. There are many kinds of resources which effectively regulate how the imagination is applied; architectural graphic standards and guidelines, building codes, typology and layout standards, and figure drawing handbooks are examples.

The term *expansive data* primarily refers to information which stimulates the generation of visual imagery. There is little limitation on the kind of information which encourages the image-making process in design. (While browsing has dubious value as a research methodology in some fields, it is a significant and valid part of the designer's approach to visual problem solving.) Influential works can be entirely textual as well as illustrated. Histories, theories, and philosophies of art are examples of texts which can inspire images or give them organization, context, and meaning.[5] For specific projects, particular library resources can be identified which match the "expansive" information needed for a specific assignment. Naturally, heavily illustrated sources are stimulating resources. In this context, the importance of browsing as an information-seeking strategy cannot be underestimated. A student interested in landscape art might browse books about that subject or artists specializing in that genre.

The sources which attempt to satisfy these information needs include nontextual as well as textual resources. The textual resources, normally found in libraries and identified in a variety of bibliographic guides, include dictionaries, encyclopedias, handbooks, bibliographies and other traditional reference works. The nontextual resources are also quite significant in the development of a design. The interplay of life experience, personal communication, exposure to works of art, and experimentation creates an important pool of information which is drawn upon in the creative process.

The Design Process

The information needs of designers, and the resources that satisfy those needs, can be placed within a larger matrix called the "design process." It is important to understand the design process as a methodic problem-solving endeavor before determining what role educators can play in helping designers acquire effective skills in using information. It is useful to equate the design process, as a problem-solving endeavor, with the creative process. The creative process, although employed in many other enterprises from writing term papers to solving mathematical equations, is in many senses the "research process" employed by designers.

The creative process has been the subject of much research from many points of view, from the humanistic to the scientific. Most scholars seem to agree, however, that the process consists of the following stages of activity, although the names for these phases vary: the exploration stage, the incubation stage, the insight stage, and the execution stage.[6]

In the exploration stage, the designer is actively engaged in seeking information relevant to some or all aspects of the design project. The scope of what information may be relevant for the design is framed by the parameters of the instructor's assignment. Activity at this phase of the creative process is a conscious and willful process. As one scholar observes,

> A great deal of the work necessary to equip and activate the mind for the spontaneous part of invention must be done consciously and with an effort of will. Mastering accumulated knowledge, gathering new facts, observing, exploring, experimenting, developing technique and skill, sensibility, and discrimination, are all more or less conscious and voluntary activities.[7]

Intermediate stages of the creative process are described to be largely activities of the unconscious mind. During the incubation stage, the designer is internally processing, synthesizing, and organizing information. During the incubation stage there exists a "preverbal intimation of approaching or potential resolution."[8] The achievement of resolution, the moment of insight, seems to occur spontaneously and involuntarily.

The final stage of execution refers to the act of bringing to reality the project in mind. During this phase, the creative product is tested, evaluated, and refined. If the creator finds at this stage that the work is "not sound and complete, he may be able to make it so, either by conscious craft or consciously directed research."[9]

The creative process, according to psychologist Carl R. Rogers, requires individuals to have certain characteristics which librarians who interact with design researchers should remember. An openness to experience is of paramount importance for the successfully creative person. This openness, or extensionality, means that closure is avoided and that ambiguity is respected. With the capacity for openness, creative individuals can handle conflicting information. A second characteristic, an internal evaluative mechanism, is the creator's need to seek satisfaction according to primarily personal, not external, criteria.[10]

Finally, creators must have the ability to experiment freely and to play spontaneously with elements and concepts. "It is from this toying and exploration that there arises the hunch, the creative seeing of life in a new and significant way."[11] Openness, experimentation, and a personal criteria for evaluation are characteristics which counter the research traits more likely experienced by librarian educators. More often, librarians encounter researchers whose goal is to prove or disprove according to an accepted methodology subject to an objective evaluative criteria.

The Design Research Strategy

The relationship between the design process and information needs becomes clearer with the introduction of another concept, the design research strategy. The design research strategy follows closely the model of the traditional research strategy which, as outlined by many bibliographic educators, generally involves matching in a systematic way an appropriate information source and an identified information need. Analyzing the research topic or question is a critical activity in the search strategy and a successful analysis charts the direction for efficient information seeking.[12]

The successful design research strategy facilitates a primary goal of artistic creation: the integration of seemingly diverse visual ideas into one meaningful and aesthetically unified concept. The strategy includes the following parts: identification of the initial contractive data, analysis of the components of the design project, identification of the information needs for each component, and application of appropriate information-seeking concepts and strategies to satisfy information needs.

To illustrate the interactions at work in the design research strategy, it is useful to follow the creation of a design project from inception to completion. Suppose an instructor has assigned an architecture class to design a public library building for Gainesville, Florida. For the student, the first stage of the research strategy is to obtain a clear understanding of the contractive data; that is, what guidelines and restrictions are provided in the assignment? What restraints, if any, are outlined by the instructor? What resources may be used to resolve the design problem? When is the project due?

The second stage of the design research strategy parallels the technique of question analysis in traditional search strategies in which different aspects of a research question are segregated with the aim of isolating specific information needs. The design problem conforms closely to what Beaubien, Hogan, and George call a "compound research topic." A compound research topic contains components of equal value and the order in which answering each component is approached is largely unimportant except for convenience.[13]

The following statement by an architectural educator helps to illuminate the design project as an intellectual inquiry involving many components:

> Design is a multifaceted problem. Each problem can be and is looked at from many different vantage points. Often each studio instructor can afford to evaluate a design problem only through a handful of perspectives: urban form, technology, environmental impact, and so on.[14]

Like many question analyses, design problem analysis requires some prior knowledge of the components of a design, although in many types of creative design these areas can be somewhat standardized. In the case at hand, the architecture student now isolates the following components of the design problem: the building type (library); the site (Gainesville, Florida) in its societal context (that is, the economic, cultural, and historical factors affecting the design); the site in its physical context (siting, soil surface, climatological, environmental concerns, etc.); client needs; and architectural design factors.

Design research strategy can also be applied to problems of studio artists. A student interested in portrait painting, for example, can conceptualize the following design components: the technique of the portrait painting, the history of portrait painting, portrait painters, and the sitter's criteria.

With the components of the design identified, the student undertakes the third part of the design research strategy, assessing what kind of information is required for each component and, finally, what course of action must be pursued to obtain the required information. The proliferation of a variety of information resources in many formats can make these final stages of design investigation a confusing and frustrating experience without the assistance of a librarian.

The Librarian's Role in the
Design Research Process

At every stage of the search strategy, the librarian can play a crucial and influential role. Bibliographic education sessions, especially those in which individual consultation is a component, can guide students through the maze of varying and proliferating information resources. That such assistance is essential is best illustrated by comparing the public library building design with examples of resources useful for different facets of the project.

An investigation of a building type often leads the researcher to many subject areas outside of the purely architectural collections. A complete inquiry into the building type includes research related to the work's function, history, and design features. A card catalog investigation about the public library building type requires the preliminary use of an array of Library of Congress subject headings. These headings, including "library architecture," "libraries—history," and "public libraries," demonstrates the need for a basic skill in using a subject thesaurus. Periodical resources identified through key indexes, such as the *Avery Index to Architectural Periodicals* (and its computerized equivalent), the *Architectural Periodicals Index*, and the *Art Index* should be augmented by material found in the information science indexes, such as *Library Literature* and *Library and Information Science Abstracts*, for a thorough study of the library structure.

The literature about the location of a projected architectural work is important supportive information which assists in placing the design within the context of the community. Information about a site from cultural, historical, and sociopolitical perspectives draws upon resources, like the building type inquiry, which extend beyond traditional architectural resources. Under the primary subject heading of "Gainesville (Fla.)" the subheadings of "History," "Industries," "Population," and "Social conditions" are among those likely to be of value. Significantly, archival material and special collections which often exist in library collections but may not be traditionally catalogued, are other resources of potential value. Similarly, the library collections of the town newspaper, public library, or historical society may be relevant. Census materials and other government documents may be particularly useful for understanding the town's population.

Researching the physical aspects of a building site requires skill at using science information tools. Site planning is an important aspect of architectural design and construction, and many pertinent materials may be found in card catalogs under the heading "Building sites." Such diverse sources as climatological data and related reference works may be located under "Florida — climate — tables." Instruction in the retrieval and use of maps and government documents may also be useful for the student investigating site details.

The reference works which treat architectural design elements incorporate both legalistic and aesthetic considerations. The subject headings "Architectural design," "Building — details — drawings," and "Building materials — standards," may yield such pertinent works as *Architectural Graphic Standards* and *Time-Saver Standards for Building Types*. Design factors are regulated or influenced by codes and specifications, and titles like the *Standard Building Code* and Hans Meier's *Construction Specifications Handbook* may be located through such subject terms as "building laws" and "building — contracts and specifications," in law collections.

The Design Product:
A Continuing Dialogue

Art, law, sociology, science, local history — these are a few of the many disciplines drawn upon to create a design. The librarian is challenged to respond comprehensively to queries from design students. Unfortunately, guidance in collecting data regarding one aspect of the design may be mistaken as the complete query. The design product, as has been illustrated, is a composite of many unique and seemingly unrelated queries. Because the solution to a design problem involves an open-ended creative act, there rarely exists one answer to a design query. The design product may inspire as many new problems and strategies as it attempts to resolve.

The integration of information resources, those both of a bibliographic and nonbibliographic nature, is an interactive process which takes place between the mind and the medium of the designer. "The biggest challenge for a designer," noted one instructor, "is to reach a design synthesis that will respond to and integrate all relevant aspects of a stated problem." The design process and its creative phases — exploration, incubation, insight, and execution — involve a continual and dynamic interchange between information received and information processed. Artistic problem solving, while appearing at one point in time, may in actuality be part of a continuing, even life-long, pursuit. As Brewster Ghiselin observed,

> Van Gogh and Kuniyoshi tell of making many paintings of the same object in order to develop and refine the insight expressed in representing it.... This process of reworking is very close to revision, but since it involves repeating virtually the whole process of production it appears more likely to preserve the spontaneous character of the initial attempt.[15]

Bibliographic Instruction for Designers:
A Model and Its Application

One can induce from the preceding examples what might constitute a model bibliographic education session for design students. At the outset it should be noted that a classroom situation is not likely to be conducive for learning to individuals who are accustomed to working freely in a studio setting. Since the visual environment is of prime importance to designers, a library instruction session in the library is likely to be more rewarding if such an arrangement is feasible.

The organization of the overall session attempts to address general bibliographic principles as well as individual needs; an ideal instructional session for designers includes four segments.[16] The first segment consists of a brief overview of what kinds of information — technical, contractive, and expansive — designers use. The librarian emphasizes that designers obtain information from a variety of sources, some of it nonbibliographic. To access information effectively, particularly library information, requires design problem analysis. The second segment of the session reviews the mechanics, with specific examples, of analyzing a design problem in order to isolate its components.

The third segment of the session identifies types and titles of library resources of value in design problem solving. How these resources are presented is greatly dependent upon the nature of the design assignment and the extent of individual variation permitted. The concept of the thesaurus and its use in catalogs and indexes plus the identification, with examples, of types of reference works are certainly key elements in the description of library resources.

The fourth segment, individual consultation, is a critical part of bibliographic education for designers. Consultation enables the librarian to provide professional expertise in the identification of resources, some of which may be inaccessible through traditional bibliographic tools.

How the instruction model is applied can be demonstrated with an example from the University of Florida. A graduate class of forty students in the College of Architecture focuses on prethesis research and is a target group each year for bibliographic education. A major part of the class assignment is to prepare a tentative research topic and preliminary bibliography for the thesis. The students have a wide range of research interests with the design of particular building types, or the adaptive reuse of existing structures, the primary research focus.

The library instruction program for the prethesis students is made up of three, and sometimes four components. The first part is an introduction to architectural resources presented by the architecture and fine arts librarian (the author) in a branch library setting. In this component, the information world of designers and design problem analysis are also covered. The second and possibly third component is fairly flexible and consists of sessions introducing students to the literature of a related discipline as encouraged by the instructor. As an example, Ray Jones, the social sciences librarian, presented two sessions: one covered social sciences reference materials of value to architects, especially those related to environmental behavior; the other focused on computer databases of importance in architectural research. The fourth part of the program, individual consultation, enabled students to meet with the architecture and fine arts librarian or the social sciences librarian to develop customized strategies for individual topics. The consultation, encouraged by the architecture instructor, allowed the student to reinforce or clarify information delivered in earlier presentations. The product of these collaborative efforts, the student's statement of research interests and accompanying bibliography, hopefully reflects an understanding of successful library research strategies.

Conclusion

Cerise Oberman has observed that

> As bibliographic education continues to develop, it must take its cue from other disciplines. For if our intention is to provide the student with a conceptual framework of principles, then we must be prepared not only to identify those concepts, but to teach them in a format which encourages retainment and transference.[17]

This chapter has attempted to place bibliographic education for designers within a theoretical context that design students can understand—the creative process. By linking the creative process to library research, and by treating design problem solving as a research strategy, it is hoped that a conceptual model has emerged which can be used to provide effective bibliographic education sessions for students in all design disciplines.

As a final note, librarians unaccustomed to working with design students should feel unrestrained in using such words as *creative, innovative, imaginative,* and *unique* for these are in the vocabulary of design. Those who are uneasy about equating artistic design with research might be mindful of this statement by Pablo Picasso: "Paintings are but research and experiment. I never do a painting as a work of art. All of them are researches."[18]

Notes

[1]The literature dealing with bibliographic education in the visual arts rarely focuses on the needs of artists and designers and is more often directed to art historians whose research methodology follows a pattern similar to other historical disciplines. Deirdre C. Stam's "How Art Historians Look for Information," *Art Documentation* 3, no. 4 (Winter 1984): 117-19, examines the art historical research process. Connie Koppelman's "Orientation and Instruction in Academic Art Libraries," *Special Libraries* 67 (May-June 1976): 5-6, 256-60, focuses on encouraging art faculty involvement.

[2]Anne K. Beaubien, Sharon A. Hogan, and Mary W. George, *Learning the Library: Concepts and Methods for Bibliographic Instruction* (New York: R. R. Bowker, 1982), 109.

[3]Ibid.

[4]Rudolph Arnheim, in Kurt Hanks and Larry Belliston's *Draw! A Visual Approach to Thinking, Learning, and Communicating* (Los Altos, Calif.: William Kaufmann, Inc., 1977), 3. Arnheim's succinct account of creative art as a rational, intellectual process can be found in Rudolph Arnheim's *Picasso's Guernica: The Genesis of a Painting* (Berkeley, Calif.: University of California Press, 1962).

[5]Russell Ferguson, reporter. "CAA/ARLIS Joint Session: 'What Do Artists Read?' " in "14th Annual ARLIS/NA Conference Proceedings," *Art Documentation* 5, no. 2 (Summer 1986): 72.

[6]Stanley Rosner and Lawrence E. Abt, *Essays in Creativity* (Croton-on-Hudson, N.Y.: North River Press, 1974). Various approaches to understanding creativity are addressed in this book.

[7]Brewster Ghiselin, *The Creative Process; A Symposium* (New York: New American Library, 1964), 28.

[8]Ibid., 14.

[9]Ibid., 30.

[10]Carl R. Rogers, "Toward a Theory of Creativity," in *The Creativity Question*, ed. Albert Rothenberg and Carl R. Hausman (Durham, N.C.: Duke University Press, 1976), 296-304.

[11]Ibid., 301.

[12]Beaubien, Hogan, and George, *Learning the Library*, 75.

[13]Ibid., 73-74.

[14]Omer Akin, "Teaching Architecture," in *Teaching Architecture: Proceedings of the 69th Annual Meeting of the Association of Collegiate Schools of Architecture*, ed. Mary C. Comerio and Jeffrey M. Chusid (Washington, D.C.: Association of Collegiate Schools of Architecture, 1981), 28.

[15]Ghiselin, *Creative Process*, 30.

[16]Systematic literature searching, as explained in Pamela Kobelski and Mary Reichel's "Conceptual Frameworks for Bibliographic Instruction," *The Journal of Academic Librarianship* 7, no. 2 (1981): 75, is the theoretical model for the instructional session.

[17]Cerise Oberman, "Question Analysis and the Learning Cycle," *Research Strategies* 1, no. 1 (Winter 1983): 27.

[18]Alexander Liberman, *The Artist in His Studio* (New York: Macmillan, 1960), 33.

CHAPTER 10

A SOCIOBIBLIOGRAPHICAL AND SOCIOHISTORICAL APPROACH TO THE STUDY OF BIBLIOGRAPHIC AND REFERENCE SOURCES
A Complement to Traditional Bibliographic Instruction

Charles A. D'Aniello

Introduction

The study of bibliographic and reference sources as reflections of the culture or period in which they were written can be an exciting complement to the more traditional approaches to bibliographic instruction. Ilse Bry, in particular, has sketched the dimensions of sociobibliographical analysis. She explores the organization of social science literature; the role of editors, "schools" of thought, and journals in the selection of material for publication; the intellectual significance of various publication formats; and the place of these considerations in tracing the evolution of a discipline. In short, she convincingly argues that bibliography is value laden and "can be investigated for a variety of scientific purposes independent of users' needs to consult ... publications."[1]

Reference sources can be studied as straightforward guides to, or compendiums of, information or knowledge once or still current. John Dillon's article on Renaissance reference books and their effect on and reflection of the state of classical knowledge during that period illustrates this point. More importantly, Dillon observes that unless the sources used by Renaissance scholars are consulted when interpreting their texts, "we may ... find ourselves viewing an earlier text through a distorting glass of our own providing."[2]

Such simple sources as yearbooks and annuals, for instance, will enable one to reconstruct past events through the eyes of their compilers. Retrospective runs of directories will enable one to identify everything from defunct publications to businesses disbanded long ago. The works used need not be of major significance; one instructor has used school yearbooks to study the period of their publication. Likewise, a chronological progression of technical dictionaries will enable one to trace the evolution of technology; a run of medical dictionaries, the advance of medical knowledge.[3]

Further, the comparison across time of bibliographies in reference sources readily illustrates the birth, persistence, and evolution of ideas. Such studies may be done using citation indexes or traditional indexes as well as other sources. Standard types of citation studies concentrate on the analysis of references made by selected sources from a total literature and on citations made to a total literature over time. Bibliographies in reference works, such as encyclopedias, can be analyzed for rate of falloff, while bibliographies and references in review journals can be used to measure the age distribution of the literature of a subject.[4]

The study of distinct and contemporaneous populations of reference sources clearly differentiates societies and periods, and even groups within a society, from one another. As Michael Keresztesi has shown, a bibliographic apparatus develops to meet the specific needs of a discipline. Its nature—the types of sources it contains—is a reflection of the level of maturity that that discipline has achieved. Therefore, given the bibliographic sources that exist, one is able to postulate the level the discipline, field, or subfield has attained. Thus the bibliographic apparatus of a discipline has a history that reflects the history of the discipline itself.[5]

Proceeding from this approach, one can study these sources in their bibliographical/historical context. For instance, it is interesting to know that some of the bibliographic tools for the social sciences have been developed by disciplinary associations while others are produced commercially and are library sponsored. The creation by the Social Sciences Research Council (SSRC) in 1928 of *Social Science Abstracts*, which ceased publication in 1932, reveals a modest research activity at that time and a lack of commitment to the use of this tool.[6] And the development of a tool which spans traditional disciplinary boundaries such as *Social Sciences Citation Index* is a realization that practitioners of most social science disciplines utilize and cite the literature of disciplines outside of their own.

Both Raymond G. McInnis and Thelma Freides have written explicitly about the need to place reference sources within a disciplinary context when offering bibliographic instruction. Implicit in the work of each is the idea that reference sources can do more than provide substantive and bibliographic information and that they can be subjects for study in their own right. McInnis suggests that "by depicting reference materials simultaneously as functional necessities and as artificial constructs designed to order scientific literature in logical coherent arrangements" their cognitive function is made clear. And Freides writes, concerning bibliographies, that they "communicate the compiler's interpretation and assessment of the subject obliquely, by means of subject headings, annotations, or, perhaps, brief introductory comments."[7]

More to the point are the insights of Elizabeth Frick. She has pointed out that "library instruction can best enrich the educational process when the librarian is able to link bibliographical skills to an awareness of the implications of the function of information in society." Specifically, she suggests that it should be made clear to students "that reference structures both open and close certain information channels" and that bibliographic instruction "can help students recognize that by understanding who generates information, who publishes it, who disseminates and classifies it, how, and for whom," will reveal the value and limitations of that information.[8]

One scholar has described the ideal general education program as one which leads the student to the creation of knowledge by utilizing substantive information with critical analysis. Knowledge then is neither facts nor information alone. It is a state of understanding which results from successfully uniting facts to one another within a broader framework or context. The study of bibliographic and reference sources as objects for sociological and sociohistorical analysis requires a knowledge of history, of cultural and intellectual traditions, and the use of analytical skills.[9] It is an exercise in cultural literacy.[10]

Illustrations of the purposeful manipulation of the record no less than images of changing paradigms, perceptions, and fashions emerge when such scrutiny is applied to these sources. Such analysis encourages students to consider how frightening the assertion by the librarian in George Orwell's *1984* truly is that "past events ... have no objective existence, but survive only in the written record and human memories."[11]

But these sources cannot speak to us clearly of the past or the present unless something of each is already understood that enables their placement in context. To examine sources in this manner, that is "to relate ... ideas ... to the socio-historical settings in which they were produced and received,"[12] requires the will to search for an underlying explanation of their nature in a critical and objective manner. Students are compelled to appreciate that behind the sources are assumptions and perceptions whose validity they may question, which may have dissolved over time, or may seem curious within a contemporary setting. They are led to the realization that "knowledge in the broadest sense is context-dependent and somehow constrained by social factors" and can only be legitimatized by appropriate institutions—academies, governments, religious bodies, or the general scholarly community.[13]

In short, the sociology of knowledge teaches us that knowledge is socially determined. Social needs determine what will be studied and valued and in non-scientific knowledge sociality controls the origin as well as the content of knowledge. As one scholar has observed, "In the case of science, tendencies arising from the social sphere induce a person to open his eyes and see; in the case of cultural studies, they induce him to open his eyes and decide what he should see."[14] Knowledge is power, that is, power is derived from the possession and control of knowledge. Knowledge determines how we interact with one another. It determines how we orient ourselves to our total environment.[15] Reference sources are the memories of our orientations.

Thus the study of bibliographic and reference sources cannot be divorced from political and sociological considerations. Societies are held together not only through coercive power but through commonly held values or the "ideological hegemony" of the state as Antonio Gramsci hypothesized. In a brief summary of the thought of Gramsci on capitalist societies, Raymond Williams observes that ideological hegemony "is the central effective and dominant system of meanings and values, which are not simply abstract but are organized and lived." Williams goes on to note, society is saturated in such a way that these meanings and values constitute "the substance and limits of common sense for most people."[16]

Obviously, however, there is more than one culture that is transmitted; counterhegemonies are continually being created and competing visions of common sense define various boundaries of reality. The power groups which create these realities include, T. J. Jackson Lears explains, "parents, preachers, teachers, journalists, literati, 'experts' of all sorts, as well as advertising executives, entertainment promoters, popular musicians, sports figures, and 'celebrities' — all of whom are involved (albeit often unwittingly) in shaping the values and attitudes of a society." But ultimately one cultural view dominates, although the membrane between dominant and subordinate cultures is not impenetrable and "contradictory consciousnesses" are ever present.[17]

Clearly, investigation along these lines requires a high level of critical thinking. The elements of critical thinking, as succinctly defined by Mona McCormick, are: the identification of main issues; the recognition of underlying assumptions; the evaluation of evidence; the evaluation of authorities, people, and publications; the recognition of bias, emotional appeals, relevant facts, propaganda, generalities and language problems; the questioning of whether facts support conclusions; questions concerning the adequacy of data; recognition of the relationship among ideas; realization of the investigator's attitudes; and a commitment to a thorough search for evidence.[18] It will also require imagination.

Finally, it must not be forgotten that economics plays a role in reference book publishing. The first books to be mass produced were "how to" books.[19] At least to some extent, in the end, financial considerations are a consequential by-product of ideological factors. The economics of reference book publishing — which sell the most, who pays for them, and who purchases and sponsors them — deserves some consideration. This is touched on only generally in what follows. Apart from their specific characteristics, the general types of reference books — popular "how-to" manuals on everything from sex to car repair to executive etiquette — cannot help but tell us something about our culture.[20]

Though reference librarians may often bemoan the underutilization of bibliographic and reference sources, these sources have always occupied a position of immense cultural importance. Whether they are the Wilson indexes or more scholarly efforts such as the *International Encyclopedia of the Social Sciences*, they shape as well as reflect society's realities. Once an opinion or a fact is honored by statement in a reference source its validity is presumed. As Richard D. Altick has noted, facts are not true because they are in print although all too often print and truth are equated as synonymous. In fact, the wider the perpetuation of a fact or interpretation, whether error or truth, the more certain we become of its validity.[21]

Reference books were, from the first, a scary thing to the academy. Textbooks are designed to exist within the hierarchy of learning and to be mediated through the skills of a teacher. Reference books stand alone. They can be revolutionary by making knowledge available to everyone. For instance, self-help wordbooks have changed our language, sometimes in opposition to more conservative linguistic elements.[22] Elizabeth L. Eisenstein has shown that the first printed reference books had a profound influence on their world by making possible the testing of knowledge by submitting multiples of the same text for review, to be followed by the publication of new and corrected editions.[23]

It is especially appropriate that we consider the social role of reference sources as we approach a time when we can at least imagine the day when all major sources, and many minor ones as well, will be searchable online. When online and computer generated sources dominate the information environment the revolution will be no less far reaching than that effected by the printing press. But because the capability will now exist for near instantaneous deletions and additions the dangers of bias and distortion will be great as well. Even more importantly, inclusion in the database will signify legitimacy, ease of access will ensure consultation, and, thus, many searchers may look no further.[24] It is, therefore, critical to remember that reference sources are not value free and, indeed, are creatures of the "moment" of their creation and all that that entails.

What follows is an overview of some of the more interesting historical aspects of topics concerning a variety of bibliographic and reference sources. It is hoped that their discussion will encourage further reflection. In many instances exercises are suggested which will help students to further explore the issues raised.

Although the exercises posed often appear daunting, they can be adapted for use at a variety of levels. For the instructor with the will and the time the overviews and exercises will serve as prototypes. Certainly, it is unlikely that this approach will be pursued with students below the advanced undergraduate level. Finally, my thoughts on this approach evolved during several years of team teaching a graduate level historical methods course. This approach should appeal especially to history students and instructors for it teaches bibliographic skills and critical thinking within a historical context. It is, of course, unlikely that sufficient time or opportunity would be available for this approach in the traditional fifty-minute session. Yet if it cannot dominate basic instructional sessions it can be "folded into" them as meaningful asides and insights.

Calendars

As librarians we are not accustomed to treating calendars as reference sources but they are one of the oldest denizens of the genre. They have been shaped not only by astronomical measures of lunar and solar cycles and corresponding religious associations but reflect politics and geography as well. In antiquity, conquerors were quick to impose their calendars on the vanquished. In more recent times, French (1793-1805) and Russian (1929-1930) revolutionaries hoped to express and effect an ideological reorientation of their societies by imposing new calendars on them. The latter two efforts failed but students might be asked to imagine a week using either calendar to appreciate the awesome power this reference source exerts on the fabric of everyday life. And, of course, an examination of the calendar(s) of a society reveals the rhythm of its religious life, the nature of its science, and famous or infamous points in its history.[25]

Encyclopedias

Encyclopedias are storehouses of essential legitimatized knowledge. The term encyclopedia is derived from the Greek word "enkykliospaideia" which translates as "circle of learning," that is, the compass of learning or state of knowledge. Other terms used for encyclopedia such as "speculum" (mirror) and "imago" (image) are clearly indicative of the source's purposefully reflective nature. Thus encyclopedias lend themselves especially well to comparisons across time, across political and cultural borders, and across class or subculture.[26]

Much has, and continues to be, written about them. Some contemporary concern has focused on racism and sexism and how the perceptions of the general public, and children in particular, are shaped and/or reinforced by their expression in encyclopedias.[27] Such studies can be easily replicated with students.

One might also have students consider an encyclopedia within its historical context. The text of Diderot's *Encyclopédie* has been a frequent subject of such investigation. It is hailed as a declaration of the infinite power of reason and, from its text to its over 3,000 illustrations, as a composite image of the Age of Enlightenment hovering on the edge of what was to be called the Industrial Revolution. Less commonly known to students are its illustrations, which despite the fact that they were actually outdated at publication, in number alone evidence a rapidly expanding interest in science and technology.[28]

The *International Encyclopedia of the Social Sciences* (*IESS*) and the *Encyclopedia of the Social Sciences* (*ESS*) are ideal yardsticks against which to measure changes in the nature of the social sciences in general and of specific disciplines in particular. Thelma Freides, in *Literature and Bibliography of the Social Sciences*, compares and contrasts these two magisterial sources. She notes that the earlier work contains many more articles on concrete social entities. In addition, many historical figures are also covered. In all respects the newer work is less descriptive and historical and more analytical, comparative, and conceptual.[29]

Overall, the earlier encyclopedia was dominated by articles with an economic focus and a Marxist slant. Its editors hoped that the social sciences would make obvious and possible reforms which would improve the human condition. It was their hope that the *ESS* would pierce and ultimately tear down the walls which isolated one social science discipline from another. Some thirty years later, the *IESS*, in some respects actually less international than the earlier work, clearly reveals that disciplinary boundaries are a long way from crumbling.[30]

There are obvious differences between the two works. The earlier work accorded history and philosophy considerable space, while the *IESS* does not include an article on philosophy and history is treated as a methodology, not as a fund of knowledge. In fact, the unifying theme of the latter work is the adoption by the social sciences of a supposedly scientific value free methodology. This reveals much about contemporary social science concerns. Language itself works against the expression of neutral social scientific conclusions; it's easy to say neutral things about natural phenomenon. However, this and the other issues that study of the work raises are not the point, because they are precisely those subjected to vigorous debate within the academy itself.[31]

The difference between the works was not unappreciated by the editors of the *IESS*. Alvin Johnson remarks in the foreword, "an encyclopedia, particularly one of the social sciences, should remain a historical document of its time and ... each generation should have an encyclopedia—new from the ground up."[32]

Since the focus of this essay is historical it is appropriate to observe in further detail that history's position in the two sources is quite different. Historian Oscar Handlin observes that in the 1930s history's position was secure "in the United States [it] was a social science, one of the group of disciplines that gave professional form to the study of the life of man in society.... It was the laboratory that churned out data and supplied information from which subsequent generalizations would arise, and that, at the same time, tested hypotheses formulated by the analytical scholars." Handlin goes on to note that this role was clearly evident in the *ESS* which "drew historical materials intimately into the whole fabric of presentation."[33] Handlin's remarks are important because they illustrate the importance the *ESS* and *IESS* have had in the scholarly enterprise and they invite students to test his conclusions.

Finally, all nature of comparisons can be made between two or more obviously perceptually diverse encyclopedias. For instance, compare essays in works representing predictably differing political, national, or religious perspectives. Comparing the essays on anti-Semitism in the *New Catholic Encyclopedia* (*NCE*) (1967) and in *Encyclopaedia Judaica* (*EJ*) (1972), as one would expect, reveals different historical perspectives. For instance, in its discussion of early Christian anti-Semitism, *NCE* observes, "The Synagogue struck the first blow" and "in the face of this hostility the attitude of Christians toward Judaism hardened."[34] *Encyclopaedia Judaica* mentions none of this but declares that "the crucial factor here was not so much Christianity's refusal to countenance any other faith, as its commitment to an ideal of redemption ... that rendered their mutual coexistence inconceivable."[35] Turning to Jewish involvement with trade and usury in the Middle Ages *NCE* explains that the Jew "set himself to his new vocation with a will. Even Jewish chroniclers criticized the riches some Jews accumulated and the high rates of interest they charged."[36] *Encyclopaedia Judaica* instead emphasizes the critical role Jewish financiers played in the expansion of commerce through their alliance with secular princes and church prelates.[37] The *Great Soviet Encyclopedia* (English trans. of Russian ed., 1970-1975) offers many points for contrast. Its political positions are generally unequivocal. The entry on Zionism proclaims that "international Zionism strives to undermine the moral and political unity of the peoples of the socialist countries."[38] One might argue for or against these contentions or attempt to reconcile them but the point here is that they are intellectually challenging illustrations of differing perspectives.

Other encyclopedia exercises approached from a historical perspective might consider the currency and persistence of an idea or simply illustrate the rapidity of change in contemporary society. Raymond G. McInnis suggests the examination of bibliographies for citations to works on "anarchism" and "eugenics" in four encyclopedias: *Encyclopaedia Britannica*, the *New Larned History*, the *ESS*, and the *IESS*. Over 100 years are spanned and throughout the comparison some works persist, new ones are added, while others vanish. Changing fashions, developing conceptualizations, and persistent or pivotal works emerge. In another work McInnis, using these sources and topics, shows how the substance and orientation of the entries themselves differ over time.[39] Finally, to illustrate how difficult it can be to keep an encyclopedia current one library science professor asks students to examine a single day's issue of the *New York Times* to identify material that ought to be incorporated into the revision of an encyclopedia entry.[40]

Biographical Dictionaries

Biographical dictionaries such as the major national sets—the *Dictionary of National Biography* (*DNB*) (1908-1909 and supplements) (Great Britain) and the *Dictionary of American Biography* (*DAB*) (1928-1937 and supplements)—are of immense importance. They list and describe a nation's most honored citizens and, through them, its most esteemed accomplishments. In addition to the actual substance of entries (information chosen for inclusion or exclusion), who is and is not listed, which professions are well-represented and which are not, all mirror values, prejudices, and history.

Specialized biographical dictionaries define discrete populations for analysis. The *Dictionary of American Negro Biography* was designed to cover a population in which the *DAB* is deficient. Its editors advise that it includes many people "largely unknown to the white public of their day, but (who) played significant roles in the separate life the Negro lived as a result of segregation." *Notable American Women* was designed to compensate for a similar deficiency. Each lends itself to internal analysis as well as to comparison with the *DAB*. And each implicitly demonstrates an assertiveness among the groups it treats.[41]

Dictionaries

Dictionaries (standard language wordbooks) list words alphabetically, giving pronunciation, spelling, and meaning. One turns to a dictionary for a definition or an indication of correct usage. This sounds innocent but put another way, standard dictionaries historically have grown out of a desire to control linguistic development by prescription, proscription, and, ultimately, by either the inclusion or exclusion of words. Artistic, scientific, and nationalistic motives led to the founding of the Académie Française (1635), parent of *Dictionnaire de la langue française*, and the compilation of Samuel Johnson's *Dictionary of the English Language* (1755). Noah Webster's *An American Dictionary of the English Language* (1828) was America's major contribution in this vein. Webster insisted that American English was different from British English but during the early national period American dictionaries with a British orientation competed with Webster's work. Patriotism and science were combined with a desire to fix language in a period when literacy was increasing, publishing was burgeoning, and old hierarchies and assumptions were increasingly being challenged.[42]

The authoritarian function of dictionaries has not escaped contemporary students of sexism. Although it is important to remember that the stereotypes and idealizations presented in contemporary dictionaries often do not reflect valid contemporary norms but are instead often vestiges of a cultural heritage, nonetheless, some linguists argue that language shapes perceptions and determines not merely how we think about things but what we can perceive. More popular is the hypothesis that language influences some kinds of thought but not others. For instance, studies suggest that language has a powerful influence on evaluative thought and affects judgments on the worth of concepts and events.[43] Critics have found few biographies of famous women in dictionaries and much sexist language in definitions and examples of usage. Men are aggressive, daring, and independent but women are emotional, foolish, and subservient.[44] Even the

Oxford English Dictionary (*OED*) is not free of discernable social and political values and the ideology of its editors.[45]

Critics have traditionally argued that dictionaries reflect middle-class male prejudices. Sexually charged words are provocative illustrations of this. One scholar, for instance, has noted that many sexual words have long been excluded from dictionaries. These include terms such as *fuck, occupy*, and even *diaphragm.* In fact, *condom* did not appear in a general dictionary until *Webster's Third New International Dictionary* (1961). The absence of these words clearly illustrates the role dictionaries have played and it also points up the inadequacy of dictionaries to faithfully sketch the linguistic environment of a period. It was not until the publication of the *American Heritage Dictionary* (1969) that *fuck* found a place in a standard dictionary.[46] Lexicographers have always had a hard time with taboo words. *Sexual intercourse*, for instance, has had a difficult time finding definition in dictionaries. It is never labeled vulgar or obscene but it is seldom fully defined either.[47]

Although some might argue that the revolutionary nature of *Webster's Third* has been exaggerated it is still illustrative to remember how excited a scholar can become about a wordbook. Historian Jacques Barzun, writing in the *American Scholar* for its board, saw *Webster's Third* as a profound reflection of the decline of western civilization. He argued that the range of words and phrases included, the refusal to make value judgments concerning usage, and even its use of a symbol to replace the word being defined in its examples of use, mirrored a general cultural decline.[48]

Linguist Robert A. Hall, Jr., took a different view, arguing that the dictionary brilliantly revealed the liberalism of contemporary American society. He saw linguistic authoritarianism as a vestige of the past, a product of "Renaissance aristocratic prejudice, seventeenth-century French academicism based on Richelieu's authoritarianism and Louis XIV's absolutism, and eighteenth-century English snobbery and social climbing."[49]

A less impassioned argument for labeling words is that we will never know what people really meant if we do not. One commentator on the principle has written "a crude notion of 'historical lexicography', which seeks to include all usages without privileging any particular form, will produce bogus results and falsify meanings. Words have been employed historically often because of their transgressive function, and a lexicon without branding labels will be impotent when it seeks to convey their force."[50]

A recent study of desk dictionaries reveals the frequent failure of dictionaries to reflect language in all its subtlety. Robert Pierson suggests that while ethnic and religious epithets are consistently labeled as offensive there appears to be no problem in calling one either a *doll* or a *queer*. Sidney I. Landau notes that terms of insult such as *white trash, hillbilly,* or *redneck*; *queer* or *fag*; and *cretin* or *retard* are equally as offensive as *wop, nigger,* and *mick* but that offended groups are relatively powerless and these words are usually not labeled in dictionaries as offensive. Landau observes that in this area, as in matters of definition, traditional dictionary practice reflects the prevailing norms and prejudices of the dominant culture. Three possible explanations are offered by Pierson: sexual preference reflects conscious decisions and thus invites prejudice; some characteristics are seemingly acceptable objects for teasing; and, finally, women are unreasonably offended by words used affectionately. Further, dictionaries fail to show that all terms are not equally offensive and that some terms which are acceptable when uttered by an insider are unacceptable when used by others.[51] Exercises which focus on this aspect of dictionaries should thus examine what is in dictionaries and what is not in dictionaries and should do this within the context of the society which they were designed to serve.

Yet another approach would focus on a study of the size of various word populations in dictionaries over time. For instance, Landau has observed that more than 40 percent of the entries in *Webster's Third* are either scientific or technical. His explanation is that this vocabulary has grown dramatically and, more importantly, science and technology are deemed most important. Another approach is to measure the length of definition for some terms as compared to others. Not the commonness of a term but its presumed importance determine its length of definition.[52]

Students of the history of racism will find much material to work with in dictionaries. Dictionaries have done a splendid job of recording racial prejudices; *black*, *nigger*, and *Jew* are powerful examples. Have students look up any of these words and the unfortunate positions blacks and Jews have occupied in Western society cannot be missed.[53]

In contemporary society, words can change their meaning seemingly over night and, needless to say, words have always changed their meanings over time. Adrian Room's *Dictionary of Changes in Meaning* conveniently illustrates this and begins with a contrived paragraph which can serve as the prototype for countless exercises. For instance, "You should avoid *accidents* when lighting a *bonfire*, or your *career* could be in danger." Possible translation using meanings no longer current: You should avoid "something that happens" (p. 16) when "lighting a fire of bones" (p. 42) or your "galloping at full speed" (p. 52) could be in danger.[54]

Exercises which require the definition of a term by period or within a chronologically qualified context illustrate this fact. In *The Art of Literary Research*, Richard D. Altick offers a series of exercises which require the citation of illustrative sentences from the *Oxford English Dictionary* to "prove" the meaning of a word at a given time.[55] Linguist Mario Pei's *Words in Sheep's Clothing* traces what he labels "weasel words"—words deliberately changed or which come to mean the opposite of what was originally intended—through the *OED* and standard American English dictionaries to illustrate the rapidity of contemporary linguistic change as made evident in the inability of dictionaries to keep up with these changes.[56] Raymond Williams's *Keywords: A Vocabulary of Culture and Society* is a sophisticated historical study of the evolution of pivotal words—for example, *racial*, *radical*, *rational*, and *sex*—and their offspring.[57]

And then there is the matter of usage books. Landau argues that these occupy an important place in a society in which individuals feel that there is a good deal of social mobility. Usage books are intended to prepare their users to speak the language of the dominant elements or, at least, of a class higher than their own.[58]

Libraries

Libraries themselves obviously reveal much about their creators. Numerous studies have been conducted from this perspective.[59]

The existence of specific types of libraries reflects the values and habits of a society. Much has been written about public libraries. I. R. Wilson looks further and suggests that the development of encyclopedic libraries is a reflection of a society's positive belief in the attainment of absolute and comprehensive knowledge. Apart from their practical benefits, he sees national libraries as a visible symbol of the state's "ultimate identity and legitimacy."[60] He sees national dictionaries and biographical sources as performing the same role. Surely the three have traditionally received much national praise and even financial support.

National and Trade Bibliographies

More encompassing than the catalog of a particular library are the components of a "national bibliography." Among these are such tools as the *American Book Publishing Record, Cumulative Book Index,* and their predecessors. Such sources contain within them the broadest outlines of publishing trends. Although one must be prepared to look beyond mere numbers, publishing trends need not solely reflect demand. For instance, in a study of the effect of copyright law on American publishing during the nineteenth century one scholar has focused on the divergence of themes between British and American novels. Because American novelists were protected by copyright law and British novelists were not, it was cheaper for American publishers to reprint British works. American novelists were more likely to deal with heroic themes to compete in an area which was neglected by British novelists who concentrated on love, marriage, and middle-class life. After 1891 the themes became the same perhaps not because the frontier was closed but because copyright law now put the authors of each country on an equal footing.[61]

In *The Popular Book*, James D. Hart studies American popular books and publishing trends within the changing context of American society. Explaining the significance of such scholarship he writes, "Literary taste is not an isolated phenomenon. The taste of the largest number of readers is shaped by contemporary pressures more than is the taste of the highly cultivated reader, who has a deeper background of aesthetic experience and knowledge to guide him. Books flourish when they answer a need and die when they do not."[62]

In light of the above, examining popular titles over time invites questions and adds a colorful dimension to the study of historical periods already long analyzed. The mid-nineteenth century saw the publication of long pressruns of numerous etiquette books; the 1920s ushered in an interest in self-improvement books that will probably never subside; immediately following World War II, popularized psychology titles became popular; and beginning in the 1970s, popular titles addressed themselves openly to sexual performance. Trade catalogs and the components of the national bibliography are the keys to this information.

Classification Systems

The classification systems used to organize libraries are of major intellectual importance and, for advanced classes, their discussion is a good complement to the mandatory comments on classification systems.[63] During the past century classification systems have been developed to respond to the qualitative as well as quantitative dimensions of the information explosion. Computerization has encouraged this search but did not initiate it. Alphabetization, a by-product of the printing press but employed before its advent, opened the door to complicated indexing systems capable of stringing together the concepts expressed in a book as well as the contents of a library. As knowledge expanded, the goal of indexing became increasingly to link and synthesize. When books were arranged systematically in early libraries it was generally by a broad and single faceted disciplinary map. Knowledge was in a sense simple. But by the nineteenth century, a wider circle of disciplines developed and, propelled by this change in the nature of knowledge itself, the Universal Decimal Classification system and Ranganathan's Colon Classification were developed. The LC classification system clearly has not been perceived as the final answer to classification.[64]

Those who would study classification systems historically would do well to remember as Jesse Shera points out "every scheme is conditioned by the intellectual environment of its age or time ... and that each generation may build upon the work of its predecessors, but must create its own classification from the materials that it has at hand and in accordance with its own peculiar needs."[65]

Still another approach is offered by Sanford Berman. He notes that by the 1960s scholars were publishing a swelling stream of work which exposed the darker aspects of Western civilization; however, much of it was findable only through Library of Congress headings which reflected the values these scholars were working so hard to eradicate.

Classification systems are customarily plagued by cultural lag, on the other hand. It is important to note that the headings Berman criticizes were created at a time when the perceptions they expressed mirrored or had recently mirrored those held by a large segment of society. While Berman explains their irony and cultural significance, he also realizes that they can be useful as well as being prejudicial. Their existence reveals important things. For instance, he urges headings such as WOMEN AS ACCOUNTANTS be changed to WOMEN ACCOUNTANTS. He faults the implied surprise but admits that the heading's existence reflects a sincere societal concern over women entering the workforce. Among other examples are: JAPANESE IN THE U.S. not JAPANESE-AMERICANS; BANKS AND BANKING-JEWS and SLAVERY IN THE U.S.—INSURRECTIONS.[66]

Statistical Sources

Organizations, governments, etc., collect statistics on what they consider to be important. Conversely, what they do not consider important they do not collect statistics on. A study of the progression of data-gathering units will reflect changing concerns and certain societies will have a phenomenon to report that is neither available nor relevant to others. Patricia Cline Cohen illustrates this in her study on numeracy in America between 1790-1820. In considering the census of

1820, she notes that among the things not counted were the number of slave-owners, black mortality, and female illiteracy. Further, it is particularly interesting that 1820 was the first census in which a household head was asked to report himself as a member of a particular sector of the economy. And, a societal interest in numeracy itself, reflected for our purposes in textbooks and traditional reference sources, indicates, as Cohen suggests, changing societal needs.[67]

One can follow this mode of analysis when discussing the U.S. census by an analysis of how questions asked in the census have changed through the years. A. Ross Eckler's *The Bureau of the Census* does this in its appendix "Population and Housing Census Questions, 1790-1970." The list is a shorthand chronicle of American history. Even before 1850 public education was an American obsession and in that year its enumeration became a census feature; as the nineteenth century ended the nation experienced massive waves of often seemingly unassimilable immigrants and the questions asked in 1890 reflect this concern; the 1940 census asked questions which poignantly described common experiences of the Great Depression; and in 1970 the 5 percent sample asked whether one's first marriage ended because of the death of one's spouse — a slightly less than obvious way of determining the extent of divorce.[68]

Margo Anderson Conk's *The United States Census and Labor Force Change: A History of Occupation Statistics, 1870-1940* focuses on the evolution of occupational classification and, like the above, shows how the way statistics are recorded defines a society. She suggests that the bureau's preoccupation with "finding" social mobility distorted and even negated evidence of actual conditions and abnormalities.[69]

Geographical Sources

The study of geography is important within a liberal education. Arthur H. Robinson observes, "any truly liberally educated person must be able to see the current scene as simply a point in the continuum of time and man's development." He goes on to advise, "the elements of cartographic history that parallel the other aspects of man's changing ideas are many: the growth to the topographic map, the changing fashions in map projections, the development of the representative fraction after the introduction of the metric system, the introduction of the thematic map as an outgrowth of the study of the social and physical world, to list but a few."[70]

Even though today maps reflect the state of geographical knowledge, it is important to remember that even commonly held knowledge, common at least among some, was, in earlier ages, slow to be published. For hundreds of years beautiful maps were published which were never geographically representative of the state of contemporary geographical knowledge. Indeed, they were more reflections of mythology and hoped for realities. Further, as mariners and travelers ventured out across the world they were hesitant for military, political, commercial, and egotistical reasons to share their findings. Mariners' charts were weighted for a quick toss into the sea. Not until the end of the eighteenth century did the British admiralty begin to systematically cooperate with commercial publishers.

The ability of students to read maps is not to be assumed; one history professor has recently written in astonishment at his students' level of map illiteracy.[71] Nothing can promise with greater certainty an ethnocentric view of the world than a total lack of geographical perspective.

In his presidential address before the annual meeting of the American Historical Association in 1983, Philip Curtin deplored the failure of American historians to acquire a broad enough perspective to escape even some of the most obvious ethnocentric pitfalls. Curtin discusses the Mercator projection, a mapping convention, as an example and potential cause of the problem. For instance, Curtin notes that the Indian subcontinent and the European subcontinent are roughly the same size but the Mercator projection, and the custom of using the Urals as Europe's eastern boundary, have "educated" us to see Europe as much larger.[72]

The Mercator projection exaggerates the size of areas in high latitudes. The North becomes larger; the South, smaller. Arno Peters's projection is one among a number of projections whose intent it is to accurately represent the relative size of the continents. The Mercator projection was used in the first mass produced atlases and, as Ian Bain observes, undoubtedly "gave imperial Britons a rosy glow of comfort at the extent of their dominion ... such as Canada." Shridth S. Ramphal explores the issue of Eurocentrism further, paying particular attention to the psychological significance of northern countries on the top of the world and southern countries on the bottom. Or the developing world occupying the bottom of the globe and the advanced nations, the top. But if nations from other parts of the world had dominated recent history would not they have viewed the world differently? For instance, during the Middle Ages it was the custom to place Jerusalem at the center of the world; in the fifteenth century Venetians put the South at the top; but by the early sixteenth century, because Western explorers lived in the North, the North was firmly established at the top.[73]

And then, of course, there is the very purposeful manipulation of geography for propagandistic ends. Maps present a precise and scientific appearance but this can belie purposeful distortion. For instance, scales, projections, and sections or extracts can present distorted images. Conventions for the amplification and simplification of geographical information can be contrived, color chosen for thematic maps can have connotative power, and typography (the size and nature of labels and symbols) can be used to convey incorrect measures of significance. John Ager gives the poignant example of pre-1914 German school atlas maps which seemingly represented Germany and the United States as the same size. German soldiers must have wondered in 1918 where all the Yanks came from![74]

Apart from these more profound questions, comparing maps of the same place over time is always fascinating. And the complementary possibilities of sources can be illustrated by using such things as census records, city directories, and photographs in conjunction with fire insurance maps and other local maps— a technique often used by historians. Since the mid-nineteenth century, fire insurance maps of incredible detail—from types of buildings to the width of sidewalks—were drawn up to provide detailed information concerning the potential fire risks of various structures. By 1924 Sanborn had published maps to 11,000 towns. The utilization of local sources usually generates considerable interest.[75]

Textbooks

Textbooks are included in this discussion because for many students they are the major "reference" book they will consistently consult. They are unquestioningly accepted as truth by too many. Although reference departments seldom have included them on their shelves, they are the primary aid in any student's "library." They have been studied in every possible way, including historically.

Some of the "problems" with textbooks become evident in a study of history texts. History is not what happened but a perception of what happened. World views and methodologies change as do social contexts, and regimes manipulate history for purely political reasons. Even more important is the unconscious manipulation of history. In short, societies and governments write the history they need to legitimatize themselves and achieve their goals, either consciously or unconsciously by either telling out-and-out lies, distorting reality, or through subtleties of interpretation. George Orwell's librarian comes to mind here perhaps more than elsewhere. Traditionally textbooks have been the most obvious medium for the transmission of official history, even if at times their context dramatically contradicts common popular knowledge; for different visions of the past exist simultaneously as official, professional, and folk history.

In discussing U.S. history textbooks, Jean Anyon writes "An ideological version of a historical period ... involves information selection and organization that provide an interpretation of social events and hierarchies that predispose attitudes and behaviors in support of certain groups."[76] The most well-known sociological study of American history textbooks is Frances Fitzgerald's *America Revised*. The author shows how elementary and secondary school American history texts have changed over time in response to a host of societal pressures. Most recently they have struggled to include nonwhites, have floundered over the Vietnam War, and customarily have shied away from questions of economic inequality. And all the time they have been designed with school board adoption foremost in the publisher's mind. One need only assemble representative texts to provide students with an exciting exercise. Fitzgerald's work should be read in conjunction with Marc Ferro's internationally focused *The Use and Abuse of History (or How the Past Is Taught)*.[77]

Textbook comparisons can powerfully and readily illustrate the social constraints on knowledge. A lecture on reference sources as historical artifacts might begin with an illustration from this genre as an "attention-getter."

Periodicals and Periodical
Abstracts and Indexes

Periodicals were made possible by the invention of the printing press. For practical purposes, indexes were made possible by this invention as well. Indexes, both author and subject, existed before printing, but the new technology clearly made their production a more reasonable undertaking.[78] The printing press led to the regular numbering of pages and the use of footnotes and title pages. Computer technology is leading to equally revolutionary changes in both publication and indexing. The call for unpredictable syntheses too numerous for manually accessed classification systems has created an environment in which only the computer can serve both economically and effectively.

Studying the development of specialized periodicals themselves vividly reveals the ever increasing specialization of knowledge. That synthetic journals should arise illustrates a recurrent concern among scholars that specialized learning must ideally be synthesized.

Bruce M. Manzer's study of the development of the abstract journal (and index and review journals as well) explores the factors which led to its development and ongoing evolution. Abstract, index, and review journals were responses to a rapidly differentiating intellectual environment. First came the abstract journal, an outgrowth of a major component of early scholarly periodicals designed to survey a manageable number of periodicals and serve a patient clientele. The abstract journal was followed in the mid-1800s by the periodical index which was designed to be more current and, in at least some instances, to respond specifically to a burgeoning population of popular periodicals. The review journal is the most recent attempt to respond to a huge and rich body of specialized periodical literature by saving users valuable time through critical synthesis. Manzer concludes with classified and chronological lists indicating the year of first issue of specific titles within each of the three types of tools. Easy access to the dates of first issuance for these tools invites one to explore the state of the disciplines they served at their appearance.[79]

The proliferation and diversity of periodical abstracts and indexes reflects contemporaneous approaches, interests, and orientations, both academic and popular. They reflect the journals they index and the journals in turn exist, as Charles Kadushin points out, "to select from the many new and old ideas those which it feels should now be talked about."[80] Today these tools exist in great proliferation because the various elements which compose our society have the right as well as the financial ability to write and publish in unprecedented freedom. Nonetheless, there exists a hierarchy of influence within the community of journals as well as within its specific segments. It should be noted that Wilson's *Social Sciences Index* and *Humanities Index* reflect this by indexing only the most major journals in each discipline.

The existence of specialized periodicals always precedes the development of tools to access them. Only after the size of the audience and body of publication are large enough, and financial resources are sufficient, are such tools developed. Or, as Michael Keresztesi suggests, only after a discipline has achieved sufficient maturity is it served by its own bibliographic and reference aids.[81] Apart from the periodicals themselves the mosaic of abstracts and indexes reveals much about a society's composition and context. For instance, only a society with strong ethnic and minority groups, free to communicate among themselves and with others, can support such sources as: *Index to Periodicals By and About Blacks*, *Index to Jewish Periodicals*, and *Women Studies Abstracts*. The statement of intent in the first issue of *Alternative Press Index* is a further reflection of a tolerant society, "We hope to help people in different regions of the country begin research on local power structures, industries, political figures, and social conditions." And later, "to help in the struggle to build a radical consciousness."

The in-depth examination of individual indexes invites more specific observations. What disciplines consider within their purview and the extent of their interest in knowledge generated by other disciplines is immediately apparent.

Through their indexes and tables of contents these tools also reflect the conceptual frameworks used to organize knowledge within the discipline. For instance, the June 1986 table of contents of *Sociological Abstracts*, compared to the table of contents of the 1963-67 quinquennial index, shows many changes. Among added divisions are: Sociology of Knowledge, Environmental Interactions, Feminist/Gender Studies, and Marxist Sociology.

Social Sciences Citation Index was the first bibliographic manifestation in the social sciences of the fact that social scientists build extensively upon the work of their colleagues. Certainly the citation indexes are the first bibliographic manifestation of a system where the literature indexes itself with an unmatched idiosyncratic precision.[82]

An interesting exercise might employ an index to create subject populations within a chronological dimension. Suggestive of what might be done is Terry David Bilhartz's content analysis of book reviews published in the *Journal of American History* over the past three decades which reveals changes in the criteria scholars use to evaluate historical works.[83] Students might be asked to identify book reviews for specific titles, selected to span a period of time, and to briefly explain how the nature of the reviews differ.

Along these lines, a periodical index might be "read" to arrive at a picture of a particular period. This would be an interesting *Readers' Guide to Periodical Literature* project. Reconstructing an event through article citations across a span of indexes can lead to a discussion of the biases evident within the group as well as when a topic was first treated and when its coverage peaked. To reconstruct history from citations rather than from the articles themselves might be a brief but interesting "archaeological" exercise.[84]

Finally, a study of the development and evolution of a particular index (or any tool for that matter) might be assigned, with a focus on its publishing history, structure, headings, sponsorship, and coverage. If done sensitively, a history of the discipline or topic it covers will emerge.[85]

Guides to Reference Books

Finally, one may wish to consider the change over time in the population of reference sources itself. Focusing on social concerns, one might trace the appearance in sources such as the *Guide to Reference Books* and its predecessors, of works on women, Afro-Americans, and other ethnic or minority groups. This approach might be extended to any number of concerns: the appearance of new indexes, by topic or by structure, or the increased publication of finely focused disciplinary dictionaries. Once a population is chosen for study, the ultimate question is why has it come into existence. It is important to remember that not all reference sources have found their way into this guide. Nonetheless, inclusion is an indication of general acceptance and presumed utility to a relatively wide audience.[86]

Conclusion

Reference sources tell us more than the information they are designed to convey. Through their content and design, they reveal much about the culture which produced them. The approach recommended in this chapter challenges students and instructors to look beyond the obvious and to consider the nature of the information they find by reflecting on the nature of the sources they use to find it. It advocates the use of reference sources as subjects on which to practice critical thinking in a sociobibliographical and sociohistorical context.

Notes

[1] Ilse Bry, "Information Storage and Retrieval: Bibliographic Issues in the Behavioral Sciences," in *International Encyclopedia of the Social Sciences*, ed. David L. Sills (New York: Macmillan/Free Press, 1968); Ilse Bry, "The Emerging Field of Sociobiology: Reassessment and Reorientation of Access to Knowledge in the Social Sciences," in *Access to the Literature of the Social Sciences and Humanities* (Proceedings of the Conference on Access to Knowledge and Information in the Social Sciences and Humanities, New York, 5-6 April 1972) (Flushing, N.Y.: Queens College Press, 1974), 11. An overview of the purposeful and unconscious manipulation of reference sources, with examples from various genres, is found in Clement E. Vose's "Information Storage and Retrieval: Reference Materials and Books," in *International Encyclopedia of the Social Sciences*.

[2] John B. Dillon, "Renaissance Reference Books as Sources for Classical Myth and Geography: A Brief Survey, with an Illustration from Milton," in *Acta Conventus Neo-Latini Bononiensis* (Proceedings of the Fourth International Congress of Neo-Latin Studies, Bologna, 26 August-1 September 1979), ed. R. J. Schoeck (Binghamton, N.Y.: Center for Medieval and Renaissance Studies, State University of New York at Binghamton, 1985), 437-50.

[3] William Graebner, "The Cold War: A Yearbook Perspective," *Magazine of History* 2 (Summer 1986): 10-14. Among instructive curiosities on the sexist heritage of the U.S. government's *Dictionary of Occupational Titles*, see Joe Morehead's "Revisions and Excisions," *Documents to the People* 4 (November 1976): 7-9. On the historical usefulness of runs of "old" documents, see Joe Morehead's "Reflections on Infant Care, Bills, and the Instructions to Depository Libraries," *Documents to the People* 7 (May 1979): 94-95.

[4] A. Sandison, "References/Citations in the Study of Knowledge," *Journal of Documentation* 31 (September 1975): 196; M. B. Line and A. Sandison, "Obsolescence and Changes in the Use of Literature with Time," *Journal of Documentation* 35 (September 1974): 311.

[5] Michael Keresztesi, "The Science of Bibliography: Theoretical Implications for Bibliographic Instruction," in *Theories of Bibliographic Education: Designs for Teaching*, ed. Cerise Oberman and Katina Strauch (New York: R. R. Bowker, 1982), 20-21.

[6] Stephen K. Stoan, "Survey of the Field," in *Sources of Information in the Social Sciences: A Guide to the Literature*, ed. William H. Webb (Chicago and London: American Library Association, 1986), 7. See also E. P. Dudley's "Reference Books Published in Britain, 1870-1914: Some Notes for a Study of Origins," in *Bibliography and Reading: A Festschrift in Honour of Ronald Stavely*, ed. Ia McIlwaine, John McIlwaine, and Peter G. New (Metuchen, N.J.: Scarecrow Press, 1983), 143-59.

[7]Raymond G. McInnis, *New Perspectives for Reference Service in Academic Libraries* (Westport, Conn.: Greenwood Press, 1978), 127; Thelma Freides, *Literature and Bibliography of the Social Sciences* (Los Angeles, Calif.: Melville Publishing, 1973), 134-35. These are briefly discussed in Sharon J. Rogers's "Research Strategies: Bibliographic Instruction for Undergraduates," *Library Trends* 29 (Summer 1980): 73-74.

[8]Elizabeth Frick, "Information Structure and Bibliographic Instruction," *The Journal of Academic Librarianship* 1 (September 1975): 14.

[9]Daniel L. Wick, "In Defense of Knowledge: An Intellectual Framework for General Education," *Change* 13 (September 1981): 8-10, focuses on the value of cultural and intellectual history and, more specifically, on the Western culture component of Stanford University's general education program. On historical methodology and the study of library history, see Orvin Lee Shiflett's "Clio's Claim: The Role of Historical Research in Library and Information Science," *Journal of Library History* 32 (Spring 1984): 390-92.

[10]E. D. Hirsch, Jr., "Cultural Literacy and the Schools," *American Educator* 9 (Summer 1985): 8-15; E. D. Hirsch, Jr., Joseph Kett, and James Trefil, *Cultural Literacy. What Every American Needs to Know* (Boston: Houghton Mifflin, 1987).

[11]George Orwell, *1984* (New York: NAL, 1961), 176, quoted in John C. Swan's "Winston the Librarian," *Library Journal* 109 (1 November 1984): 1994.

[12]Lester Coster, "Sociology of Knowledge," in *International Encyclopedia of the Social Sciences*, 428.

[13]Nico Stehr and Volker Meja, "Introduction: The Development of the Sociology of Knowledge," in *Society and Knowledge: Contemporary Perspectives in the Sociology of Knowledge*, ed. Nico Stehr and Volker Meja (New Brunswick, N.J.: Transaction Books, 1984), 1.

[14]Werner Stark, "Sociology of Knowledge," in *Encyclopedia of Philosophy*, ed. Paul Edwards (New York: Macmillan, 1967), 477.

[15]Norbert Elias, "Knowledge and Power: An Interview by Peter Ludes," in *Society and Knowledge*, 251-91.

[16]Raymond Williams, *Problems of Materialism and Culture: Selected Essays* (London: Verson, 1980), 37-38, discussed in Michael H. Harris's "State, Class, and Cultural Reproduction: Toward a Theory of Library Service in the United States," in *Advances in Librarianship*, vol. 14, ed. Wesley Simonton (Orlando, Fla.: Academic Press, 1986), 224-25. My consideration of cultural transmission is heavily indebted to this essay.

[17]T. J. Jackson Lears, "The Concept of Cultural Hegemony: Problems and Possibilities," *American Historical Review* 90 (June 1985): 572, 574.

[18]Mona McCormick, "Critical Thinking and Library Instruction," *RQ* 22 (Summer 1983): 339-42. Among other useful works are Harvey Siegel's "Critical Thinking as an Educational Ideal," *Educational Forum* 45 (November 1980): 7-23; Robert H. Ennis's "A Concept of Critical Thinking: A Proposal Basis for Research in the Teaching of Critical Thinking Ability," *Harvard Educational Forum* 32 (November 1980): 81-111; and Edward

D'Angelo's *The Teaching of Critical Thinking* (Amsterdam: B. B. Gruner N.V., 1971), 7-15.

[19]L. P. V. Febvre and H. J. Martin, *The Coming of the Book* (London: NLB, 1976), 109-27.

[20]James D. Hart, *The Popular Book: A History of America's Literary Taste* (New York: Oxford University Press, 1950), 285.

[21]Richard D. Altick, *Librarianship and the Pursuit of Truth*, Richard Shoemaker Lecture, no. 2/2 (New Brunswick, N.J.: Rutgers University Graduate School of Library Service, 1974).

[22]Tom McArthur, *Worlds of Reference: Lexicography, Learning and Language from the Clay Tablet to the Computer* (Cambridge: Cambridge University Press, 1986), 62-63, 81-89.

[23]Elizabeth L. Eisenstein, *The Printing Press as an Agent of Change*, vol. 1 of *Communications and Cultural Transformation in Early-Modern Europe* (Cambridge: Cambridge University Press), 9-10, 52-53, 108-13.

[24]Parker Rossman, "The Coming Great Electronic Encyclopedia," *Futurist* 16 (August 1982): 55-56.

[25]Frank Parise, ed., *The Book of Calendars* (New York: Facts on File, 1982).

[26]Sidney L. Jackson, "What a History of the Encyclopedia Could Show," *Library Review* 19 (1963/64): 398-401.

[27]For instance, June L. Engle and Elizabeth Futas's "Sexism in Adult Encyclopedias," *RQ* 23 (Fall 1983): 29-39; Linda Kraft's "Lost Herstory: The Treatment of Women in Children's Encyclopedias," *Library Journal* 98 (15 January 1973): 218-27; and Beryl Caroline Graham's "Treatment of Black Women in Children's Encyclopedias," *Negro History Bulletin* 39 (May 1976): 596-98.

[28]Charles Coulston Gillispie, ed., *A Diderot Pictorial Encyclopedia of Trades and Industry: Manufacturing and the Technical Arts in Plates Selected from L'Encyclopédie, ou Dictonnaire Raisonné des Sciences, des Arts et des Métiers of Denis Diderot* (New York: Dover, 1959); *Diderot Encyclopédie: The Complete Illustrations, 1762-1777* (New York: Abrams, 1978).

[29]Thelma Freides, *Literature and Bibliography of the Social Sciences* (Los Angeles, Calif.: Melville Publishing, 1973), 99-102.

[30]"The New *ESS*," *Newsweek*, 1 April 1968, 66.

[31]Ralph Ross, "On the *International Encyclopedia of the Social Sciences*," *American Political Science Review* 70 (September 1976): 939-51.

[32]Alvin Johnson, "Introduction," in *International Encyclopedia of the Social Sciences*, xiii.

[33]Oscar Handlin, *Truth in History* (Cambridge, Mass.: The Belknap Press of Harvard University Press, 1979), 6-7.

[34]*New Catholic Encyclopedia*, vol. 1 (New York: McGraw-Hill, 1967), 634.

[35]*Encyclopaedia Judaica*, vol. 3 (New York: Macmillan, 1972), 96.

[36]*New Catholic Encyclopedia*, vol. 1, 635.

[37]*Encyclopaedia Judaica*, vol. 3, 102.

[38]*Great Soviet Encyclopedia*, 3d ed., vol. 23 (New York: Macmillan, 1973), 745. On the second edition's treatment of American history, with references to changes from the first edition, see William Benton's "The *Great Soviet Encyclopedia*," *Yale Review* 47 (Summer 1958): 552-68; on the third edition, with comments on missing biographies and Vietnam, see Patricia K. Grimsted's "The *Great Soviet Encyclopedia*: Détente on the Reference Shelves?" *Wilson Library Bulletin* 49 (June 1975): 728-40.

[39]Raymond G. McInnis, "Integrating Classroom Instruction and Library Research: An Essay Review," *Studies in History and Society* 6 (Winter 1974/75): 39; Raymond G. McInnis, "History," in *Social Science Research Handbook*, ed. Raymond G. McInnis and James W. Scott (New York: Barnes & Noble, c1974; repr., New York: Garland, 1984), 89-92. See also John MacGregor and Raymond G. McInnis's "Integrating Classroom Instruction and Library Research: The Cognitive Functions of Bibliographic Network Structures," *Journal of Higher Education* 48 (January/February 1977): 17-38, and Eugene Garfield's "Primordial Concepts, Citation Indexing, and Historio-Bibliography," *Journal of Library History* 11 (July 1967): 235-49.

[40]Dorothy Ethlyn Cole, "The Characteristics of *Americana* and *Britannica*," *RQ* 12 (Spring 1973): 226.

[41]*Notable American Women, 1607-1950* (Cambridge, Mass.: Belknap Press of Harvard University Press, 1971); *Dictionary of American Negro Biography*, ed. Rayford W. Logan and Michael R. Winston (New York: W. W. Norton & Co., 1982), vii. In addition to indexes, which will be mentioned later, these two groups have also been underrepresented in quotation books, as described in Elaine McPheron's "Dictionaries of Quotations: A Comparative Review," *Reference Services Review* 12 (Winter 1984): 26-27, 29.

[42]Sidney I. Landau, *Dictionaries and the Art and Craft of Lexicography* (New York: Charles Scribner's Sons, 1984), 59-64; McArthur, *Worlds of Reference*, 93-101; Donald A. Wells, *Dictionaries and the Authoritarian Tradition* (The Hague and Paris: Mouton, 1973).

[43]Benjamin Lee Whorf, *Language, Thought and Reality: Selected Writings of Benjamin Lee Whorf*, ed. John B. Carroll (Cambridge, Mass.: M.I.T. Press, 1956). Critical of this hypothesis is Eleanor Rosch in "Natural Categories," *Cognitive Psychology* 4 (May 1973): 328-50. On evaluative thought, see Donald G. MacKay's "Language, Thought and Social Attitudes," in *Language: Social Psychological Perspectives*, ed. Howard Giles, W. Peter Robinson, and Philip M. Smith (New York: Pergamon Press, 1980), 89-96.

[44]H. Lee Gershuny, "Sexist Semantics in the Dictionary," *ETC: A Review of General Semantics* 31 (June 1974): 159-69. On racism, see William Walter Duncan's "How 'White' Is Your Dictionary?" *ETC: A Review of General Semantics* 27 (March 1970): 89-91. For a combination of racism and sexism, see Patricia Bell Scott's "The English Language and Black Womanhood: A Low Blow at Self-Esteem," *Journal of Afro-American Issues* 2 (Summer 1974): 218-21.

[45]Hans Aarsleff, "The Early History of the *Oxford English Dictionary*," *New York Public Library, Bulletin* 66 (September 1962): 417-39; Raymond Williams, *Keywords: A Vocabulary of Culture and Society*, rev. ed. (New York: Oxford University Press, 1985), 18-19. See also Robert DeMaria's *Johnson's "Dictionary" and the Language of Learning* (Oxford: Clarendon Press, 1986).

[46]Ethel Strainchamps, "Our Sexist Language," in *Women in Sexist Society: Studies in Power and Powerlessness*, ed. Vivian Gornick and Barbara K. Moran (New York: Basic Books, 1971), 353-57.

[47]Landau, *Dictionaries*, 184-85.

[48]Jacques Barzun, "What Is a Dictionary?" *American Scholar* 32 (Spring 1963): 181.

[49]Robert A. Hall, Jr., "*Webster's Third New International Dictionary*: A Symposium," *Quarterly Journal of Speech* 48 (December 1962): 435.

[50]Pat Rogers, "The *OED* at the Turning-Point," *TLS* (9 May 1986): 488.

[51]Robert Pierson, "Offensive Epithets in Six Dictionaries," *Reference Services Review* 12 (Fall 1984): 41-48; Landau, *Dictionaries*, 186-88.

[52]Landau, *Dictionaries*, 133; see also 17-18; on definition length, 250, 302-3.

[53]Insight into the evolution and connotation of "Black" is offered in Winthrop Jordan's *White Over Black: American Attitudes Toward the Negro, 1550-1812* (Chapel Hill, N.C.: The University of North Carolina Press for the Institute of Early American History and Culture, 1968), 257-59. See also Duncan's "How 'White' Is Your Dictionary?" 89-91.

[54]Adrian Room, *Dictionary of Changes in Meaning* (London: Routledge & Kegan Paul, 1986), 1.

[55]Richard D. Altick, *The Art of Literary Research*, 3rd ed., rev. by John Fenstermaker (New York: W. W. Norton & Co., 1981), 255-56.

[56]Mario Andrew Pei, *Words in Sheep's Clothing* (New York: Hawthorn Books, 1969).

[57]Raymond Williams, *Keywords: A Vocabulary of Culture and Society*.

[58]Landau, *Dictionaries*, 211-16.

[59]Insight into the significance of such study is offered by Alan Gribben in "Private Libraries of American Authors: Disposal, Custody, and Description," *Journal of Library History* 23 (Spring 1986): 300-314.

[60]I. R. Wilson, *On the History of Libraries and Scholarship*, Viewpoints Series, no. 4 (Washington, D.C.: Library of Congress, 1980), 0001-26.

[61]Wendy Griswold, "American Character and the American Novel: An Expression of Reflection Theory on the Sociology of Literature," *American Journal of Sociology* 86 (January 1981): 740-65.

[62]Hart, *The Popular Book*, 285. See also Alice Payne Hackett and James Henry Burke's *80 Years of Best Sellers, 1895-1975* (New York and London: R. R. Bowker, 1977).

[63]For a concise historical synopsis of classification systems, see Fritz Machlup's *Knowledge: Its Creation, Distribution, and Economic Significance*, vol. 2 of *The Branches of Learning* (Princeton, N.J.: Princeton University Press, 1982).

[64]David Batty, "Information Science and Information Science Techniques as an Approach to Synthesis and Interpretation," in *Knowledge Structure and Use: Implication for Synthesis and Interpretation*, ed. Spencer A. Ward and Linda J. Reed (Philadelphia, Pa.: Temple University Press, 1983), 313-42.

[65]J. H. Shera, "Classification as the Basis of Bibliographic Organization," in *Bibliographic Organization*, ed. J. H. Shera (Chicago: University of Chicago Press, 1951), 77; discussed in Norman Stevens's "The History of Information," *Advances in Librarianship* 14 (1986): 21. A relevant foreign study is Christian Amalvi's "Catalogues historiques et conceptions de l'histoire," *Storia della Storiografia* 2 (1982): 77-101.

[66]Sanford Berman, *Prejudices and Antipathies: A Tract on the LC Subject Heads Concerning People* (Metuchen, N.J.: Scarecrow Press, 1971).

[67]Patricia Cline Cohen, *A Calculating People: The Spread of Numeracy in Early America* (Chicago: University of Chicago Press, 1982).

[68]A. Ross Eckler, *The Bureau of the Census* (New York: Praeger Publishers, 1972).

[69]Margo Anderson Conk, *The United States Census and Labor Force Change: A History of Occupation in Statistics, 1870-1940* (Ann Arbor, Mich.: UMI Research Press, 1980).

[70]Arthur H. Robinson, "The Potential Contribution of Cartography in Liberal Education," in *Geography in Undergraduate Liberal Education; A Report* (Washington, D.C.: Association of American Geographers, 1965), 39-40. Among the many interesting sources of examples see Wilma George's *Animals and Maps* (Berkeley, Calif.: University of California Press, 1969); Norman J. W. Thrower's *Maps and Man: An Examination of Cartography in Relation to Culture and Civilization* (Englewood Cliffs, N.J.: Prentice-Hall, 1972); P. D. A. Harvey's *The History of Topographic Maps: Symbols, Pictures and Surveys* (London: Thames and Hudson, 1980); Leo Bagrow's *History of Cartography*, rev. and enl. by R. A. Skelton (Cambridge, Mass.: Harvard University Press, 1964); and Rodney W. Shirley's *The Mapping of the World: Early Printed World Maps, 1472-1700*, Holland Press Cartographica, vol. 9 (London: Holland Press, 1983).

[71]James D. Ryan, "The Problem of Map Illiteracy," *History Teacher* 19 (November 1985): 9-14.

[72]Philip D. Curtin, "Depth, Span, and Relevance" *American Historical Review* 89 (February 1984): 7-8. The fact that most chronologies neglect the non-Western world illustrates the ethnocentrism and nonintegrative focus of much contemporary historiography; see Stephen W. Rogers's "Selected Historical Chronologies," *Reference Services Review* 11 (Summer 1983): 17.

[73]Iain Bain, "Will Arno Peters Take over the World?" *Geographical Magazine* 56 (July 1984): 342-43; Shridath S. Ramphal, "A World Turned Upside Down," *Geography* 70, no. 307 (April 1985): 193-205; "The World Upside Down, Inside Out," *Economist* 293, no. 7373/7374 (22 December 1984): 19-21, 24.

[74]John K. Wright, "Map Makers Are Human: Comments on the Subjective in Maps," *Geographical Review* 32 (October 1942): 527-44; Richard Muir, "The Slickness of the Map Deceives the Eye," *Geographical Magazine* 46 (May 1974): 436; John Ager, "Maps & Propaganda," *Society of University Cartographers, Bulletin* 11, no. 1 (1977): 1-15.

[75]Robert A. Sander, "The Use of Sanborn Maps in Reconstructing 'Geographies of the Past': Boston's Waterfront from 1867 to 1972," *Journal of Geography* 79 (November 1980): 204-13. For an example of an exercise which requires the use of city directories, tax lists, and maps, see Edward Orser's *If All the World Were Baltimore: Social History Documents from the 100 Block of W. Lee St. and Welcome Alley* (Baltimore, Md.: Department of American Studies, University of Maryland—Baltimore County, 1983).

[76]Jean Anyon, "Ideology and United States History Textbooks," *Harvard Educational Review* 49 (August 1979): 363.

[77]Frances Fitzgerald, *America Revised: History Schoolbooks in the Twentieth Century* (Boston: Little, Brown, 1979); Marc Ferro, *The Use and Abuse of History (or How the Past Is Taught)* (London: Routledge & Kegan Paul, 1984).

[78]Charles B. Osburn, "The Place of the Journal in the Scholarly Communications System," *Library Resources & Technical Services* 28 (October/December 1984): 315-24.

[79]Bruce M. Manzer, *The Abstract Journal, 1790-1920: Origin, Development and Diffusion* (Metuchen, N.J.: Scarecrow Press, 1977).

[80]Charles Kadushin, *The American Intellectual Elite* (Boston: Little, Brown, 1974), 56. Of special interest to historians is Margaret F. Stieg's *The Origin and Development of Scholarly Historical Periodicals* (University, Ala.: University of Alabama Press, 1986).

[81]Keresztesi, "The Science of Bibliography."

[82]Frick, "Information Structure and Bibliographic Instruction," 13.

[83]Terry David Bilhartz, *Good History vs. Bad History: The Changing Art of Book Reviewing* (Bethesda, Md.: ERIC Document Reproduction Service, 1984). ED 235 094. Terry David Bilhartz, "In 500 Words or Less: Academic Book Reviewing in American History," *History Teacher* 17 (August 1984): 525-36.

[84]On the importance of this source, see C. Paul Vincent's "How about the *Readers' Guide?" Research Strategies* 3 (Spring 1985): 87-89.

[85]Though lacking perception and depth, suggestive of what might be done as a brief project is Herbert B. Lundau's "*Engineering Index*, 1884-1984," *Special Libraries* 75 (October 1984): 312-18.

[86]On a relevant analysis of history sources in *American Reference Books Annual*, see Michael Keresztesi's "Trends in Historical Bibliography," *Association for the Bibliography of History, Newsletter* 7 (June 1984): 1-2. Although not dealing with reference sources, an interesting group of books is defined in C. Maury Drevine, Claudia M. Dissel, and Kim D. Parrish, eds., *The Harvard Guide to Influential Books* (New York: Harper & Row, 1986).

CHAPTER 11

TEACHING THE ART OF LITERARY RESEARCH

Maureen Pastine

Introduction

The purpose of this chapter is to provide a conceptual framework for the librarian teaching the art of literary research. Focus is on recognition and use of primary and secondary sources, as most literary research begins with the reading of an original text (the primary source) and is followed by an interpretation of that text, assisted by the reading and examination of secondary and tertiary sources (that is, literary criticism, biographical accounts, and fact-finding and further explanatory materials). Teaching methodologies using primary/secondary sources as the conceptual framework can easily be adapted for undergraduate, upper division, and graduate level courses. Sources covered can be narrowed to include those relating to a particular author's work, a national literature, a genre, a theme, an historical period, or a literary movement. The model presentation in this chapter will be for American literature, but sources noted are representative samples available for the study of any literature. However, it should be mentioned that bibliographical coverage and control of a literature varies greatly depending on the time period, nationality, genre, theme, literary movement, or particular authors under study. Early American literature, for example, is under much better bibliographical control than is contemporary American literature.

Literary Research Guides

Bibliographic instruction is most effective if all students have access to the same published literary research guide in each targeted course, although different course titles may require different literary research guides. There are a number of excellent guides in print. The literary guide for student use in the recommended course is Valmai Kirkham Fenster's *Guide to American Literature.*[1] Students do not always recognize the significance of the guides to the literature. Thus, it is highly recommended that great emphasis be placed on defining the purpose of Fenster's guide, a summary of its coverage, and how to locate similar guides to the literature in this and other disciplines. Specialized guides to southern literature, western American literature, Native American literature, Afro-American poetry, etc., should also be mentioned. These guides provide excellent overviews of types of reference sources available, specific reference titles, and general or esoteric information regarding the reference sources included.

Primary/Secondary Sources as Conceptual Framework

Generalizations regarding publication sequence should be introduced early in bibliographic instruction presentations. For example, once an idea is conceived for a creative work (e.g., a poem, play, short story, essay, novel), it may be some time (months or years) before it becomes an actual publication. A handwritten manuscript (perhaps several drafts of it) may still exist in the special collections area of the library specializing in collecting materials by and about that author, along with further illumination of its shaping prior to publication in the author's letters to friends, family, and publisher and/or in diary or journal entries. This type of creative, original work, along with the first publication and variant editions in book, journal, broadside, and similar forms, is considered primary source material.

Secondary sources come after the primary sources in the publication sequence. Examples of secondary sources are literary criticism, biographical accounts, and other explanatory sources. Much of the instructional session will focus on bibliographic tools which give access to secondary sources. Primary/secondary sources as a conceptual framework allow for a discussion of access tools in relation to the nature and importance of the material for which they provide listings.

Although various conceptual frameworks can be used to provide a meaningful experience for students conducting literary research, use of primary/secondary sources allows for a structure in which comparisons to library organization, publication sequence in the humanities, and type and purpose of reference sources can be easily explained. This framework also allows for comparisons with social scientific and scientific research development. Further breakdowns of the conceptual characteristics of American literary research can include discussions of search strategies and resources accessible by nation or region, chronological period, genre, or theme, and how research strategies differ among humanities scholars, scientists, and social scientists. And it can include interdisciplinary sources useful to all.

Research strategies of humanities scholars are often quite different than those employed by scientists and social scientists. First of all most humanities scholars work alone and tend to use libraries more often than scholars in other disciplines. But humanities scholars also rely heavily on their own files and their colleagues to provide needed literature citations. There is a greater need for retrospective materials and less need for current information, unless the focus of study is a writer who has only recently gained critical acclaim. Since most research conducted by the literary scholar is not based on an initial key experiment from which new studies build and develop previous knowledge, citations to the secondary literature may not be necessary. Thus, there is more reliance on the primary sources, the original texts, than on journal literature. But literary scholars do, often, focus on critiques of particular works of authors that may relate to the scholars' work. A. Robert Rogers in *The Humanities: A Selective Guide to Information Sources* provides an excellent summary of how humanities scholars differ from scientists and social scientists.[2]

There are fewer abstracting services available in the humanities than in the sciences and social sciences. Although attendance and presentation of papers at conferences is a common occurrence, few literary research scholars consider conference proceedings papers as valuable in their own research—unlike the sciences and social sciences.

Even though computer searching is not as extensive as it is in the sciences, the linguistic ability of the literary scholar is usually greater than the scientist and social scientist. An excellent discussion of "The Computer and the Humanities" is included in Rogers's guide.

PRIMARY SOURCES

Primary sources (works by a particular author such as manuscripts, diaries, letters, and first, subsequent, and variant editions of novels, short stories, poems, plays, and other original creative works) are usually identified and located through author, title, and/or subject approaches. It is far easier to conduct a search on author, title, or genre in literature than it is to locate fictional works on a particular subject or theme. For instance, there is no subject access to novels, plays, or other literary works in typical library catalogs.

To gain increased subject or thematic access, the student must be made aware of the specialized subject oriented guides and bibliographies to works of fiction. Some excellent examples for American literature include Virginia Terris's *Woman in America: A Guide to Information Sources*, which provides an excellent listing of fictional works on women in American literature, Sam Bluefarb's *The Escape Motif in the American Novel: Mark Twain to Richard Wright*, Leslie A. Fiedler's *Love and Death in the American Novel*, Edmund Wilson's *Patriotic Gore: Studies in the Literature of the American Civil War*, Roger O. Rock's *The Native American in American Literature: A Selectively Annotated Bibliography*, Elsa L. Radcliffe's *Gothic Novels of the Twentieth Century: An Annotated Bibliography*, and Betty Rosenberg's *Genreflecting: A Guide to Reading Interests in Genre Fiction.*[4] The latter is a fascinating listing of fictional accounts on topics such as mining, the range war, bad men and good men, the singular woman, disaster, spy-espionage, soap opera, new wave, immortality, mythology and legend, reincarnation and possession, and monsters.

When searching for editors/compilers and titles of collections of short stories, poetry, drama, and essays, it is usually better to consult an index to the genre first. For example, *Granger's Index to Poetry* provides bibliographical citations to specific poems by author's surname, title of poem, subject, and first line.[5] After identifying the anthology which includes the specific poem, it is necessary to check the library's catalog for inclusion in that library's holdings or collections. Similar indexes exist for other poetry, short story, essay, and drama titles published in anthologies. Most of these indexes provide citations to anthologies of works *by* and *about* particular authors' works.

SECONDARY AND TERTIARY SOURCES

This section deals with secondary sources, such as book reviews, biographies, and literary periodicals, as well as access sources to secondary material such as indexes and bibliographies. Already established popular and well-known authors with a large reading audience waiting for the next publication are usually easy to research as published interviews and book reviews appear on or near publication release. Within a few months, the reviews and interviews are usually indexed in publications such as the *New York Times Index* and *Readers' Guide to Periodical Literature*. As publications gain popular interest, book reviews increase in newspapers and magazines. Reviews in scholarly journals are slower to appear and these are usually limited to authors of substantive literary merit and/or popularity.

BOOK REVIEWS

The Book Review Digest (which indexes about eighty general periodicals and a few scholarly journals) and *Book Review Index* (which indexes over 200 journals) provide citations to more reviews as they appear. Unlike some indexing reviews, *Book Review Digest* provides excerpts from the reviews. For those that provide citation only to the original review, use guides to the literature to find other book reviewing citation sources. And remember that a book published in 1985 is not going to be reviewed in a 1960 index volume. Major American authors are frequently reviewed, and citations to reviews of their works are found not only in the general book reviewing sources, but in published book length bibliographies by and/or about the author, and in bibliographies of major writers of particular literary movements or time periods, genre bibliographies, and national or regional bibliographies. Appearance of these bibliographical publications may, however, be produced years after the works indexed are published.

The Reader's Advisor: A Layman's Guide to Literature is an excellent source for information relating to textual variations and different editions of one title.[6] The first volume of this work has a chapter on general reference books related to literature, including American literature.

BIOGRAPHICAL SOURCES

Biographies of authors are usually produced only after an author has produced a substantial body of writings and is considered a key literary figure. Frequently the best and most accurate biographies are those published by the critic considered the expert on the life and works of a particular literary personality. Officially authorized biographies may be more accurate than those not sanctioned by the author or family members.

Guides, bibliographies, and indexes to biographies and obituaries are extremely useful in tracing the importance of an author during his/her lifetime, as a long-standing, reputable literary figure, or in relation to other literary figures over a period of time. *The Dictionary of Literary Biography* is an excellent source of biographical information on literary figures. *Biography Index* and *Current Biography* assist in gleaning information regarding contemporary literary personalities, though *Contemporary Authors* includes more names of literary figures. In American literature, the Twayne's United States Author Series and the University of Minnesota Pamphlets on American Writers Series are extremely valuable in determining the current "giants" and gaining detailed biographical and critical information from the experts' perspectives.

It is much more difficult to trace the literary output and subsequent reviewing, bibliographical, and biographical (i.e., the secondary source) material published on lesser-known authors, or those authors whose popularity was great during their own lifetime but whose works did not withstand the test of time. Secondary access sources including published bibliographies and biographical and other indexing/citation sources may omit them in favor of including more prominent literary figures. Another problem for literary scholars is the blatant omission of women and minority authors in secondary access tools. However, a number of reprint publishers are attempting to address this need through publications of original works in both book and/or microfiche format. An example of this is *Gerritsen Collection of Women's History*, 1543-1945, reproduced by University Microfilms on microfiche and microfilm. A number of publishers have also solicited writers and editors to produce new secondary access resources to works by and about long forgotten or neglected writers. Lina Mainiero's *American Women Writers: A Critical Reference Guide from Colonial Times to the Present* helps to fill the gap in inadequacy on coverage of American women writers.[7]

BIBLIOGRAPHIES

An excellent historical account of the development of bibliographies in American literature is Vito Joseph Brenni's *The Bibliographical Control of American Literature, 1920-1975*.[8] Although uneven in coverage, Jacob N. Blanck's *Bibliography of American Literature* is one of the best literary history bibliographies available, and it will be the most comprehensive when completed.[9] Jacob N. Blanck died in 1974 and the seventh volume was completed by Virginia L. Smyers and Michael Winship in 1983. The eighth volume, being edited by Earle E. Coleman, will complete the set. It covers over 300 major American authors up to 1930. Another comprehensive bibliography, with a separate section on American literature, is the *M.L.A. International Bibliography of Books and Articles on the Modern Languages and Literatures*.[10] Entries are arranged, under nationality, in chronological periods with further subdivisions under author and work. It is available in print and through online access. Beginning in 1981, the bibliography changed from three to five volumes per year, the first of which is on British, American, Australian, English-Canadian, New Zealand, and English-Caribbean literature.

LITERARY PERIODICALS

There are a number of guides to literary periodicals. One by Donna Gerstenberger and George Hendrick, the *Fourth Directory of Periodicals Publishing Articles in English and American Literature and Language*, lists over 600 scholarly journals, providing manuscript and subscription information.[11] The

M.L.A. Directory of Periodicals: A Guide to Journals and Series in Languages and Literatures is a companion to the bibliography giving complete bibliographic citations to the approximately 3,000 journals and series indexed in the bibliography.[12] Many of the literary research guides and Gerstenberger and Hendrick provide specific lists of periodicals devoted to more specialized areas of literary study. William A. Wartman's *A Guide to Serial Bibliographies for Modern Literature* will provide a listing of bibliographies on literatures of various countries which are published at regular intervals either as separate publications or as part of scholarly journals.[13]

INDEXES

Specialized indexes to a specific group of periodicals can be consulted by author, title, and/or subject for citations by and about certain authors, their works, or subjects such as "courtly love," "Afro-American fiction," or "psychological themes." Some of these continuing indexes cover all time periods and literatures. Others have ceased publication and include only eighteenth or nineteenth century writings, and others cover only little magazines. There is some duplication among many of these indexes and some inadequacies due to limited numbers of periodical titles indexed. The *American Humanities Index* and *Arts and Humanities Citation Index* are more general in scope and cover a greater time period than some of the more specialized indexing sources. All are necessary to comprehensive coverage of periodical literature.

The genre indexes to poetry, drama, fiction, short stories, and essays range from those devoted to index citations to original works to those specifically addressed to citations of literary criticism and explication. An example of the former is the *Short Story Index: An Index of Stories in Collections and Periodicals*, which is now published annually.[14] An example of the index to literary criticism is Patricia E. Sweeney's *William Faulkner's Women Characters: An Annotated Bibliography of Criticism, 1930-1983*.[15] The literary guides are excellent sources for titles, coverage, and limitations of these indexes.

DICTIONARIES AND GLOSSARIES

Other reference tools for the study of literary research in American studies abound. Specialized dictionaries and glossaries provide a means of tracing word origins and date of first recorded usage, definitions of literary terminology and allusions, and other fascinating information on literary characters and literary writing styles. An example is Clarence H. Holman's *A Handbook to Literature Based on the Original Edition by William Flint Thrall and Addison Hibbard*.[16] *Current Contents* (specialized periodical guides to contents pages of recent issues of journals in many disciplines, including the humanities) is an excellent source when researching a contemporary novelist.

HANDBOOKS AND ENCYCLOPEDIAS

A number of literary one-volume and multiple-volume handbooks and encyclopedias exist to provide brief explanations, plot summaries, articles and biographies on writers and philosophers, literary terms, character identifications, chronological outlines of historical periods, literary societies and awards, and literary movements and styles of thought. One of the best is James D. Hart's *The Concise Oxford Companion to American Literature*.[17] Some are more specialized dictionaries to fictional characters, place-names, and poetry and poetics.

LITERARY SURVEYS

Literary surveys are useful in placing literary contributions in context and in analyzing the historical, political, and social contexts and contributions of specialized groups of writers or individual women and minority authors. These literary surveys are divided into historical surveys, genre surveys, regional surveys, general ethnic surveys, women and feminist surveys, general surveys, and individual critical approaches. An example of an historical survey is the four-volume *Cambridge History of American Literature*.[18]

Bibliographic Control

The proliferation of publications of new literary works, reviews of works, literary criticism, in print and nonprint format, and development of newer technologies (electronic publishing, videotext, and laser disc) for creative publication makes bibliographical control more difficult. The media materials such as films, documentaries, short story video creations, poetry reading video productions, and video interviews, are often treated as special materials located in instructional media service areas. Many libraries do not catalog and classify these items under traditional classification schemes, thus access to them is more limited. In addition, the reviewing sources are not through the traditional indexes, but through special indexes for audiovisual materials and in media journals. The indexing that exists is by no means comprehensive and quality of reviews is uneven.

Access to criticism of longer works and critiques of these works, primarily novels, is much better than to shorter works such as poetry, short stories, and essays. There is much less published criticism available on poetry and short story publications, and since much poetry and short fiction is never published in anthologies, it becomes more difficult to locate this original literature, much less critique it. Since a majority of such work is published in little magazines and fine art reviews, and indexing to these is limited, much of recent literature is lost to the researcher.

Critical approaches in the study of literature may require other conceptual frameworks needed for teaching literary research methodologies. For example, social, political, and economic forces of certain historical periods may be studied in relation to specific literary works (e.g., *Uncle Tom's Cabin*, *All the King's Men*, *One Flew Over the Cuckoo's Nest*). Thus, someone studying *One Flew Over the Cuckoo's Nest* may need instruction in historical research to discover the time period when lobotomies were an acceptable surgical practice, or medical research strategies to determine the details of that surgery and the effect on motor and psychological/emotional functioning and reactions. The importance of government publications and newspaper reporting and accuracy might be considered in a political approach to the study of *All the King's Men*. A comparative analysis of social and literary reaction to *Uncle Tom's Cabin* would require interdisciplinary research methodologies from both an historian's and a literary scholar's viewpoint, requiring different research methodologies—i.e., one a study of literary style and human values, one a study of current social milieu and thought, each requiring different search strategies and source material.

Summary

Regardless of conceptual frameworks utilized in bibliographic instruction for literary research, close liaison between teaching faculty and librarian is a necessity for effective and successful learning to take place. Objectives must be clear and consideration given to critical approaches to the literature covered. Students should be encouraged to purchase an appropriate literary research guide to the nationality, time period, genres, and/or thematic coverage of the course. These guides are excellent and invaluable for referral. Evaluative statements regarding variant editions and secondary source material are often an important part of the literary guides. Students should also be encouraged to browse in appropriate call number areas of reference, circulation, and current serials areas to search for new books and articles on a topic or author, not yet indexed by existing reference sources.

The importance of subject bibliographies, retrospective and current, is to be emphasized over locally produced handouts to ensure comprehensiveness of research and knowledge of key resources not held locally but available through interlibrary loan.

Students should be encouraged to make use of secondary access services in their computer-accessible forms to speed up their research and allow for interdisciplinary and boolean-logic-operator capability not accessible through traditional manual search practices.

And of great importance is the follow-up of effectiveness of bibliographic instruction, as perceived by librarians providing individual reference desk assistance, by faculty teaching the course, and by students enrolled in the course. An examination of sources cited in completed research will also lend insights into the students' ability to do research. Continually review, revise, and test effectiveness of instruction provided. Keep a log of problems encountered, questions asked, questions not answered, and number of students actually using the information presented whenever possible. Review these lists periodically to improve and enhance the library user education program. Publish the results of efforts, successes and failures, and implications needing further study so that other institutions and librarians will benefit.

Encourage students and faculty to discuss research interests, concerns, and problems with you. Ask questions to determine strengths and weaknesses of your instruction, the library's organization and staff competency (so further education can be undertaken in-house if necessary), and the strength and weakness of published resources (print and nonprint) in specified areas of literary study. Act on the data collected to enhance the institution's ability to meet student needs and obtain relevant lifelong learning skills.

And whenever appropriate and within existing time constraints, introduce new concepts, sources, and ideas to faculty members and students in literary research. If possible, build the liaison through helping a faculty member maintain current awareness of new resources, teaching methodologies, and research interests in his/her field. Read or scan the professional literary journals and higher education journals. Ask to meet with teaching faculty at their regular departmental meetings to keep them informed and to obtain their perspectives of student library research abilities. Attend subject related professional association activities to ensure that you are aware of key issues of importance to teachers and scholars and to remind them of the need for bibliographic instruction. And notify publishers and scholars of inadequacy of bibliographical control in certain areas, or to suggest ideas for further publications in the field.

One of the most effective library assignments for literary research instruction is to require students to prepare a bibliographical essay for publication. The essay should focus on an evaluation of bibliographical control of the works by and about a particular author (can be limited further if necessary), a particular literary genre, a particular regional literature, literature by or about a specific ethnic group, literature regarding a recent literary movement, or literature published about a political event or on a particular theme. Such an assignment requires gaining a familiarity with primary and secondary or tertiary sources; scope, coverage, and limitations of sources; duplication and overlap of sources; strengths and weaknesses of secondary sources; and errors, omissions, and similar information. The student would be asked to select an appropriate journal for manuscript submission. Final papers could be critiqued by other students, faculty, and librarian acting as an editorial board prior to actual submission. The librarian's role would be to evaluate sources consulted and accuracy of strengths and weaknesses of secondary sources evaluated. For example, the student could trace a recent novel from its first publication to appearances of plot summary, book reviews, criticism in journals, biographies of the author, and primary literature and secondary literature indexing and abstracting citations in serial bibliographies in the humanities, noting the adequacy of coverage in traditional reference sources, thus predicting the potential for the work to become a classic or the author a major literary influence. The librarian would, thus, evaluate the student's knowledge of sources and expertise in conducting literary research.

The most frequent type of literary research done by students is that of tracing a particular author's productivity or the critical analysis completed on a specific work of an author. Students can gain a thorough knowledge of how information is generated, reproduced, and analyzed, and how to access this published material by using the conceptual framework of primary and secondary sources to teach research methodologies in literature. By linking publications *by* (primary sources) and *about* (secondary sources) an author to types of reference tools and appearance of those access tools in print, it is possible for students to gain the bibliographical expertise needed, not only to access the literature on a particular author or work, but to evaluate the literary reputation of that author and the bias in the publishing and literary world in promoting or neglecting certain authors, themes, genres, etc. Information gained should encourage students to transfer what is learned about communication to other disciplinary research.

This chapter by no means lists all of the relevant sources to the study of literary research in American literature. Titles listed are only examples of what is available. Even to cover all of this information in one course will require more than one fifty-minute presentation to students enrolled in a survey course on American literature. Thus, it is important to work closely with the teaching faculty to ensure that bibliographic instruction is an integral part of the entire course and assignments help build on previous learning.

Notes

[1] Valmai Kirkham Fenster, *Guide to American Literature* (Littleton, Colo.: Libraries Unlimited, 1983).

[2] A. Robert Rogers, *The Humanities: A Selective Guide to Information Sources* (Littleton, Colo.: Libraries Unlimited, 1979).

[3] Ibid., 268-83.

[4] Virginia Terris, *Woman in America: A Guide to Information Sources*, American Studies Information Guide Series, vol. 7 (Detroit: Gale, 1980); Sam Bluefarb, *The Escape Motif in the Novel: Mark Twain to Richard Wright* (Columbus, Ohio: Ohio State University Press, 1972); Leslie A. Fiedler, *Love and Death in the American Novel* (New York: Criterion Books, 1960); Edmund Wilson, *Patriotic Gore: Studies in the Literature of the American Civil War* (New York: Oxford University Press, 1962); Roger O. Rock, *The Native American in American Literature: A Selectively Annotated Bibliography* (Westport, Conn.: Greenwood Press, 1985); Elsa L. Radcliffe, *Gothic Novels of the Twentieth Century: An Annotated Bibliography* (Metuchen, N.J.: Scarecrow Press, 1979); Betty Rosenberg, *Genreflecting: A Guide to Reading Interests in Genre Fiction*, 2nd ed. (Littleton, Colo.: Libraries Unlimited, 1986).

[5] *Granger's Index to Poetry*, 8th ed. (New York: Columbia University Press, 1986).

[6] *The Reader's Advisor: A Layman's Guide to Literature*, 13th ed. (New York, R. R. Bowker, 1986).

[7] Lina Mainiero, *American Women Writers: A Critical Reference Guide from Colonial Times to the Present* (New York: Frederick Ungar Publishing, 1979).

[8] Vito Joseph Brenni, *The Bibliographical Control of American Literature, 1920-1975* (Metuchen, N.J.: Scarecrow Press, 1979).

[9] Jacob N. Blanck, *Bibliography of American Literature* (New Haven, Conn.: Yale University Press, 1955-).

[10] *M.L.A. International Bibliography of Books and Articles on the Modern Languages and Literatures* (New York: Modern Language Association, 1921-).

[11] Donna Gerstenberger and George Hendrick, *Fourth Directory of Periodicals Publishing Articles in English and American Literature and Language* (Chicago: Swallow Press, 1974).

[12]Eileen A. Mackesy, Karen Mateyak, and Diane Siegel, comps., *M.L.A. Directory of Periodicals: A Guide to Journals and Series in Languages and Literature* (New York: Modern Language Association, 1979- , biennial).

[13]William A. Wartman, *A Guide to Serial Bibliographies for Modern Literature* (New York: Modern Language Association, 1982).

[14]*Short Story Index: An Index of Stories in Collections and Periodicals* (New York: H. W. Wilson, 1953-).

[15]Patricia E. Sweeney, *William Faulkner's Women Characters: An Annotated Bibliography of Criticism, 1930-1983* (Los Angeles, Calif.: ABC-Clio, 1985).

[16]Clarence H. Holman, *A Handbook to Literature Based on the Original Edition by William Flint Thrall and Addison Hibbard*, 4th ed. (Indianapolis, Ind.: Bobbs-Merrill, 1980).

[17]James D. Hart, *The Concise Oxford Companion to American Literature* (New York: Oxford University Press, 1986).

[18]*Cambridge History of American Literature* (New York: Putnam, 1917-1921).

Part 4
SCIENCES

INDEX STRUCTURE AS A CONCEPTUAL FRAMEWORK FOR BIBLIOGRAPHIC INSTRUCTION IN CHEMISTRY

Pamela G. Kobelski

Developing a multisession course on the literature of chemistry or any other discipline requires careful selection of a conceptual framework. Conceptual frameworks are the basic ideas used to organize the content of an educational presentation. They provide the structure for the information presented. Such structures are particularly important when the material covered is unfamiliar, appears unorganized, or lacks any sort of context for students. Conceptual frameworks are critically important in bibliographic instruction, giving students a foundation for assimilating the material presented.[1]

Academic and Industrial Chemists

Selecting conceptual frameworks for instructional presentations begins with a thorough understanding of what information students need and how they will use the material presented. Individual frameworks stress different aspects of the literature. The choice of which framework to use to organize classes has to be based on the kinds of literature problems students will encounter both during their school years and their professional careers. Undergraduate chemistry majors tend to use the literature to supplement experimental work. They are rarely required to do the kind of extensive term papers required in other fields of study. Graduate study and day-to-day job responsibilities in the chemical profession often require that extensive literature searches be performed before experimental work begins.

Bibliographic instruction in the chemical literature is thus important to both students pursuing academic careers and those interested in industrial positions. The American Chemical Society's Committee on Professional Training Guidelines recommends formal instruction in the chemical literature as part of the undergraduate curricula in chemistry and there have been numerous studies and symposia on such instruction.[2] While attempts have been made to include bibliographic instruction within the core courses in chemistry, most of the discussion has centered around individual courses in the chemical literature, usually at the advanced undergraduate or graduate level.

In many ways those planning industrial careers need even more detailed instruction in the use of the literature than those pursuing academic careers. W. A. Hendrickson noted:

> In essence, the research changes that occur in moving from academics to industrial work changes the type of library searching techniques needed and broadens the variety of literature that must be checked. The major point that I think needs to be stressed is that industrial research is fast paced and any and all techniques to get into the library and out again rapidly should be used. A solid foundation in library searching is needed to succeed in industry.[3]

While chemists in an academic environment may meet all their information needs searching the chemical literature, industrial chemists must often search the literature in applied chemistry fields such as coatings, corrosion, textiles, ceramics, etc. In addition to needing a good background to use a wide variety of literature tools, industrial chemists must also have the background to learn to use patent and proprietary literature systems that are rarely used by academic chemists. Patents, used only occasionally as a source of information by academic chemists, are of prime importance in an industrial setting. Patents provide protection for new ideas/products that come out of industrial research. It is important to know whether or not there are existing patents on products or processes before research is begun. In addition to the published literature, most private companies have extensive collections of proprietary information, laboratory research, technical reports, internal correspondence, etc. Industrial chemists are expected to access this information and use it for planning research projects.

Index Structure

Index structure is an excellent framework for meeting the needs of those training to become chemists. This framework concentrates on the indexing process and how various sources index the bibliographic literature. It is designed to allow students to learn how to use effectively diverse tools. By emphasizing how indexing choices are made and how indexes are structured, students can learn fairly sophisticated searching techniques. Index structure concepts can also be applied easily to new indexes and abstracts not covered in the classroom.

F. Wilfrid Lancaster describes subject indexing as comprising two steps:

1. Deciding what a document is about (i.e., its subject matter);

2. Translating this conceptual analysis into index terms which act as shorthand symbols, or labels, for the subject matter of the document.[4]

Instruction organized around index structure covers the various types of subject indexing used in bibliographic tools. The focus is on the different ways to describe and represent the content of a publication. The differences between indexes and abstracts using author designated subjects or indexer-generated subjects are stressed. The index structure framework also concentrates on how these subjects are translated into indexing terms and concepts and organized into bibliographic tools. By understanding how indexes and abstracts are structured, students learn to use them effectively to meet their information needs.

The initial step in using this framework for bibliographic instruction is to develop a list of the main types of indexes and abstracts to be covered. Class sessions are arranged by increasing complexity of index structure. Indexes and abstracts can then be arranged in a logical sequence by index structure within class sessions designed around these structures.

The general indexing structures that should be covered in bibliographic instruction include keyword indexes, controlled vocabulary indexes, and specialized vocabulary indexes. There are many examples of each type of index in chemical literature.

Keyword Indexes

The simplest form of keyword index is the keyword title index. This form of indexing starts with the assumption that the best description of the content of a document is the title chosen by the author. Words (keywords) are taken from the title and compiled into an index either individually — keyword out of context (KWOC) — or with surrounding words — keyword in context (KWIC). Individual keywords are used to index *Current Contents: Physical Chemical & Earth Sciences* while *Chemical Titles* uses the keyword in context approach. Concentrating on the index structure alerts students to the difference between just being able to find articles with an individual word in the title, i.e., xylene, and finding other words that indicate the subject of the article, i.e., production of xylene from benzene. It is no accident that keyword title indexing is the indexing form used in both of these current awareness publications as it is a very quick way to generate a subject index and allows for timely publication. Another form of keyword indexing uses keywords from the title or abstracts or assigns keywords. There is no attempt to standardize the words used. This form of indexing is used in the weekly issues of *Chemical Abstracts*. Again the use of keyword indexing, even assigned keywords, allows for very rapid indexing of publications. This is a major benefit of keyword indexing.

Note that starting with keyword indexing also means starting with the tools that would first cover a chemical publication. Conceptual frameworks are not mutually exclusive. In this case information on publication sequence is easily included in classes structured using the index structure as the conceptual framework.

Controlled Vocabulary Indexes

Controlled vocabulary subject indexing is the form of indexing with which most students are familiar. The subject of a publication is determined by an indexer and terms describing this subject are chosen from a set list or thesaurus. Students are probably familiar with indexes using this approach, including tools such as the *General Science Index* or *Chemical Abstracts* "General Subject Index." *General Science Index* covers the major scientific journals. *Chemical Abstracts* "General Subject Index" covers broad subject areas within chemistry. The other indexes covering separate but related disciplines such as *Index Medicus* or *Physics Abstracts* can also be introduced to teach this form of index. Some of these tools use cross-references to guide users to the correct terms. Others have printed thesauri to guide users to the correct terms. Class sessions should stress the difference between a cross-reference, which merely takes the user from one heading to another, and a thesaurus, which outlines how the subject is handled and gives additional search terms. The thesaurus for the *Chemical Abstracts* "General Subject Index" is the *Index Guide*.

Specialized Indexes — Chemical Nomenclature

In addition to controlled vocabulary indexes using general terms, there are indexes which use the specialized chemical nomenclature. Much of the chemical literature is oriented toward describing, as precisely as possible, the structure of molecules. Most molecules can be named in a number of ways, all equally "correct." *Chemical Abstracts* has developed its own nomenclature for chemical compounds. The *Index Guide* serves as a thesaurus to this nomenclature going from common to *Chemical Abstracts* names. Another thesaurus to *Chemical Abstracts* nomenclature is the *Registry Number Handbook*, a numeric listing of registry numbers giving *Chemical Abstracts* name and molecular formula. Registry numbers are unique numbers assigned to each chemical compound and are often given in abstracts and within the text of articles. Figure 12.1 shows sample entries for the antibiotic "spectinomycin."

Index Guide

Spectinomycin
    See 4H — -Pyrano[2,3-b][1,4]benzodioxin-4-one,
        decahydro-4a,7,9-trihydroxy-2-methyl-6, =
        8-bis(methylamino)-, [1695-77-8]

Registry Number Handbook

1695-77-8   4H-Pyrano[2,3-b][1,4]benzodioxin-4-one,
    decahydro-4a,7,9-trihydroxy-2-methyl- = 6,8bis(methyl-
    amino)- $C_{14}H_{24}N_2O_7$

Fig. 12.1. Sample entries for spectinomycin.

Understanding the concepts *Chemical Abstracts* used to develop this naming system and how it differs from other chemical nomenclature systems is important for understanding how to use the literature. In addition to chemical nomenclature, *Chemical Abstracts* also provides an index to chemical names by ring systems. Chemical formulas are used directly to index the literature for compounds with under twenty references. For compounds with a larger body of literature, the formula index cross-references the *Chemical Abstracts* chemical nomenclature. Both types of entries are shown in figure 12.2.

Formula Index

C14H24N2O7
    Glycine, N-[(1,1-dimethylethoxy)carbonyl]-
        anhydride [51499-90-2], 6922y,198762r

    4H-Pyrano[2,3-b][1,4]bensodioxin-4-one,
        decahydro-4a,7,9-trihydroxy-2-methyl-6,8-=
        bis(methylamino)- [1695-77-8] For general
        derivs. see *Chemical Substance Index*

Index of Ring Systems

C_4O_2-C_5O-C_6
    4,10a-Epoxy-10aH-1-benzoxocin

    4H-Pyrano[2,3-b][1,4]benzodioxin

Fig. 12.2. Index entries by ring systems.

The section on nomenclature indexes can also easily accommodate other sorts of reference works. While they are not primarily thought of as indexes and abstracts, such tools as *Dictionary of Organic Compounds* and *Merck Index* easily fit into a discussion of chemical nomenclature. They are organized by chemical name, using different naming conventions than *Chemical Abstracts*. Both include extensive cross-references and formula indexes. More importantly, both provide access to the bibliographic literature by giving references to journal articles on the identification, synthesis and toxicity of the compounds listed.

There are a number of different types of specialized vocabulary indexes in the chemical literature. Molecular formula indexes are part of both *Beilstein's Handbuch der Organischen Chemie* and *Gmelin's Handbuch der Anorganischen Chemie*. In addition *Beilstein* has a complex system number organization that also describes the structure of the compound being indexed. These two reference works are part of the older literature tradition of compiling encyclopedic sources to journal references. Both Beilstein (organic compounds) and Gmelin (inorganic and organometallic compounds) include a large amount of numeric and synthetic data as well as comprehensive literature references to all compounds covered. Despite the fact that both are in German, they are standard sources for chemical literature prior to 1950. Another specialized vocabulary index would be the Wiswesser line notation index to *Current Abstracts of Chemistry*.

Specialized Indexes—Patents

In addition to the specialized indexes devoted to chemicals, indexes to patents would fall into the category of specialized vocabulary indexes. Patents are legal documents conferring monopoly rights to products or processes within the country issuing the patent. Most large companies will apply for patents within a large number of countries. Thus the same information may be contained in a number of patents which are essentially the same. *Chemical Abstracts* covers a patent only in the first country of issue. A patent number/patent concordance index comes with each volume. As can be seen in figure 12.3, reference is made from the first patent to all subsequent patents and from subsequent patents to the first patent covered. Patent numbers are preceded by a two-letter code for the country that grants them.

```
US (United States of America)
    4183856 A,   See DE 2818947 A1          cross-reference
    4183956 A,   See DE 2433837 A1            ”         ”
    4183983 A,   92:133271k                 abstract number
        FR   2433588 A1                     equivalent

        GB   2028379A                         ”        ”
```

Fig. 12.3. Sample patent entry in *Chemical Abstracts*.

The Derwent *World Patent Index* also includes listings of patent equivalents. While they are not generally available in university libraries, Derwent patent indexes are used extensively in industry and should be covered. The *U.S. Patent Office Gazette* is a numeric listing of U.S. patents indexed by author and patent classification code (a code to describe the use of the invention). It is available in most large public and university libraries.

Specialized Indexes—Citation Indexes

The last major form of specialized vocabulary index is the *Science Citation Index*. Understanding the concept of describing the subject of a paper by the references cited is hard for most students. Organizing the class around index structure allows considering citations as subject descriptors to be covered in depth. The inclusion of citations to patents, as well as articles in most of the major chemical journals, makes *Science Citation Index* an important chemical reference source.

Other Areas

In addition to the sessions devoted to indexing structural concepts, additional class sessions including information on library use, proprietary databases, online searching, and current literature developments would be useful. Proprietary information systems will probably have to be discussed conceptually as few organizations will make such systems available to outsiders. Such systems vary widely as each company often takes a unique approach to handling internal information.

> A major portion of the resources of an industrial chemical information system must be directed to internally generated information. Since most of the information is of a proprietary nature, all efforts to store, index and retrieve it must, of necessity, be done internally. This requires that internal indexing and retrieval systems be developed and made an integral part of the information system.[5]

It is important that students know such systems exist.

Online searching is a natural extension of the index structure framework. From a conceptual view, it is nothing more than using a computer to manipulate the index terms introduced in covering the various indexes and abstracts. For students already aware of online searching and search systems, the individual databases could be introduced as the printed tools are covered. For other students introducing the concept and basics of searching is best done in a separate session.

The class schedule might resemble the outline in figure 12.4, page 154, which illustrates how the index structure framework might be adapted to structure a course or series of presentations on the chemical literature. Actual classes will include different materials depending on what is in the library collection and any special interests of the students. While they are not a main focus, reference books can easily be accommodated in this framework. In many cases they are used not so much as a source of data, but as an entry point to the literature. As such, their structure and how they serve to index bibliographic literature are important class topics.

1   Library organization, use of serials, card catalog, basic bibliographic techniques, journal abbreviations, *Chemical Abstracts Service Source Index.*

2   Keyword indexing, *Current Contents, Chemical Titles, Chemical Abstracts*—weekly issues.

3   Controlled vocabulary subject indexing, *Chemical Abstracts*—General Subject Index, *General Science Index, Physics Abstracts, Index Medicus.*

4   Chemical nomenclature indexing, *Chemical Abstracts*—Formula Index, Substance Index, Registry Number Handbook, *Dictionary of Organic Compounds, Merck Index.*

5   Reference works, dictionaries, handbooks, data collections.

6   Specialized vocabulary indexes and reference sources, *Beilstein, Gmelin, Current Abstracts of Chemistry.*

7   Patents, *Chemical Abstracts*—Patent Index, *World Patent Index, U.S. Patent Office Gazette.*

8   Citation indexing, *Science Citation Index.*

9   Online and proprietary information systems.

Fig. 12.4. Class schedule.

Class Assignments/Exercises

In addition to their use in structuring bibliographic instruction presentation, conceptual frameworks must also be used to structure class assignments. It is important that assignments be an integral part of the instruction. They should be used to stress the framework used in the class(es).

The importance of well-designed assignment/exercises in bibliographic instruction cannot be stressed too often. They should focus on the major points covered in class presentations as well as give students practical experience in using the tools covered. The value of library exercises in the chemical literature is easy to explain to students majoring in chemistry as a large part of their time is spent in laboratory exercises illustrating the major lecture points.[6]

As laboratory exercises mirror the sorts of problems students will encounter as practicing chemists, library assignment should function as mini-exercises in literature use. Their structure should mirror the structure of library problems students will encounter. Most published problem sets use a series of unrelated questions with only a single "right" source/answer. This may be an effective way to teach future reference librarians, but it has little in common with the way most other professionals use their literature.

Whether preparing class papers, research projects, or proposals most chemists use literature to find a number of papers on a single topic. Class exercises should be designed in a similar manner, such as minibibliographies. Topics should be chosen which might be of interest to students. In general compounds that are commonly used or classes of compounds are good choices. This allows questions to be framed such as, "Check a recent issue of *Chemical Titles* and give the citations to two articles on benzene?" It is important to check each question to make sure there are citations fitting the question in one or two current issues of the index or abstract being covered. In covering index structure, include questions asking students to give the index terms used for the articles they record. This stresses the differences in how subjects are indexed. Specific references can also be requested in more than one index to alert students to these differences.

This type of exercise has a number of advantages in addition to seeming "useful" to students. By looking up the same topic in different tools, it serves to illustrate the differences in index structure discussed in class. Because students are not looking for a single answer, the same assignment given to different students will produce different answers. This makes it unnecessary to have individual exercises for each student and makes copying another student's answers readily apparent. Thus it is only necessary to develop one set of exercises for every five students rather than try to develop an individual assignment for each student. Choosing topics that are of current interest to students should make for a "fun" exercise rather than drudgery.

Conclusion

Overall index structure is a very effective framework for covering chemical literature. Its only limitation is some awkwardness in covering data sources and library structure within the framework. These topics can be easily included in class sessions without seriously disrupting flow. The lack of any text structured around this framework is also a minor problem.

The advantages of using the index structure framework include the ability to incorporate indexes and abstracts from other fields of study as well as proprietary information systems. This framework can be used to introduce discussions of search strategy as well as online searching. It provides an excellent introduction for sessions in end-user searching. Index structure concepts are oriented toward accessing the journal literature which is of major importance in both school assignments and professional careers.

Notes

[1] Pamela Kobelski and Mary Reichel, "Conceptual Frameworks for Bibliographical Instruction," *The Journal of Academic Librarianship* 7 (May 1981): 73-77.

[2] Arleen N. Somerville, "Chemical Information Instruction of the Undergraduate: A Review and Analysis," *Journal of Chemical Information and Computer Science* 25 (August 1985): 314-23.

[3]W. A. Hendrickson, "Library Searching: An Industrial User's Viewpoint," *Journal of Chemical Education* 59 (December 1982): 999.

[4]F. Wilfrid Lancaster, *Information Retrieval Systems: Characteristics, Testing, and Evaluation* (New York: John Wiley & Sons, 1968), 3.

[5]Carlos M. Bowman and Paula B. Moses, "Evolution of Industrial Chemical Information Systems," *Journal of Chemical Information and Computer Science* 25 (August 1985): 197-202.

[6]George Gorin, "An Approach to Teaching Chemical Information Retrieval," *Journal of Chemical Education* 59 (December 1982): 991-94.

CHAPTER 13

MEDICAL SUBJECT HEADINGS
A Conceptual Framework for Bibliographic Education in the Health Sciences

Alice C. Wygant

Introduction

Medical Subject Headings (*MeSH*),[1] the controlled vocabulary developed by the National Library of Medicine (NLM), is the cornerstone on which all of the biomedical bibliographic systems in the United States rest. *Index Medicus, Abridged Index Medicus, International Nursing Index, Cumulative Index to Nursing and Allied Health Literature*, and *Hospital Literature Index* as well as their corresponding online files all rely on *MeSH* for their subject indexing access. In addition, most public catalogs in medical libraries are based on *MeSH*. Medical libraries also have a long history of online searching experience, more so than the libraries of most other disciplines. Therefore, medical researchers are, out of necessity, more accustomed to considering their research in terms of a controlled vocabulary system. For these reasons it is impossible to effectively use medical library resources without understanding *MeSH* and, as a result, *MeSH* automatically provides an obvious conceptual framework on which to base bibliographic instruction in a health sciences center.

The usefulness of *MeSH* as a conceptual framework arises from two factors. First, it is a controlled vocabulary of medical terms that provides access to worldwide medical literature. The explanation of *MeSH* leads to the notion of subject access through controlled vocabulary which is a dominant mode of access in libraries and other information retrieval systems. Second, it acts as a link among periodical indexing services such as *Index Medicus* and *Hospital Literature Index*, online systems such as Medline, and medical libraries' catalogs that provide access to monographic and audiovisual literature in medicine. *MeSH*, therefore, can be viewed as a hub to which the spokes of a wheel are joined. Consequently, this chapter provides a description of *MeSH* and its use in medical literature as well as how *MeSH* is used as the foundation for an effective teaching approach.

Using *MeSH*

MeSH is composed of approximately 14,000 controlled vocabulary terms and seventy-six topical subheadings. The topical subheadings are attached to *MeSH* terms to make them more specific. For example, the topical subheading "drug therapy," abbreviated "dt," is attached to the *MeSH* "asthma" to separate the citations about drug therapy from all the other asthma citations. A few of the other topical subheadings are "adverse effects," to be used with drugs and chemicals; "chemical synthesis," to be used for the chemical preparation of molecules in vitro; and "history," to be used for the historical aspects of any subject. There are also numerous form subheadings available only to catalogers. These include "abstracts," "anecdotes," "audiotapes," "statistics," "models," and "programmed instruction" among many others. Subheadings of both kinds can be very useful to medical library patrons. For instance, someone interested in the epidemiology of leukemia could check the library's catalog under "leukemia-statistics," "leukemia-occurrence," "leukemia-mortality," and "leukemia-tables."

The *MeSH* system is a carefully constructed, interlocking unit. This unit is presented to its users in four different forms: an alphabetic list which appears as Part Two of the January issue of *Index Medicus*, the *Annotated Alphabetic List*, the *Tree Structures*, and the *Permuted Medical Subject Headings*. These four parts provide three different ways of approaching the National Library of Medicine's controlled vocabulary system.

The first two are obviously alphabetic listings of all the *MeSH* terms. Part Two of the January issue of *Index Medicus* is sometimes called the "Black and White" *MeSH* as it always has a black cover with white lettering. It contains only the major descriptors found in *Index Medicus*. *The Annotated Alphabetic List* provides extra information about many of the terms as well as both major and minor descriptors. This extra information includes a term history, allowable subheadings, "see" references, definitions, and hints for searchers and catalogers. Figure 13.1 illustrates some of the special instructions included in the annotations.

FOOT
  A1.378.592.350+

  vertebrates only: for invertebrates use EXTREMITIES: TN
117; /abnorm permitted but note FOOT DEFORMITIES, ACQUIRED;
dis of foot = FOOT DISEASES; skin dis on foot = FOOT
DERMATOSES; neopl of foot: use neopl coords (IM) + FOOT
DISEASES (IM); foot ulcer: index under FOOT DISEASES (IM) +
SKIN ULCER (IM) but not LEG ULCER; foot prints (like finger
prints) = PLANTAR PRINTS

Fig. 13.1. Sample entry from the *Annotated Alphabetic List*.

The *Tree Structures* is a hierarchical arrangement which shows each term and its relationship to other terms (see figure 13.2). Terms are located by using an alphanumeric designator listed with each term in the alphabetic *MeSH* listings.

Notice that the tree number for FOOT is the same as the number given in the example from the *Annotated Alphabetic List* in figure 13.1.

LEG	A1.378.592
ANKLE	A1.378.592.116
FOOT	A1.378.592.350
HEEL	A1.378.592.350.377
TOES	A1.378.592.350.792
HALLUX	Al.378.592.350.792.456
HIP	A1.378.592.467
KNEE	A1.378.592.586
THIGH	A1.378.592.867

Fig. 13.2. Sample entry from the *Tree Structures*.

Finally, as shown in figure 13.3, the *Permuted Medical Subject Headings* is a keyword-in-context index to all *MeSH* terms.

FOOT
    ATHLETE'S FOOT see TINEA PEDIS
    FOOT
    FOOT-AND-MOUTH DISEASE
    FOOT-AND-MOUTH DISEASE VIRUS
    FOOT DEFORMITIES, ACQUIRED
    FOOT DERMATOSES
    FOOT DISEASES
    FOOT JOINT see TARSAL JOINT
    FOOT ROT
    HAND, FOOT AND MOUTH DISEASE see under
        COXSACKIEVIRUS INFECTIONS
    IMMERSION FOOT
    TRENCH FOOT
FOOTBALL
    FOOTBALL

Fig. 13.3. Sample entry from the *Permuted Medical Subject Headings*.

MeSH is like a very elegantly designed puzzle in which each individual piece is a separate entity as well as a part of the whole picture.

Most researchers and librarians use the *Annotated Alphabetic List* because of the extra information given there. In addition, each year of the "Black and White" *MeSH* is applicable only to that particular year of *Index Medicus* while the *Annotated Alphabetic List* is good for the current year plus all the past years. Although Part Two of the January *Index Medicus* does contain the *Tree Structures*, it does not have the *Permuted Medical Subject Headings*. Since most library patrons only use the "Black and White" *MeSH*, they do not have access to this valuable tool.

MeSH, as was stated earlier, is used as a controlled vocabulary for a number of the print indexes to medical literature such as *Index Medicus, Abridged Index Medicus, International Nursing Index, Cumulative Index to Nursing and Allied Health Literature*, and *Hospital Literature Index*. These printed bibliographic tools have only two access points: by author and by subject through *MeSH. Index Medicus* and *Abridged Index Medicus* use *MeSH* in an unadulterated form. All of the other indexes mentioned use *MeSH* in a modified form that is enhanced for their particular subject matter. For this reason a knowledge of *MeSH* is absolutely necessary for the researcher who needs to use any of these indexes.

All of these indexes categorize articles under the most specific term available. This makes the *Tree Structures* indispensable to researchers. They use the *Alphabetic List* to identify the term and then look it up in the *Tree Structures* in order to place that term in the NLM hierarchy and to check to see that there is not a more specific term available. The latter is extremely important since most of the indexers follow the "Principle of Specificity." In other words, they choose the most specific index term available and do not use the more general term in addition to the specific term. For example, an article about toes would be indexed under "toes" but not "foot" or "leg," as well.

Several of the MEDLARS (Medical Literature Analysis and Retrieval System) databases produced at NLM also use *MeSH* as one of the many access points. Although *MeSH* is only one of a number of access points available for these online files, it is a very important one. Database searchers almost always can increase and clarify their retrieval by using the controlled vocabulary terms.

The Moody Medical Library's online catalog, MEDICAT, and its card catalog are typical of the catalogs of medical libraries in the United States. *MeSH* is the basis of the subject access to both catalogs. Some Library of Congress subject headings have been added for areas not covered by *MeSH*. Patrons find MEDICAT somewhat easier to use than the card catalog because subject headings are presented in an array which makes it unnecessary to determine the form and topical subheadings that may be attached to the *MeSH* term. In figure 13.4 the patron sees all of the available headings at once rather than card by card.

There are some rather pointed differences between using *MeSH* in the online files and in the printed indexes or library catalogs. In the first place, the online files enable researchers to search through more than one year at a time. In fact, the entire online database of MEDLINE from 1966 to the present can be searched all at once through the BRS file, MESZ. Secondly, there are many more searchable access points online so specific words from *MeSH* terms may be searched as well as the entire term. Thirdly, the online files are carefully maintained and in most cases if a term is changed then the backfiles are corrected, too. This is, of course, impossible to do in the printed versions of the indexes so each form of the term must be searched for the appropriate year(s). Fourth, several *MeSH* headings can be combined and searched online. Fifth, all "see" references are mapped to the appropriate *MeSH* term online. These differences of using *MeSH* and of teaching *MeSH* for the online and for the print versions of the various indexes should certainly be discussed, but the instructor should not allow them to obscure the major similarities in the way the terms are applied in each instance.

Controlled vocabulary systems often are not used by the library's patrons for a number of reasons. Many times they are simply unaware that any special system is being used to index journal articles and books. Also, they usually do not understand the complexities involved in indexing. A large part of the time spent in

45   SUBJECT SEARCH   PAGE 1 of 5

S/PATHOLOGY

ITEM NUMBER   NUMBER OF CITATIONS

Item	Subject	Citations
1.	PATHOLOGY	181
2.	PATHOLOGY/ADDRESSES	1
3.	PATHOLOGY/ATLASES	21
4.	PATHOLOGY/BIOGRAPHY	4
5.	PATHOLOGY/CASE STUDIES	3
6.	PATHOLOGY/CATALOGS	3
7.	PATHOLOGY/COLLECTED WORKS	2
8.	PATHOLOGY/CONGRESSES	15
9.	PATHOLOGY/DICTIONARIES	2
10.	PATHOLOGY/EDUCATION/CONGRESSES	1

OPTIONS: 1.   TYPE ITEM NUMBER FOR LISTING OF
                      TITLES ON SUBJECTS LISTED ABOVE
      *2.   3.   TYPE F TO PAGE FORWARD
      4.   TYPE I TO RETURN TO INDEX
      5.   ENTER NEW SEARCH HERE:
          THEN PRESS ENTER KEY :

*If the option of paging backwards is possible, the message,
"TYPE B TO PAGE BACKWARDS" appears as option number 2.

Fig. 13.4. Sample entry from MEDICAT.

bibliographic instruction classes is taken up with trying to explain these indexing systems in the library's catalog as well as indexes and abstracts. Patrons have to be shown the advantages of knowing and using controlled vocabulary systems. Since the use of controlled vocabulary is sometimes perceived as an extra and somewhat unnecessary step by library patrons, instruction librarians must convince them that the extra step is worth the time and trouble it takes. Education librarians in health science centers are fortunate to have such a closely connected system of research tools which are all built using *MeSH* to make this job easier.

Obviously if the library user does not know or stumble on the proper *MeSH* term when using the printed indexes or the catalog he or she probably will not find the materials for which he or she is looking. This alone can be a powerful incentive for learning at least the rudiments of *MeSH*. For end-user searchers the importance of *MeSH* is harder to demonstrate. The MEDLINE database is so large that any search, no matter how crude, will usually yield some citations. Novice searchers tend to think of their retrieval as 100 percent of the material available. Instruction librarians must clearly demonstrate the advantages of controlled vocabulary searching before end users feel that it is worth the extra trouble. An example which uses the acronym "DRG" to search for "diagnosis related groups" can be very effective as this group of characters also turns up articles on "dorsal root ganglion." A further search using the *MeSH* term, "case mix," for "DRGs" reinforces this concept.

Many times patrons and librarians have had bad experiences with other controlled vocabulary systems that were not consistently applied or maintained. A reiteration of some of the strengths of MEDLARS and *MeSH* can help to overcome these negative feelings and at the same time demonstrate that *MeSH* is extremely reliable.

Medical Subject Headings is one of the most consistently applied controlled vocabulary systems in use today. One reason for this consistency is the sophisticated computer system used by the indexers at the NLM. It automatically prevents them from making certain common errors and automatically assigns certain terms under a specific set of circumstances. Age groups are routinely applied to the indexing for any article that deals with human subjects. All articles are also routinely designated either human or animal. These "check tags" do not appear in *Index Medicus* or the other printed indexes, but they are extremely useful to online searchers. There are other "check tags" besides the age groups or human/animal such as "pregnancy" or "case report." Extensive documentation about NLM's indexing policies is also available to users of *MeSH* and serves to clarify various points about NLM's indexing policy.

MeSH is not a static concept set in stone. Rather it is a flexible, dynamic system that is incredibly responsive to one of the most rapidly changing and developing fields in scientific research. Biomedical research is also composed of many different and varied fields from cell biology to psychiatry to drug interactions. To be of use with such a broad field of research the development of *MeSH* must keep pace and allow for the introduction of new terminology and the replacement of outmoded vocabulary. Terms are changed to reflect new developments and deleted when they become obsolete.

Paradoxically, the flexibility which makes *MeSH* useful also makes it more difficult to use and to control. Indexers at the NLM follow a rigid set of rules which are based on an interpretation of *MeSH*. The more researchers, either patron or professional, know about how these rules are applied, the more successful their search will be. This is especially true for the average library patron. *MeSH* is considered a worthy adversary for the most skilled information professional, and it can be overwhelming for the unsophisticated user. This is a complicated tool which is used to index a complex system of knowledge. That, coupled with the idiosyncrasies of indexing and the vast amount of documentation available, makes *MeSH* a real challenge for instruction librarians. It is up to the instruction librarian to act as a buffer and as a communications link between the user and *MeSH* by explaining and simplifying the NLM documentation and the complexities of the system.

The NLM has a history of online access to its files which goes back to the early 1960s. This long and unusual experience has improved the print products, and at the same time it has increased access online. *MeSH* is revised and updated every year. This degree of currency, which is one of its major strengths, makes the systems, whether in print or online, more flexible and more receptive to change. All MEDLARS files are carefully maintained to correspond with changes in *MeSH* whenever possible. While this does not affect the printed indexes it does make online searching much easier and more consistent.

The proof of the usefulness of *MeSH* has been its widespread use by all the major health science bibliographic tools in the United States. The fact that it is widely used is also a powerful teaching tool. Researchers can learn one controlled vocabulary system and use it to gain access to a number of different sources. The same *MeSH* term can be used to search the library's catalog, *Index Medicus*, and MEDLINE. Also the fact that *MeSH* has been adapted for use in *International Nursing Index*, *Cumulative Index to Nursing and Allied Health Literature*, and *Hospital Literature Index* makes it an even more valuable system.

Medical Subject Headings is an excellent vehicle for understanding the process of retrieving medical literature. As a conceptual framework it provides a basis for retrieval of all kinds of health sciences literature from many different places. Furthermore, material for different levels of sophistication and expertise can be retrieved. Techniques by which students are taught to retrieve the simplest and most basic information are equally viable when used for answering the most complex biomedical research question. Since there is much overlap between the different sources in which *MeSH* is used students usually find that a thorough understanding of *MeSH* serves as a framework for remembering specific features of the various sources.

Instruction librarians in health sciences centers find their in-depth knowledge of *MeSH* both necessary to do medical reference work and useful in teaching *MeSH* as a conceptual framework. Once *MeSH* is learned there is a great degree of transfer of learning from it to all the sources in which it is used. In addition, the consistency of the system makes it extremely reliable for developing examples and practice exercises.

Use of *MeSH* in
Bibliographic Instruction

In 1983 the Moody Memorial Library received a grant to produce a videotape and a programed instruction workbook on *Medical Subject Headings*. The product, *MeSH ... A Key to Library Resources*, explains *MeSH* and its relationship to *Index Medicus*, *Abridged Index Medicus*, and the online files. The videotape also offers instructions on the use of *Index Medicus* and online searching.

The videotape uses the analogy of *MeSH* and the telephone directory to explain the relationship of the *Annotated Alphabetic List* to the *Tree Structures*. The alphabetic listing functions like the white pages of the telephone book; if the name of a particular Italian restaurant that serves good pizza is already known, then going directly to the listing for that restaurant in the white pages is the most efficient way to find its telephone number. With *MeSH*, the researcher may find the appropriate subject heading by using the *Annotated Alphabetic List*. If a specific restaurant is not known, then using the Yellow Pages to identify Italian restaurants is the more efficient way to locate one that serves pizza. The *Tree Structures* can function like the Yellow Pages since all the subject headings are arranged by subject in relation to each other.

This videotape has been very useful in formal bibliographic instruction programs as well as with individual patrons. It is used in most of the library's seminars and has been part of several class assignments.

In a typical bibliographic instruction seminar at the Moody Medical Library the instruction librarian will begin the class with a thorough explanation of the workings of *MeSH*. He or she begins by defining it and listing all the biomedical sources that use it as a controlled vocabulary. This is followed by a detailed explanation of the various parts of *MeSH*, the *Alphabetic List*, and the *Tree Structures*, and how they relate to each other.

At this point the lecture is interrupted to show the videotape described earlier, *MeSH ... A Key to Library Resources*. The videotape goes over an explanation of the workings of *MeSH* again and then ties *MeSH* to the various indexes and online files mentioned earlier. It also presents a detailed explanation of MEDLINE which includes a step-by-step explanation of a computer printout of a MEDLINE search.

After the videotape the instructor begins an explanation of all the relevant bibliographic tools. The information presented in the lecture and the videotape lays an excellent foundation on which to place further explanations of the catalog, both the online and card versions, and the various indexes.

During this final phase of the seminar it is necessary to caution students about the minor differences among the different versions of *MeSH*. For instance, the *Cumulative Index to Nursing and Allied Health Literature* uses *MeSH* as a basis for its controlled vocabulary but also adds "non*MeSH*" terms which will not be found in *Index Medicus* or the *International Nursing Index*.

All of these instructional activities stress the use of *MeSH* as a foundation for health sciences information retrieval. *MeSH* is especially suited to be used as a conceptual framework. Its widespread use in a variety of bibliographic resources and its consistency and timeliness make it an extremely useful tool for researchers.

In each class or seminar taught by the Moody Medical Library, participants fill out a formal evaluation sheet. The form asks them to rate each component of the class according to the following scale: "not at all useful," "not very useful," "useful," "very useful." In dozens of classes over the last six years the ratings for *MeSH* and *MeSH ... A Key to Library Resources* have been overwhelmingly "very useful." This endorsement has been confirmed by verbal feedback from patrons. Many of them comment on the elegance of the system, and others wonder how they ever got along without knowing about *MeSH*.

Copies of the "Black and White" *MeSH* are kept near the MEDICAT terminals. Patrons frequently consult them. In fact, they have been stolen, perhaps one of the highest compliments that can be paid a reference work. End-user searchers are certainly the most sophisticated users of *MeSH*. Judging from some of the questions that are asked the teacher of "the basics of searching MEDLINE," at least a few of them have become very sophisticated users.

Conclusion

Instructional librarians in medical libraries have a prefabricated conceptual framework available in *MeSH* and its relationship to most of the other health sciences research tools. It provides a perfect lead-in to access to books through the card catalog and to journals through abstracts and indexes as well as online. Few disciplines are lucky enough to have such a standardized controlled vocabulary that is applied to so many different sources.

Notes

[1]*Medical Subject Headings* (Washington, D.C.: National Library of Medicine, 1963-). Annual.

CHAPTER 14

PUBLICATION SEQUENCE
The Use of a Conceptual Framework for Library Instruction to Students in Wildlife and Fishery Management*

Louise W. Greenfield

Introduction

The instruction session described in this chapter was developed for students enrolled in "Introduction to Wildlife and Fisheries Ecology," a required course of the Division of Wildlife, Fisheries, and Recreation Resources, School of Renewable and Natural Resources, at the University of Arizona.[1] This session is one of four units (library research skills study units), which were presented once a week for four weeks to students in this required course. The development and design of the project was done under the auspices of the Office of Management Studies, Association of Research Libraries, as part of the Public Services and Research Libraries research projects. The project objective was to assess the library instruction needs of students in a selected science discipline and to develop a program to meet those identified needs.

The selection of the Division of Wildlife, Fisheries, and Recreation Resources was based on criteria which included: the department is research oriented; all undergraduate course levels are represented; the process of developing a program for this department could be transferrable to other disciplines; faculty in this division believe librarians have a role in teaching and evaluating student research skills, and students in the division have a need for library instruction.

The library research skills study units included sessions on distinguishing between popular and scholarly articles, selection and use of indexes and abstracts, locating federal and state government documents, and doing known-item searching. Students completed a basic workbook outside of class, which ensured that they had been brought up to designated library skills levels. During

---

*Adapted from the Library Research Study Unit of Public Services in Research Libraries Research Project, Office of Management Studies, Association of Research Libraries, Washington, D.C., January 1985.

the sessions and through handouts, they were introduced to reference sources relevant to their field. A representative list of sources is included at the end of this chapter. Assignments followed each lecture and a final assignment, which required students to apply the skills, concepts, and information gained in the four classes, was designed to simulate a professional management situation. Students were to assume that they were in a work situation where their supervisor had asked them for life history information on a specific species. For example, students could study mortality factors for mountain lions or population regulation mechanisms for mule deer. The students were to explain why such information would be important for wildlife or fishery managers. They were directed to summarize recent findings, offer management recommendations, and identify future research needs. Students were required to examine two scholarly or scientific articles, two government documents, and one conference report. They were given written guidelines for documenting both the sources they used and the sources that they examined but did not use. Their papers were read and graded by both librarians and faculty. Librarians assessed the students' research skills, while faculty evaluated the content. The final grade was a combination of both scores.

The first of the four units employed the conceptual framework "publication sequence" and had the following objectives: students would recognize the difference between popular and scholarly articles as well as the difference between primary and secondary literature; students would be introduced to the sequence in which information appears in publication in the sciences; and students would learn how publication sequence reflects communication in the field. Several factors were taken into consideration when designing the unit. Students in this discipline make much use of the "invisible college," so an understanding of both the formal and informal information network was important. This knowledge was also important because much emphasis is placed on "key people and key research," and because much material in the discipline, such as conference proceedings, is difficult for libraries to collect.

A major in wildlife and fisheries science prepares students for a professional career with state or federal fish and game departments, or other natural resource management agencies. Course offerings include: limnology, wildlife management, fishery management, nutrition, ornithology, mammalogy, and current problems in wildlife ecology.

Wildlife management requires the application of information from many fields and disciplines. "The principles of wildlife management include some that are specific to the profession and many that are shared with other professions and sciences."[2] Traditionally, students of wildlife and fisheries management need to become familiar with the literature of a variety of scientific disciplines, including ecology, soil science, and meteorology. Recently, educators in the field have stated there is also the need for wildlife professionals to gain information in areas not traditionally in the purview of fish and wildlife managers such as sociology, psychology, and economics. Therefore, developing skills which allow them to find information in a variety of fields and disciplines is essential.

Wildlife managers participate in conservation efforts, a process which includes professionals as well as lay people. They need to supply information to agencies, community groups, political groups, private factions—the groups that will influence the final course of an action on, for example, an environmental law or a resource policy. There is a need to broaden public awareness and interest in wildlife values.

Another important need for effective research relates to the students' roles as problem solvers and decision makers; they need to get the results of wildlife research which help serve as a basis for management and administrative decision making. Wildlife principles change. According to James Bailey, author of the college textbook *Principles of Wildlife Management*, "Principles are neither unchallengeable nor unchanging. They may be widely accepted today, and become expanded, modified, or discarded and replaced, as new knowledge provides new insight."[3] So decisions demanded by management and land use situations should be made with a thorough knowledge of the most recent research available.

Research skills can be presented as being relevant to these students by introducing the following main points: the diversity of information from which wildlife managers must draw; their responsibility to make the public aware of wildlife issues and values; their future roles as problem solvers and decision makers; and their need for a knowledge of current wildlife principles and practices.

The model of publication sequence is effective in introducing students to new information and concepts. Ideas such as how people in a field communicate with each other and the point at which information moves from the informal information network to a published format and is available in the library collection are important to students' understanding of the organization of information in their field. The distinction between popular and scientific literature is emphasized by wildlife faculty because of these students' future roles as educators and advocates.

Tracing an Idea—Journal Articles

This unit makes use of two diagrams, as well as two articles provided to the students in class. The diagrams illustrate publication sequence for scholarly journals and the sequence followed for popular literature. The first diagram, shown in figure 14.1, Tracing an Idea—Journal Articles, uses the conceptual framework of publication sequence. The term conceptual framework is used in the fields of education, library science, and psychology to identify organizing principles. For most people, libraries are complex places, and the reasons for how information is organized, stored, and retrieved can seem rather confusing or senseless to them. Publication sequence provides a framework or structure upon which to bring together what may appear to be unrelated or meaningless facts, so they will have an order and be given meaning.

1. *Ideas—Sources for Research*. Where do research ideas come from? There is no one answer. Ideas may come from informal conversations with colleagues or attendance at a conference or meeting which sparked an idea which warrants further investigation.

2. *Research and Investigation*. Here the researcher may request informal comment and evaluation from colleagues or may send a copy of his work-in-progress to a subject expert familiar with this type of research.

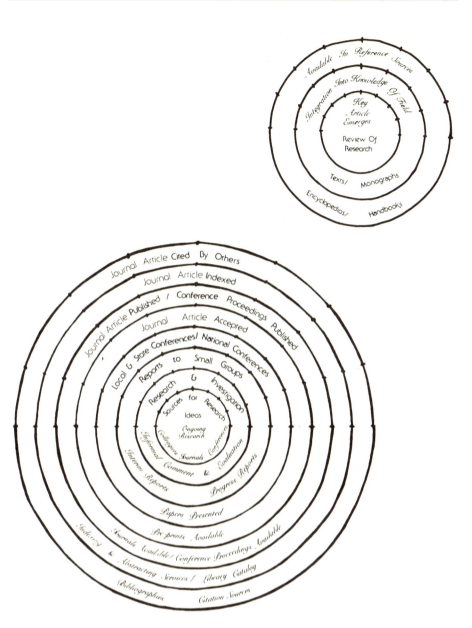

Fig. 14.1. Tracing an idea—journal articles.

3. *Reports to Small Groups.* At this point, the information may be in the form of an interim or progress report. It may go to a sponsoring agency, perhaps the organization which funded the research. It could be reported at a departmental meeting within the researcher's own institution. (The above is part of the informal information network. While this information exchange is going on, the information is not available in most library collections.)

4. *Local, State, or National Conferences.* A paper may be presented on the subject. There may be a call for papers, and, perhaps, if a professor is doing work within the guidelines of the conference theme or if he or she is an established researcher doing serious research in an area, he or she might be asked to contribute to the program. This process introduces the ideas to the larger scientific community. On the other hand, the person doing the research, the speaker, or author may learn of other related work being done—perhaps similar work or work which would be relevant to his or her study.

5. *Journal Article Accepted.* Once a journal article is accepted, preprints are available. This is the manuscript. Often there is a significant time lag between the time the information/article is accepted and when it makes its way into print (six months to a year).

6. *Journal Article Published.* The sixth step is the publication of the journal article. This is the point at which it comes into the formal information network, and is available in libraries and to subscribers.

7. *Journal Article Indexed.* However, not until a journal article is indexed does it become more systemically available. Individuals familiar with a particular subject or author can now easily gain access to the work.

8. *Journal Article Cited by Others.* Once a journal article has been read and analyzed, it may appear in the notes or bibliography of other researchers. The ideas, conclusions, or projections on an issue or concept may have been read by another researcher and examined or referred to in his or her own paper and documented in the bibliography, references, or literature cited sections.

9. *Key Articles Emerge.* Eventually the information on a subject may be brought together in the form of a review of the research which brings together current thinking and research on a particular topic. Scientific reviews also put current thinking into its historical context by providing background information on the topic.

10. *Integration into Knowledge of the Field.* Finally, one may find that certain ideas, concepts, or principles become accepted by the authorities in the field and are integrated into the established knowledge (i.e., textbooks).

11. *Available in Reference Sources.* Access to such information is available through reference sources such as handbooks and encyclopedias.

After outlining the general conceptual framework of publication sequence, it may be helpful to introduce students to a concrete example. Publication sequence can be further explained by identifying an idea presented in a journal article and following it through the formal publication sequence. For example, Val Geist, at the time a Ph.D. candidate at the University of British Columbia, wrote an article discussing the relationship between dominance and horn size in male bighorn sheep. His article "The Evolutionary Significance of Mountain Sheep Horns" appeared in 1966 in *Evolution, International Journal of Organic Evolution.*[4] In this article Geist reported results of research which investigated and verified that rams can distinguish horn sizes. Large horned individuals dominate smaller horned rams irrespective of age. Geist followed this publication up with his thesis, published in 1967, and several other articles published between 1967 and 1968 on evolution and behavior in bighorn sheep.[5] In 1971 he published *Mountain Sheep: A Study in Behavior and Evolution*, considered to be the authoritative book on bighorn behavior.[6]

In a 1974 scientific review article in *Evolution*, S. J. Gould of the Museum of Comparative Zoology at Harvard discusses Geist's work and cites the 1966 article as well as his book:

> Geist's work on Mountain Sheep has provided impressive confirmation for a belief that horns and antlers of most bovids and cervids function primarily as "visual dominance-range symbols."
>
> Geist demonstrated that mountain sheep 1) display their horns; 2) can distinguish horn size; and that large horned rams 3) dominate small horned individuals; and 4) gain reproductive advantage over them.
>
> It is, Geist writes, "this ability to predict rank from horn size without combat that allows rams to live in an open society."[7]

Grzimek's Animal Life Encyclopedia, published between 1972 and 1975, is a thirteen-volume set arranged by animal groups, with four volumes devoted to mammals. The evolution of each group of animals is described including physical description, feeding habits, etc. Val Geist's work is referenced in the description of bighorn sheep. The text states:

> The social life of bighorn sheep has recently been studied by Val Geist in the Canadian Rocky Mountains. According to his findings, the horn size is significant for rank order among rams. Only rams with horns of approximately equal size fight with each other.[8]

The Desert Bighorn, published in 1980, is a collection of contributed essays from noted biologists who have studied bighorn sheep extensively. It provides an overview of the general life history and management of bighorn sheep. In his article on behavior, Norman M. Simmons cites Geist when discussing social dominance and leadership of bighorns.[9]

Geist's original idea has been traced beginning with its initial appearance in a journal article. Geist reported on additional studies in several journal articles and his thesis. His book, *Mountain Sheep*, was published in 1971. His work was cited in a scientific review article in 1974, and his work was referred to in an article in a comprehensive animal life encyclopedia. It was traced further through an overview volume on bighorn sheep published in 1980.

Additional confirmation of Geist's idea's acceptance into the established body of knowledge in the field of bighorn sheep study comes from the following two examples.

The *Annotated Bibliography of Desert Bighorn Sheep Literature, 1897-1983* is a current and comprehensive bibliography designed to highlight the scientific studies that have been completed on desert bighorn sheep.[10] Geist's 1966 article is included, as well as the 1971 monograph, *Mountain Sheep*, which is described as "the authoritative book on bighorn sheep behavior." In *Principles of Wildlife Management*, a 1984 textbook currently being used in college and university wildlife management courses, several of Geist's articles on bighorn sheep behavior published between 1967 and 1968 are cited.[11] His 1971 book is also cited.

Popular vs. Scholarly Articles

The above description traced an idea through the scholarly information sequence. As stated earlier, publication sequence is a convenient model for explaining other concepts. The popular literature diagram (figure 14.2) was used to point out to students that information may sidestep the normal scholarly publication sequence. It may appear in print — books, press releases, newspaper articles and magazine articles — from any point in the publication sequence. Therefore it does not have the benefit of the scientific community's response or evaluation. It has not been modified or refined. Conclusions can be reported prematurely. It may not be presented by an authority. It may have been popularized and simplified (difference in language use and vocabulary). It may not be interpreted accurately or reported accurately. It may be emotional, with issues highly dramatized. Because it is important that students be able to distinguish an article written for a popular audience from one intended for the scholarly community, the instructor may want to compare two articles which have similar topics, one appearing in a scholarly or scientific journal, and one appearing in a popular magazine. Two such articles on northern elephant seals were used during the library research skills study unit to illustrate the differences between a popular and scholarly treatment of similar issues.

The objective of the *Behavioral Ecology and Sociology* article entitled "Mother-Pup Separation and Adoption in Northern Elephant Seals" was to examine the reproductive consequences of raising pups, under crowded, low density breeding conditions.[12] On the other hand, the title and tone of "Sex, Violence, and Plenty of Rest" in *Science News* leave little doubt that it is popular literature.[13] It is an overview of the factors which have influenced successful breeding of the northern elephant seal which was almost extinct 100 years ago.

There are several ways of identifying the scientific article. Generally it reports the results of investigation, includes methodology, reports data collection, makes reference to earlier studies, and is written by a subject expert. The popular article is written for the nonscientist or the nonexpert. It is designed to be

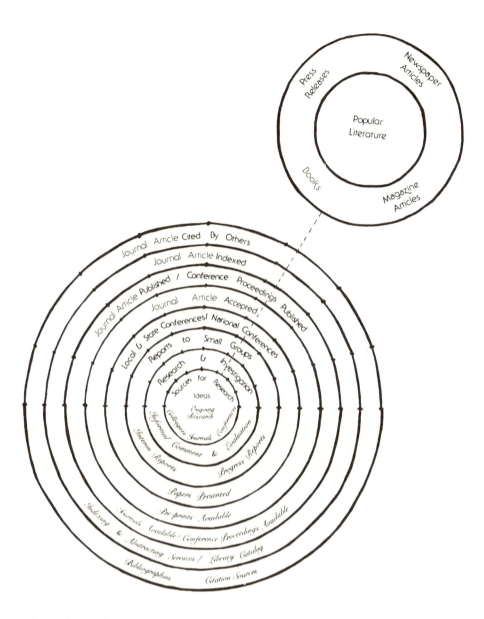

Fig. 14.2. Popular literature.

more easily understood by a general audience and is generally descriptive in nature.

Most scholarly or scientific journals include a written statement of guidelines for contributions. For example, *Behavioral Ecology and Sociobiology* states clearly that it accepts only original contributions dealing with quantitative analysis and experimental analysis. *Science News*, on the other hand, publishes articles by professional journalists who rewrite the work of scientists. It is kind of a scientific *Reader's Digest*.

Looking at the authors' credentials is revealing. Joel Greenberg, the author of "Sex, Violence and Plenty of Rest," is a journalist. The authors of "Mother-Pup Separation and Adoption" are affiliated with a recognized research institution—the Center for Marine Studies, University of California Santa Cruz.

There is a difference in how background information is presented. Greenberg's article states "For more than a decade scientists from UCSC and elsewhere have ventured into this natural oceanfront laboratory to study and record the behavior of the massive mammals."[14] Riedman and Le Boeuf tell us that adoption and fostering behavior have been reported previously in northern elephant seal breeding rookeries and give a long list of references to other published reports.

The article "Mother-Pup Separation and Adoption" clearly states the research methodology used. It describes the study area, identifies methods used for marking and identifying the pups and females, and identifies methods used for recording the behavioral observations. The results are reported as well as the conclusions drawn from the results. In contrast, Greenberg's article is purely descriptive rewriting of other's findings.

The use of publication sequence has proven successful in introducing students to the distinctions between popular and scholarly articles. It is an effective framework from which to describe the organization of literature in the field, and to explain how researchers in wildlife and fisheries science communicate. Once students are introduced to this framework it serves as an effective model to which they can always refer back. While proven successful for this discipline, the conceptual framework of publication sequence can be used effectively when teaching other courses in the applied sciences.

Reference Sources in Wildlife and Fisheries

INDEXES AND ABSTRACTS (PROFESSIONAL LITERATURE)

Aquatic Sciences and Fisheries Abstracts. vol. 1- . London: Information Retrieval, Ltd., 1971- .

Issued monthly, this is "an international information journal for the science, technology and management of marine and freshwater environments." Covers approximately 5,000 primary journals and a wide variety of other source documents. Includes literature in disciplines related to aquatic sciences. Access through author, subject and taxonomic indexes.

Biological Abstracts. vol. 1- . Philadelphia, Pa.: Biosciences Information Service, 1926- .

Issued semimonthly, this is the most comprehensive indexing and abstracting service for the life sciences. Abstracts 165,000 research papers. It covers over 8,000 journals and serials from over 100 countries. Access through subject, author, biosystematic and concept indexes. Abstracts of the articles are provided. Main concept headings for abstracts include forestry and forest products, ecology and social biology.

Biological Abstracts/RRM. vol. 17- . Philadelphia, Pa.: Biosciences Information Service, 1980- .

Biological Abstracts/RRM (Reports, Reviews, and Meetings) provides content summaries of 125,000 books, book chapters, bibliographies, reports, reviews, and meetings published annually in biology and biomedicine. Previously titled *Bioresearch Index* (1965-1979).

Biological and Agriculture Index: A Cumulative Subject Index to Periodicals in the Fields of Biology, Agriculture, and Related Sciences. vol. 1- . New York: H. W. Wilson, 1916/1918- .

Index to English language periodicals in biology and agriculture. Coverage includes environmental science, forestry, animal husbandry, soil science, and zoology. Published monthly (except August) with a bound cumulation each year.

Current References in Fish Research. vol. 1- . Eau Claire, Wis.: University of Wisconsin, 1976- .

A title listing of published scientific papers of fish research. Author, keyword and scientific name indexes provide access to the citations. Covers over 350 scientific journals that publish fish research.

Keyword Index of Wildlife Research. vol. 1- . Zurich: Swiss Wildlife Information Service, 1974- .

Indexes approximately 400 wildlife periodicals. Keyword index provides reference numbers leading to the citation in the author-title index. A thesaurus and an alphabetical and systematic species list in the back of each volume provide guidance in using the keyword index.

Wildlife Abstracts: A Bibliography and Index of the Publications Abstracted in Wildlife Reviews. Washington, D.C.: U.S. Fish and Wildlife Service; distr., Washington, D.C.: Government Publications Office, 1935- .

A five-year cumulation of citations and articles appearing in *Wildlife Review.* Arrangement is in two sections, one contains the citation, the other contains the author, geographical, subject and systematic indexes.

Issued quarterly, *Wildlife Review* "serves to alert wildlife biologists of current worldwide literature of wildlife management and conservation. Each issue contains separate author, geographic, taxonomic and subject indexes." Beginning in 1981, an annual index volume with accumulated author, geographic, taxonomic and subject indexes has been issued.

Wildlife Disease Review. vol. 1- . Fort Collins, Colo.: Wildlife Disease Review, 1983- .

"*Wildlife Disease Review* is a monthly index to world literature of wildlife diseases arranged by family and taxonomically by species within the family. It covers international literature of diseases in both captive and free-ranging wildlife." *Wildlife Disease Review* is a specialized publication for the veterinarian, biologist, researcher or student. Over 6,000 international scientific journals are searched monthly. Includes subject, author and geographic index.

Zoological Record ... Being the Record of Zoological Literature Relating to the Year ... vol. 1.- . 1864- . London: Zoological Society of London, 1865- .

"The world's largest taxonomic index to the zoological literature. The object of *Zoological Record* is to give in an annual volume an index to the zoological publications which have appeared worldwide the preceding year." Every yearly volume consists of twenty-seven separately issued sections dealing with different taxonomic classes, plus two sections—one covering general zoological literature and the other, listing new generic and subgeneric names indexed in the other sections. Each section has five indexes: author, subject, geographical, paleontological and systematic. Subject access is by broad subject headings and subdivisions (e.g., feeding—feeding behavior—food sharing).

INDEXES (POPULAR LITERATURE)

Biology Digest. vol. 1- . Medford, N.J.: Plexus Publishing, 1974- .

Organizes, summarizes, and indexes worldwide scientific literature in the life sciences. It is designed to assist "students and educators at the secondary school and undergraduate college levels." Covers 200 foreign and domestic periodicals. Abstracts of up to 325 words are provided. Keyword and author indexes provide access. Published monthly (except June, July, and August).

General Science Index. vol. 1- . New York: H. W. Wilson, 1978- .

This index provides access to popular science magazines (*Audubon, International Wildlife, Oceans,* etc.) as well as scholarly journals (*American Midland Naturalist, Journal of Wildlife Management,* etc.). Subject arrangement. No author entries. Issued monthly, except June and December.

INFOTRAC. Belmont, Calif.: Information Access Co., 1984- .

The INFOTRAC database is a computerized (laser disc) research tool which consists of references to articles from approximately 1,000 business, technical and general interest magazines and journals. Coverage begins in January 1982, and the database is updated every thirty days. Information from the *New York Times* and the *Wall Street Journal* is also included for the most recent sixty days. Indexes such magazines as *Marine Fisheries Review, Natural History,* and *Audubon.*

Readers' Guide to Periodical Literature. vol. 1- . New York: H. W. Wilson, 1905- .

"A cumulative author/subject index to periodicals of general interest published in the United States." Includes such titles as *Audubon, Field & Stream,*

Outdoor Life, and *Wilderness*. Subject headings include Wildlife Conservation, U.S. Fish and Wildlife Service, Wetlands, and Wildlife Management. Published monthly or semimonthly.

INDEXES (LITERATURE OF RELATED DISCIPLINES)

Business Periodicals Index. vol. 1- . New York: H. W. Wilson, 1958- .
   A cumulative index to English language periodicals in business and related fields. Coverage includes accounting, advertising and public relations, economics, management and personal administration. Relevant subject headings: Environmental Policy, Fishery Management, Values, Wilderness Areas. Published monthly, except August.

Education Index. vol. 1- . New York: H. W. Wilson, 1929- .
   A cumulative subject/author index to educational publications in the English language. Subject areas indexed include administration, higher and adult education, teaching methods and curriculum. Relevant subject headings: Animals, Extinct; Fishes-Habits and Behavior; Geographical Distribution of Animals and Plants; Population (Biology); Wildlife Conservation. Published monthly, except July and August.

Psychological Abstracts. vol. 1- . Arlington, Va.: American Psychological Association. 1927- .
   Covers the world's literature in psychology and related disciplines. Published monthly. Indexes scholarly journal articles and books. Provides nonevaluative summaries. Relevant subject headings: Consumer Attitudes, Conservation (Ecological Behavior), Ecology, and Environmental Attitudes, Management.

Public Affairs Information Service (PAIS) Bulletin. vol. 1- . New York: Public Affairs Information Service, Inc., 1915- .
   Published quarterly since 1972, it covers issues on public policy, with emphasis on factual and statistical information. It is a selective subject index of the latest books, pamphlets, government publications, reports of public and private agencies, and periodical articles relating to business, economic and social conditions, public administration, and international relations. Relevant subject headings: Animals, Fisheries, Hunting, Wilderness Areas, and Wildlife Conservation.

Social Sciences Index. vol. 1- . New York: H. W. Wilson, 1974- .
   A cumulative author/subject index to English language periodicals. Fields covered include anthropology, economics, environmental sciences, geography, law and criminology, planning and public administration, and political science. Relevant subject headings: Rare Animals, Fishery Laws and Legislation, and Wildlife Conservation. Published quarterly.

ONLINE DATABASES

There are hundreds of databases now accessible by computer. BIOSIS, for example, is the online counterpart of both *Biological Abstracts* and *Biological Abstracts/RRM*. There are also databases for which there are no print equivalents. Directories are available which describe the subject, sources, scope and coverage, producers, etc. of these services. Two examples are *The Encyclopedia of Information Systems and Services* (Gale Research Company, 1981) and *The Computer Data and Database Source Book*, by M. Lesko (Avon Books, 1984). Informational directories are also available from database vendors such as DIALOG Information Services, Inc. (Palo Alto, Calif.) and BRS Information Technologies (Latham, N.Y.).

INDEXES (PROCEEDINGS)

Directory of Published Proceedings: Series SEMT-Science/Engineering/Medicine/Technology. vol. 1- . White Plains, N.Y.: Interdok Corp., 1965- .

The *Directory of Published Proceedings* is a bibliographic directory of preprints and published proceedings of congresses, conferences, symposia, meetings, seminars, and summer schools that have been held world-wide from 1964 to date. Issued monthly, with annual cumulations, it is arranged chronologically by the date of the conference. Information includes the name of the meeting, the principal sponsors—including universities. Bibliographic information includes publisher or distributor, order of information, title and series of journal of publication. Indexing is by keyword in the name of the conference, sponsors, and the title.

Index to Scientific and Technical Proceedings. vol. 1- . Philadelphia, Pa.: Institute for Scientific Information, Inc., 1978- .

Published monthly with semiannual cumulations, the *Index to Scientific and Technical Proceedings* indexes conference literature in science to the article level. Nearly 90,000 papers published in 3,000 volumes of proceedings are indexed annually. International coverage for proceedings published in books, reports, or journals. Arranged in seven sections, the table of contents of each proceedings is reproduced in the main section. The remaining six sections index the information by author's name, conference sponsor, subject category, meeting location, title words, and author's organizational affiliation.

Index to Scientific and Technical Proceedings provides a number of ways to locate the proceedings: Use Meeting Location Index if you know where it took place; use Sponsor Index if you know the organization which put it on; use Category Index if you know the general subject; use Permuterm Subject Index if you know a key word from the title; use Author/Editor Index if you know an author of the paper or the editor of the proceedings; use Corporate Index if you know a presenter's organizational affiliation.

CITATION SOURCES

Science Citation Index. vol. 1- . Philadelphia, Pa.: Institute for Scientific Information, 1961- .

"An international, interdisciplinary index to the literature of science, medicine, agriculture, technology and the behavioral sciences." Issued quarterly with annual and five-year cumulations. Includes citation, source, and permuterm subject index.

REVIEWS OF RESEARCH

Index to Scientific Reviews. vol. 1- . Philadelphia, Pa.: Institute for Scientific Information, 1974- .

Issued semiannually with annual cumulation. "An international, interdisciplinary index to review literature of science, medicine, agriculture, technology and behavioral sciences." Includes citation, source, and permuterm subject index.

ENCYCLOPEDIAS

Grzimek's Animal Life Encyclopedia. Bernhard Grzimek. New York: Van Nostrand Reinhold, 1972-1975, 13 vols.

The English edition of a German publication. Arrangement is by animal group. Text describes evolution and behavior of each animal group and includes detailed color illustrations. Text avoids all foreign words and technical expressions not understandable to the layman.

Notes

[1]Louise Greenfield, Jean Pfander, Chris Sherratt, and Karen Williams, *University of Arizona Library. A Final Report from the Public Services Research Projects. Assessing the Instructional Needs of Students in a Selected Scientific Discipline at the University of Arizona. One of a Series of Self-Studies and Research Projects* (Tucson, Ariz.: University of Arizona Library, 1985).

[2]James A. Bailey, *Principles of Wildlife Management* (New York: John Wiley & Sons, 1984), 7.

[3]Ibid.

[4]Val Geist, "The Evolutionary Significance of Mountain Sheep Horns," *Evolution* 20 (1966): 558-66.

[5]Geist, "On the Behavior and Evolution of American Mountain Sheep" (Ph.D. thesis, The University of British Columbia, 1967); Geist, "A Consequence of Togetherness," *Natural History* 76 (1967): 24-31; Geist, "On the Delayed Social and Physical Maturation in Mountain Sheep," *Canadian Journal of Zoology* 46 (1968): 899-904.

[6]Geist, *Mountain Sheep: A Study in Behavior and Evolution* (Chicago: University of Chicago Press, 1971).

[7]Steven J. Gould, "The Origin and Function of Bizarre Structures: Antler Size and Skull Size in the 'Irish Elk,' Megaloceros Gigantes," *Evolution* 28 (June 1974): 214.

[8]Bernhard Grzimek and W. G. Hepnerd, "Goats and Sheep," in *Grzimek's Animal Life Encyclopedia*, vol. 13 (New York: Van Nostrand Reinhold, 1972-1975), 514.

[9]Norman M. Simmons, "Behavior," in *The Desert Bighorn*, ed. G. Monson and L. Sumner (Tucson, Ariz.: University of Arizona Press, 1980).

[10]J. R. Krausman, P. R. Mogart, and M. Chilelli, *Annotated Bibliography of Desert Bighorn Sheep Literature, 1897-1983* (Phoenix, Ariz.: Southwest Natural History Association, 1984).

[11]Bailey, *Wildlife Management*, 351.

[12]Marianne L. Riedman and B. J. Le Boeuf, "Mother-Pup Separation and Adoption in Northern Elephant Seals," *Behavioral Ecology and Sociology* 11 (1982): 203-15.

[13]Joel Greenberg, "Sex, Violence and Plenty of Rest," *Science News* 125 (1984): 120-23.

[14]Ibid., 120.

Part 5
AUTOMATED SYSTEMS

CHAPTER 15

END-USER INSTRUCTION
Emphasis on Concepts

Joan K. Lippincott

Introduction

When teaching end users to search bibliographic databases, whether to emphasize skills or concepts is a significant issue. While this distinction in emphasis can be applied to any form of library instruction, it seems an especially pressing issue to resolve in regard to online systems. Some institutions, in fact, describe their overall program as a library *skills* program. In contrast, the program which will be described here is a component of an "information literacy" program, one which emphasizes developing concepts which will enable students to come to terms with the world of information. In addition, some practical skills are taught.

An educational curriculum, one which emphasizes concepts, is developed by selecting elements having the greatest potential interpretive value. A training or skills curriculum is based on an analysis of functions.[1] If the goal of the end-user curriculum is that students will be able to transfer their knowledge and make use of a wide variety of electronic information systems, then it is important that the curriculum be developed around concepts. This kind of nonspecific transfer, the transfer of principles and attitudes that can be used as a basis for dealing with subsequent problems of the idea originally mastered, is dependent on the mastery of the structure of the subject matter, according to Jerome Bruner.[2] If the goal is specific transfer—to teach students to perform highly similar searches on a specific system—then a skills approach would be more suitable.

End-user searching generally refers to situations in which the actual user of the results of a computer search performs the search him or herself. Online searching in libraries has been strongly centered on intermediary (librarian performed) searching as opposed to end-user searching. However, with the advent several years ago of menu-driven and simplified command systems such as BRS After Dark and DIALOG's Knowledge Index, the potential for end users to perform their own searches was greatly expanded. The low rates of these off-peak hours systems meant that it was more acceptable for infrequent, slower, and less experienced users to perform searches which formerly were only cost-effective when run by an efficient, experienced librarian.

While end-user searching, as stated above, has generally been applied to teaching systems such as BRS and DIALOG, the same principles can be applied to other electronic information systems, such as online catalogs and CD-ROM bibliographic databases. The concepts which will be described later are becoming increasingly important in online catalog instruction as those catalogs begin to incorporate more sophisticated features such as keyword and Boolean searching. Up to this point, many instruction programs for online catalogs have emphasized skills, not concepts. For example, students are taught the system protocols for entering author, title, and subject searches, or a specific transfer of skills used in the card catalog. One of the most frequent problems encountered with the use of online catalogs is students' lack of understanding of the role of the Library of Congress subject headings. Perhaps if the concept of controlled vocabulary was emphasized in instruction, students would better understand the nature of subject searching in online catalogs. The importance of teaching concepts and not just procedures of online catalog use is defended in Betsy Baker's article on a model for instruction in the use of the online catalog.[3] Objectives for library instruction of online systems developed by the Reference and Adult Services Division of the American Library Association also pair concepts and skills as jointly important elements.[4]

Practical reasons for emphasizing concepts over skills in an end-user searching program are that new systems are continually coming on the market and students will need to use a variety of information systems, each with a different system protocol, until front-ends and gateways become more highly developed and widespread in use. Students should be able to approach a new information system and analyze it based on a conceptual framework, and quickly understand how to use it.

End-user instruction is one component of an information literacy program. Narrowly considered, it addresses the retrieval of information. Other components of information literacy include an awareness of the power, variety, and uses of information, the organization of information, and the management of information. Some of these topics can be included in class sessions emphasizing information retrieval. The variety of formats of information — print, online, floppy disk, CD-ROM, unpublished manuscript, etc. — can be described. The use of online information systems in future professional careers can be described; current awareness and performing literature reviews for components of grant proposals are two good examples. The creation and management of personal files of information can be described in particular using references downloaded from a computer search as the core of a small database. These examples provide students with a better understanding of how information is perceived and used in the academic and professional worlds. Rather than a simple exercise to retrieve references for one term paper, the instruction session on end-user searching can broaden students' awareness of information in today's society.

In addition to cognitive goals in end-user searching programs, affective goals are also important. Students should be motivated to use electronic information systems and they should not be fearful of computer technology. These goals can often be successfully realized by tailoring class presentations to students' needs and providing an opportunity for unpressured hands-on experience with the system.

What follows is a discussion of what concepts need to be emphasized in instruction of electronic information systems. This is based both on knowledge of the structure of online bibliographic database systems and experience in instructing over 2,500 end users (undergraduates, graduate students, faculty, and staff) at the Albert R. Mann Library of Cornell University. The program, now in its fourth year, prepares students to search the BRS After Dark system, but CD-ROM bibliographic retrieval systems and a local online catalog will be added in the near future. By stressing concepts rather than systems, we feel that we are preparing students to be efficient searchers and informed consumers of electronic information systems of all types.

The Concepts

For a sophisticated understanding of any electronic bibliographic system, users need to develop understandings in the following conceptual areas:

- What a database is.

- What a bibliographic record, its fields, and access points are.

- How to divide a topic into component parts (sets) for development of a search strategy.

- How to effectively use controlled vocabulary and free text terms.

- How Boolean operators or connectors are used to link terms or sets.

THE DATABASE

Information users need to be aware of the wide variety of databases available for searching and they need to have an understanding of what a particular database covers. Since many individuals regard the computer as an all-encompassing monolith, they often believe that they can search the entire record of knowledge through one simple online transaction. It is not generally apparent to them that they are searching a limited set of bibliographic records which are usually constricted by subject, date, and/or publication type. It is important to define a database, e.g., "a collection of information items — facts, observations, bibliographic references, abstracts, etc. — organized for future access."[5]

Building on that concept, the librarian can then describe the content of those databases to be emphasized in a particular class and to specify that only bibliographic databases will be described in this class session, if that is the case. It is useful to include information on the subject areas covered by the database, the types of publications included (e.g., periodicals, government documents, dissertations, reviews, books), the dates covered, languages included, and the reputation of the database or database producer. All of these factors can help searchers determine what gaps remain if they are attempting to conduct a comprehensive review of the literature. If the database only covers periodicals, then searches must be made of other sources for other types of materials. If the subject is inter-disciplinary or in an area covered only in a peripheral manner by a database, then other sources will be needed to complement the search.

A clear understanding of the database content also has implications for developing a search strategy. Searchers of the PsycInfo database may want to develop a strategy that will exclude dissertations from the search result; Biosis searchers may want to limit the search to English language publications.

A general area of user confusion is over the dates of coverage of a database. This has been particularly true of online catalogs but is also an issue in other technologies. The CD-ROM systems appearing on the market will undoubtedly add to the confusion, since they may not be as up-to-date as print or online sources. Users will probably expect that this newest technology will have the most recent information and therefore will need instruction on its limitations.

Since there are myriad bibliographic databases available in a given subject area, the librarian should guide users to those considered most standard or comprehensive in a field while describing the special uses of other subject related databases. In addition, it is helpful to describe the relationship of the database(s) to manual tool(s): they may be equivalent in content (e.g., P.A.I.S.), they may combine access to separate printed publications, (e.g., ERIC, one database which includes references from *Current Index to Journals in Education* and *Resources in Education*), they may provide more than the printed source (e.g., the abstracts in MEDLINE which are not included in *Index Medicus*), or they may provide less (e.g., the absence of abstracts in *Chemical Abstracts* on BRS and DIALOG).

Eventually, gateways or expert systems may guide users to the most appro-priate databases for their search. Since the software of this type that is currently available is in limited use and not very sophisticated, the users of information systems will need to make informed choices on appropriate databases to search for their topics. Therefore, it is important that they understand the concept of a database and then learn to apply standard criteria to determine their scope and usefulness in a particular situation.

It is also important that students perceive that individual databases are part of a larger system of information. Users will often form an incorrect mental model of the system; many students are not easily shaken from the notion that the BRS databases reside on the local campus mainframe. Instruction can emphasize both the systems available from particular vendors and the broader concept of the universe of information and the library's systems for providing efficient access to it.

THE BIBLIOGRAPHIC RECORD

One of the reasons that computer searches of online information systems are more powerful than manual searches in a print equivalent is that the computer greatly increases the access points available in the bibliographic record. In order for students to understand that distinction, they must have an awareness of what a bibliographic record and its fields are. Useful definitions and graphic repre-sentations are provided by T. Cooney: a field is a "specific category or type of data; may be comprised of one or more distinct words or groupings of letters, numbers, and symbols"; a record is "a collection of one or more fields or types of data on a related subject."[6] Examples of fields in bibliographic data are such elements as title, author, and abstract. The record is the complete bibliographic citation, which would include an abstract in some databases.

Often students have given little thought as to what fields are represented as access points in manual tools. For example, many students are unaware that they can search books by title in the card catalog. Therefore, it can be useful to display a typical database record on a computer projector screen or on a duplicated handout and review its fields or component parts. In online catalogs, it is particularly important that students understand whether access to a field is by keyword or by phrase. The difference in access points between the online and print versions should be emphasized. The power of a keyword system can be demonstrated by choosing a record that has an important term in the abstract or title that would not be easily retrieved through the print source. For example, when looking for information on the teaching method "guided design" in ERIC, the computer will retrieve items where the term is used in the title or abstract. Since "guided design" is not an ERIC descriptor and has not been consistently assigned as an identifier, comprehensive retrieval on this topic through the printed sources would be cumbersome and probably incomplete.

In developing sophisticated search techniques, understanding the structure of the bibliographic record is critical. Limiting a search to a particular field is one method of heightening the precision of a search. Using the logical operators "with" and "same" is also dependent on an understanding of fields.

While reviewing the bibliographic record can be a convenient time to point out how to find out if the library owns the particular item. Differences in format — e.g., monograph, serial, government document, and their implications for searching appropriate library finding aids (catalogs, serials printouts, etc.) — can be described. The portion of the bibliographic record used to check serials holdings can be identified and sources for locating complete titles for periodical abbreviations can be mentioned.

THE SETS

Sets are the building blocks of a search strategy in most online information systems. Prior to actually creating sets, students must go through an analytical process to determine the relevant component parts of their topic. The capability of students to do this independently is often erroneously taken for granted by the instructor. Students can get some practice in this area by devoting some of the class time to small group work on sample topics. If the class is relatively small, the instructor can prepare several sample search topics representing different areas of interest of the class. Each group of three to four students can be given a topic, a thesaurus or photocopies of appropriate pages, and a volume of the appropriate print index or abstract. The group identifies the concepts and chooses appropriate terms to form sets. The instructor circulates among the groups, discussing strategies and advising on the likely outcomes of various approaches.

Generally we can describe sets as groups of things with like characteristics. Often, in online searching, we describe sets as groups of synonyms, e.g., "aged, elderly, senior citizens." However, the terms in a given set do not have to be synonyms; they can be a group of items or concepts that you would like to see in relation to another group of concepts. For example, the set "corn or wheat or oats or barley" is not a group of synonyms but a group of different varieties of grains. A set could be created to represent different social policy issues, e.g., "health care services or housing or welfare" and relate those concerns to a set consisting of various minority groups, e.g., "Asian Americans or Chinese Americans or Vietnamese Americans." It is important to stress the logical relationships among terms in the set rather than definitional relationships.

Broadening or narrowing a search can be covered in the treatment of sets. Adding more terms to a set (and linking them with "or") broadens the search while adding additional sets which will be linked by "and" to other sets will narrow the search. The topics of sets, controlled vocabulary, and Boolean operators are intertwined and can often best be covered in a discussion or examples covering all areas.

CONTROLLED VOCABULARY/FREE TEXT TERMS

Effective use of controlled vocabulary and free text terms is a key factor in performing a successful online search in most bibliographic systems. If students understand the concepts of controlled vocabularies and the rationale for their use, they might be more motivated to use them. It can be explained that use of controlled vocabularies can save time and improve efficiency. For example, if "adolescents" is a thesaurus term for a particular database, it saves the user from having to key in "adolescents or teenagers or teens or youth." The enhanced retrieval rate as a result of using controlled vocabularies can be illustrated through contrasting a search using common speech terms and a search utilizing controlled vocabulary terms. If a database does not use controlled vocabulary, the importance of using synonyms, variant forms of words, and truncation should be stressed.

While students seem ready to accept an either/or situation of using controlled vocabularies in databases with thesauri and and free text terms in databases without controlled vocabularies, they seem to have difficulty in dealing with intermediate situations. For example, a database may have excellent controlled vocabulary terms for one set or concept but none for a second aspect of the topic. It is fully appropriate to devise a strategy with controlled vocabulary terms in one set and free text terms in another; even individual sets can include a mixture of terms. To promote students' understanding of this complex situation, it is useful to relate the concepts of controlled vocabulary and free text terms to the concept of the fields of the bibliographic record. The relationship of the controlled vocabulary terms to the descriptor field can be described and the process of searching for the free text terms throughout the bibliographic record can be noted. For example, in a MEDLINE search on the topic of nutrition programs for the aged, "aged" is a *MeSH* descriptor and can be searched either solely in the descriptor field or through all fields of the record. However "nutrition programs" is not a descriptor and therefore will never be found in that field (or as an index term in *Index Medicus*). One of the powerful capabilities of the computer search is that it will check such fields as title and abstract for terms that are not descriptors. To mix descriptor and nondescriptor terms in this case would probably be a good strategy.

BOOLEAN OPERATORS

Most librarians have been taught about Boolean operators through the use of Venn diagrams, and most impart the information to their students in the same manner. These conceptual representations of sets are interlocking circles which are then usually shaded to show the result of linking sets with particular Boolean operators. This tried and true method of explaining both sets and Boolean operators still seems to be the most useful model available.

In the discussion of Boolean operators, students need to understand the uses of "and," "or," and "not" in building sets and in broadening and narrowing search results. Sophisticated students may ask about nesting sets, which can be described. However, most students have a better conceptual understanding of the search strategy if each set is input separately as a search statement; this also allows for greater flexibility and less rekeying if the search needs to be modified.

The Skills

An end-user instruction program that totally ignores skills would certainly be detrimental to novice users. Some of the skills which can be taught include:

- Logging on and off the system.

- Keyboard mechanics.

- Input and output procedures.

- Locating materials identified through the search.

LOGGING ON

Whether to teach log-on and log-off procedures will be dependent on such factors as complexity of the system or telecommunications software, security, and staffing. If the telecommunications software requires a number of steps and alternate procedures if one network is not working, it may be more complex to teach the log-on than the entire search process. Also, if password security is an issue and the telecommunications software does not mask the password, it will be best if users do not sign themselves on the system. However, if the user is not taught the log-on procedure, staff will have to be readily available to sign on the end users. If users will log themselves on and off the system, a set of step-by-step printed instructions is probably the best approach.

KEYBOARD MECHANICS

Searching electronic information systems may be some students' first exposure to personal computers or computer terminals, or they may be used to a different brand of equipment. The instructor should explain some fundamental mechanics of the equipment the students will be using for searching, including the location of the return key and shift key, procedure for backspacing and correcting errors, and in some cases turning the hardware on and off.

INPUT AND OUTPUT

The procedure for typing in the search request should be reviewed, emphasizing the importance of using the return key to send the message. If some menu choices or prompts are confusing, they should be explained. How to print out or download search results should be reviewed, and if citations are available in a variety of formats, they should be displayed. These items could be demonstrated in the class session or could be described on printed handouts.

LOCATING MATERIALS

Students' expectations are often high after they have completed an online search. The proper procedure to use to locate the materials identified on the printout should be described and could be reinforced through a worksheet. If interlibrary loan is an option, its use should be explained.

Conclusion

Emphasizing concepts rather than skills in an end-user searching program gives students an awareness of the structure, power, and intricacies of electronic information systems. Particularly in academic libraries, it seems important that students have an intellectually curious approach to information systems, rather than a push-button mentality.

An underlying issue related to end-user instruction is whether electronic information systems should require any formal instruction at all. Some individuals feel that a system should be designed in such a way that searching is either self-evident or clearly explained through prompts, menus, and help screens. While everyone wishes that the means of proceeding through a particular system be as clear as possible, this does not address the conceptual issues involved in end-user instruction.

For example, a novice user might walk up to an online catalog and type in a subject search "effect of welfare reform on single parent families." When queried, the user might add that he or she is looking in particular for periodical articles on the topic. This type of situation, which occurs daily in many libraries, illustrates that it is often not system design but conceptual deficiencies on the part of the user which can cause failure in online searching. If the student understood the nature of the online catalog database, he or she would not have searched there for periodical articles. If the user were searching in an appropriate database, he or she would need to understand the concepts of sets, Boolean operators, and often controlled vocabularies to retrieve information on his topic.

We will better prepare our students for the information society if we structure our teaching to the conceptual framework of the subject. The information age is upon us and is ever-changing. It is our role to equip our students for it.

Notes

[1]Mauritz Johnson, "Definitions and Models in Curriculum Theory," *Educational Theory* 17 (April 1967): 127-40.

[2]Jerome Bruner, *The Process of Education* (New York: Random House, 1960).

[3]Betsy Baker, "A Conceptual Framework for Teaching Online Catalog Use," *The Journal of Academic Librarianship* 12, no. 2 (1986): 90-96.

[4]Dennis Hamilton, "Library Users and Online Systems: Suggested Objectives for Library Instruction," *RQ* 25 (Winter 1985): 195-97.

[5]Charles L. Gilreath, *Computerized Literature Searching* (Boulder, Colo.: Westview Press, 1984), 166.

[6]T. Cooney, "Anatomy of a Database," *The Compiler* 4 (Summer 1986): 6-9.

CHAPTER 16

THE ONLINE CATALOG
AND INSTRUCTION
Maintaining the Balance
on the Log

Betsy Baker and Beth Sandore

The card catalog may be only a transitory stage in the evolution of the catalog, for there are some annoyances and disadvantages connected with it, but it is, at the present stage, absolutely necessary.

Harriet B. Gooch[1]

Introduction

In the latter part of the nineteenth century, President James Garfield characterized the precarious nature of education with a quip about Mark Hopkins being balanced on one end of a log and a student on the other. Although much time has elapsed since this comment was made, we find ourselves still grappling with the dilemma of balancing the simplicity of curiosity or the spirit of inquiry with the complexity of teaching. Within the library world, our current educational challenge includes not only maintaining curiosity and developing sound teaching methods, but also keeping a step ahead in the face of constant innovation. In that light, the added element of technological innovation presented by the online catalog and other online systems has posed yet another balance to maintain — balancing instruction about the procedural aspects of searching with instruction about the conceptual aspects of searching. Our interest in achieving such a balance is a result of our experience with online catalogs and online catalog users, which is reinforced by a growing body of literature on user behavior with online systems.

With the introduction of the first online catalogs in the early years of this decade, a debate began within the profession regarding the necessity for instruction.[2] Now, there is general agreement that various instructional methods are valuable accompaniments to online systems. Just as our perspective of the value of online catalog instruction has evolved with our increased level of experience, so might our current basis for determining the content of online catalog instruction benefit from a fresh assessment.

This chapter traces developments that have influenced and shaped our online catalog instructional efforts. We review relevant research in online catalogs and information retrieval systems, which emphasizes the importance of using conceptual frameworks in instruction. We discuss analogies that have been used thus far in online catalog instruction, distinguishing between the use of analogies and the use of models in instruction. We close by stressing the value of providing a realistic framework for users so they will be able to develop an accurate mental model of system structure.

How Online Catalog Instruction
Has Been Shaped—Historical Overview

After nearly a decade of experience with online catalogs and online catalog users, it is easy to trace the sources that fueled the early debate over instruction. Initial online catalog development concentrated on the goal of including all instruction in system use as part of its interface. Many felt that this should be all that even the most naive user would need to know to use a system effectively. In this light, efforts to develop an instructional program for the online catalog suggested that the catalog was not fulfilling its purpose, that its design was flawed. With this logic, any attempts by public services staff to provide additional instruction in online catalog use was viewed as wasted effort as well as an implicit criticism of the designers.[3]

A pervasive atmosphere of support in academic libraries for user education activities in general prompted others to embrace the contrary view—that formalized instruction must be given to all online catalog users.[4] Although instructional programs had been successfully integrated into many public service areas of libraries, instructional efforts had yet to be negotiated for the online catalog. This was a result of the relatively slow involvement of public service librarians in online catalog design and implementation, a phenomenon which resulted from development that was initially concentrated in technical service areas and caused public service librarians to be faced with the dual challenge of educating themselves as well as their users to a new and integral information resource. This challenge was understandably met with a mixture of enthusiasm and reluctance.[5]

Many of the early efforts to educate online catalog users reflect these personal attitudes of the designers. For example, the fascination by librarians with the online catalog served as a catalyst for the establishment of one of the first approaches used—a stand alone workshop devoted exclusively to online catalog instruction. The low attendance at these sessions prompted librarians at many institutions to evaluate their effectiveness and appropriateness as a forum for educating online catalog users.[6] These attitudes toward online catalog instruction are explored at length in a recent article by Betsy Baker.[7] Among other observations, she points to the changes triggered by technology, and how our attitudes toward these changes reflect the way we introduce new services to our users. In instructional programs, the opportunities to convey these attitudes are numerous. Recently, librarians began exploring programs that strive to integrate the online catalog into the user's full complement of research skills and processes.

A number of conflicting recommendations regarding user performance, their perception of their performance, and the value of instruction also emerged from several seminal research projects sponsored by the Council on Library Resources (CLR) in the early 1980s. While these research projects evaluated and reported overall positive user responses to online catalogs, they nevertheless documented high user error rates and subminimum searching proficiency levels. They also revealed that while users admitted benefiting from instruction, they were reluctant to invest much time in instructional activities.[8]

Now, we rarely encounter a simple yes or no response to the complex issue of how to approach online catalog instruction. Rather than debating instruction, public service librarians, technical service librarians, and system designers are all identifying common goals to which they all contribute different, but equally important, perspectives to online catalog development. The need for different methods of instruction to online system use is now recognized in a variety of efforts, such as user-friendly online interfaces, printed materials, organized and individualized instruction sessions, and computer assisted tutorial programs. This cooperation is coupled with the realization that the perfect online catalog does not exist (and may never exist). As such, the development of methods of instruction and the perfection of online catalogs are no longer considered mutually exclusive efforts.

While there may be a growing support for instruction, the content of such instruction remains an issue of contention. Should instruction be designed around procedural matters, conceptual matters, a combination of both, or something completely different?

Research on Online Catalog Use

The early CLR projects mentioned above serve as a basis from which we can draw much of our knowledge about online catalog user behavior. Within the past several years, additional research has been completed. Much of it provides useful insight into users and their experience with online catalogs. Virtually all of these studies have revealed that users have positive feelings about the online catalog. But, many of these also show that users experience both procedural and conceptual searching problems.[9]

Work done by Patricia Sullivan, Peggy Seiden, and Christine L. Borgman summarizes some of the common problems users experience with online catalog searching.[10] Sullivan and Seiden identified four general areas where users experienced conceptual problems in searching: awareness of search options; understanding of search options; confusion over too many options; and effect of prior experience on choice of subsequent searching options. They also differentiated between procedural training (e.g., using commands, manipulating information within a search) and conceptual training (teaching users the concepts they need to construct searches successfully when using a system), noting that "good user training must provide some understanding of the system architecture, either abstractly or through analogy."[11] Teaching an understanding of system architecture is especially important in the case of systems with user-friendly front-end interfaces. While an interface greatly facilitates searching for novice users, it also masks the workings of the system to the user, making error diagnosis difficult.

Borgman's own work and her reviews of other research have further identified areas of user search problems and also confirmed that lack of conceptual understanding hinders successful system use.[12] Some of the findings Borgman highlights are: the need to determine what factors make computers difficult to learn and use;[13] that users find the concept of Boolean searching difficult;[14] that users tend to make mistakes in clusters, and that an error is likely to be followed by another error in online searching;[15] that users usually quit after receiving an error message, instead of requesting either online or human assistance.[16]

Another CLR funded online catalog research effort attempted to provide some understanding of the instruction question.[17] This project had as its goal to develop and evaluate a model for instruction in online catalog use that could be adopted by other libraries and modified to fit their specific instructional needs. The instructional program, which included printed materials and a workshop, was implemented at Northwestern University.

One of the fundamental teaching objectives was to provide an overview of how an online system is structured. From the outset of this study, the researchers believed that instruction should provide users with some understanding of database structure and information retrieval in order to determine how search strategies might work in an online catalog. The workshop method included this conceptual information, organized around a card catalog analogy.

Highlights of the findings of this study revealed that students who responded favorably to using the online catalog did not necessarily perform satisfactorily on a test. Also, in the evaluation of teaching methods, it was found that students who were provided with a workshop session performed significantly better on the tests than those who had no training or those who received only printed instructional materials. While the workshop approach did offer the added advantage of interaction between student and teacher, the project's conclusions provide further impetus for adopting some method of conceptually based instruction which aids students in developing the skills to use online systems.[18]

In the early 1960s, F. W. Lancaster's research demonstrated yet did not articulate a need for such concept based instruction. Lancaster's early research in assessing the ability of users to successfully manipulate command-driven systems offers further support for focusing an instructional program on concepts. In Lancaster's work with MEDLARS, he discovered that most users had little difficulty with commands, which have been the primary focus in the development of user-friendly systems. Instead, he found that users encountered the greatest difficulty in conceptualizing and formalizing their information needs, selecting appropriate terminology, and developing search strategies that could exploit the interactive power of an online system.[19]

Trends and Indicators

What trends have surfaced as a result of this research? First, there is strong documented support for modeling online catalog instruction around system concepts.[20] Second, it is important that users be observed to determine their searching behaviors. Users may not necessarily achieve the same objectives librarians believe are necessary to demonstrate a minimum level of searching competence, or they may not learn this information in the order expected. Observation will help librarians adapt their instruction to focus on strategies that maximize users' success. Third, learning about information retrieval concepts is becoming an increasingly important element of library use. Therefore, an effective program to teach online system use must be grounded in an understanding of the psychology of human/computer interaction.

In her book *The Second Self: Computers and the Human Spirit*, Sherry Turkle devotes considerable attention to the psychology of the human/computer interaction.[21] She observes that the way an individual approaches and uses a computer reveals his or her conceptual and psychological orientation to both the tool and the task to be completed. Just as some individuals interpret Rorschach ink blots differently than others, Turkle suggests it is possible to identify the cognitive learning styles of computer users by the way they use the computer and for what purpose they use it. This idea might be used in observations of how users approach and search online systems. Identifying groups of users by their cognitive styles could aid the development of more powerful and flexible instructional programs—programs that draw on concepts and cognitive skills that library patrons commonly use in other aspects of their daily lives. Tapping these existing skills will help users make the necessary transfer of knowledge to search among different online catalogs, bibliographic databases, and other automated services.

Although the projects discussed here do not have the same research objectives, their collective focus enriches our own experimentation with different approaches to research on online system instruction and use. H. Rudy Ramsey and Jack D. Grimes address this issue in a recent review article:

> We are entering not only a new era in user-interface technology but a new growth stage in our profession, in which psychological models of the user will be more effective than they have been and in which they will be a subject of both research and engineering concern. However, this is also an era in which a failure to adapt our research method, and even to alter the focus of those efforts, may well undermine our future effectiveness in molding systems to the needs and capabilities of their users.[22]

Our view of the library's catalog in a transitional phase is certainly not novel when we consider Harriet Gooch's remarks about the cumbersome characteristics of the card catalog at the beginning of this century. Another important part of that statement, however, is the fact that librarians will always maintain some representation of library holdings, and this information will remain part of the integral function of library service, despite its form or scope. An ongoing ability to interpret the catalog to users, and to assist them in efficient and successful use, is a central component of our professional responsibility. As Ramsey and Grimes point out, another aspect of librarians' professional commitment encompasses understanding online systems so that they can continue to guide their development to meet the needs of users.

Analogies and Models: Tapping Users' Familiarity with the Library

Given the focus in the literature on the value of conceptual frameworks in instruction, what direction can librarians take in online catalog instruction? Within a relatively short time period, librarians have gone through a rapid evolution of thinking in regard to content of online catalog instruction.

In addition to reconsidering the appropriateness of the isolated workshop as a viable instruction means, instruction librarians are distinguishing between operational (procedural) training and educational (conceptual) training for online systems. Judith Wanger suggests that educational programs have two aspects that distinguish them from training programs. First, an educational program strives to develop concepts and related foundations for the underlying principles of the subject being taught. Second, educational programs use models and analogies to teach the processes, rather than teach a set of procedures.[23]

In this light, librarians have experimented with several analogies for teaching the online catalog. In using any analogy or model, one must consider whether it will trigger a familiar association for users with other relevant or related concepts. Before discussing the use of analogies and models, some clarification of their definitions is offered.

Often, the term *model* is used synonymously with *analogy*. An analogy points to similarities and also helps to establish an initial link between the familiar and the unfamiliar. Once the important link is established, it is important to move beyond the analogy to a model. For example, in an instructional setting one may say that the card catalog is similar to the online catalog. However, while they may share the same function, they do not have the same structure. A model need not have the same function as the system being taught, but it will represent the same structure as the system being taught. As such, a model provides the necessary framework one needs to build an understanding of a system's structure. The crucial difference between analogies and models is that a model allows a user to move beyond partial, sometimes nonreinforcing similarities, to a foundation that provides a picture of what the structure of the new system will be. Rather than checking the new system against the old system, a conceptual framework enables the user to apply a set of general guidelines in constructing his or her own mental model for the operation of the system.

We will examine some analogies that have been used by instruction librarians, and discuss their usefulness in developing a link to sound mental models for users of online catalogs. We will then suggest a conceptual framework for online catalog instruction—based on the model of a database—that has evolved from early work with analogies.

CARD CATALOG ANALOGY

Early on, the card catalog analogy emerged as a means of moving beyond procedurally oriented instruction presentations. Many felt it provided the clearest transition from printed cards to an online file. The fact that the card catalog and the online catalog essentially serve the same function in the library made this a natural parallel. For certain segments of the library user population, the card catalog analogy may still be the most viable means of introducing the online catalog. For example, older clientele such as senior faculty members, returning students may be most familiar with information seeking in the library via the card catalog.

This analogy may take advantage of what students already know about catalogs in general. For instance, an instructional session might draw comparisons between online catalogs and card catalogs, noting four similar characteristics: their coverage and scope; their status as union catalogs; filing arrangement; and cross-reference provision. These comparisons can be drawn to make students aware of both the similarities of the two files and of how search strategies must be adjusted depending on which file is approached. This background provides a subtle means of conveying what may well be new information about the card file in a way that is not patronizing.[24] However, the day is fast approaching when librarians will encounter users whose only library experience has been with an online file. Also, the similarities between the card file and the online file may diminish rapidly after the basic comparisons have been made. As systems become more sophisticated, the differences will outweigh the similarities.

INDEX ANALOGY

Similarly, the index analogy has been useful as a simple illustration of an integrated author, title, and subject file. With the index analogy, one has the implicit understanding of access points, frequent updating, and dynamic change that may not be conveyed by the card catalog. Its dual applicability in an online environment and as a familiar library tool has been its strength.

Librarians at Carnegie-Mellon have experimented with designing instruction based on such an analogy. The online catalog is described to users as an access index tool similar to standard printed indexes but providing additional access points such as keyword searching.[25] According to the researchers at Carnegie-Mellon, those students who are familiar with computing concepts appear able to associate the idea of an index more readily with the structure of the online catalog.

For scholars whose research involves extensive use of current periodical literature (e.g., those in the sciences and engineering), this analogy may serve as a meaningful link to the way the online catalog operates. However, care must be exercised to make the distinction that periodical titles *only* may be retrieved using the online catalog, while with other user-ready online systems in the library such as INFOTRAC, BRS After Dark, and Search Helper, just the opposite type of retrieval power applies.

ANALOGIES: BRIDGES TO MODELS

Those institutions which adopted online catalogs in the early 1980s were on the vanguard of innovations in library automation. At that time, the card catalog analogy was comfortable to both librarians and users. Any other approach involving more in-depth computer understanding would not have been appropriate for the times, as both librarians and users had not achieved the degree of computer literacy that now exists. And, the use of any conceptual focus in instruction was significant in the face of the initial tendency to concentrate on system procedures. For many, the conceptual approach was controversial because it questioned the adequacy of detail laden programs that lacked an overriding instructional theme.

The card catalog and index analogies are useful bridges for those who may be unfamiliar with online systems. When we use card catalog and index analogies, we are assuming, however, that the users have actually developed a correct understanding of how to use these seemingly familiar library tools, and that they understand the principles on which they are built. All too often, this may be an incorrect assumption. If so, it is a rather tenuous basis for an introduction to a resource by which much of the information we now use is made available. Although users may appear "comfortable" with the card catalog analogy, we may unfortunately be perpetuating their own limited understanding of using these tools and incorrectly assuring them that this is a valid base for learning to search the online catalog.

This is not to suggest that these analogies are no longer useful. But, it is important to recognize that they contribute only a small part of the necessary conceptual framework a user needs to understand and move between online systems. Once the initial recognition of that link has been established, the usefulness of the card catalog and the index analogies begins to diminish. Their greatest drawback, however, may be that they do not appeal to the majority of users. Many users do not consult these tools regularly, while others feel they are already reasonably proficient in their use. The danger of emphasizing these is that they reinforce the user's perception that they do not need new skills or models to use online systems.

DATABASE MODEL: RATIONALE
AND DISCUSSION

As online systems become increasingly sophisticated, the card catalog and index analogies become less applicable. As public service librarians, our responsibility to users includes continual evaluation of the manner in which new services are presented to them. As such, librarians must not continue to use old frameworks of reference simply because they are comfortable with them and believe users understand them.[26]

A new framework of reference is gaining momentum based on the growing importance placed on information and how technology has changed its packaging. In the early 1960s, Peter Drucker predicted that within twenty years over half of our workforce and gross national product would be devoted to the "knowledge industries"—businesses whose focus is to produce and distribute ideas and information rather than goods and services. Figures supplied by the U.S. Bureau of Labor Statistics in 1980 confirm this projection, showing that computer related occupations such as computer analysts are among the fastest growing occupations in the United States, and will continue to be during the 1980s.[27]

In an essay on the impact of the database on the publishing and information sector, James Ducker provides statistics that document the astronomical proliferation of new databases for both reference and source (full-text) materials. Ducker notes that between 1978 and 1983, the number of electronic publicly available databases grew from 300 to 2,000. Ducker also identifies the increasing trend toward primary source or full-text databases (50 percent of all databases in 1983), which makes databases more likely to be used directly by the general public without intermediary assistance from librarians or information specialists.[28]

As the use of computers and databases becomes more prevalent, both within and beyond library settings, instruction planners at some institutions are taking steps to broaden their teaching focus to include popular microcomputer applications, such as database management systems, word processing programs, and end-user searching services into their programs to create an ongoing link with new technology and library research.[29]

If librarians wish to provide meaningful instruction for users, broadening online catalog instruction to include other systems might be most effective. Linking instruction with other database uses provides the benefit of widespread appeal, increasing familiarity, and providing a readily transferable model to the structure of the online catalog. The underlying teaching model for both microcomputer and online catalog structures is the concept of the database. As such, employing this model in online catalog teaching may offer great potential for communicating a correct mental model of the system to the user.

While some questions may remain about how widespread society's familiarity with microcomputer applications is, its uses are increasing rapidly in all areas of daily lives. Even those individuals whose lives are not yet directly affected by computers are aware of their growing importance. If students see that the database model cuts across routine aspects of their daily lives, of which library research is one component, they will be more inclined to readily internalize and use it.

TEACHING WITH THE DATABASE MODEL

Using the database model in instruction and thinking about our own experience in searching a variety of online systems may make it clear how skills can be transferred almost automatically between databases, using generic concepts. For instance, reference and public services librarians use similar skills whether they are searching a local online catalog, a commercially produced database, or a bibliographic utility. The concept is consistent. As long as the user is aware of the fact that content, protocols, and searching commands will inevitably be different for each system, he or she will be better prepared to adapt to searching mechanics quickly and embrace the most exciting aspect of database searching—retrieving the information that is sought.[30]

The same may be true for our users, many of whom encounter databases regularly in their daily routines—indirectly via automated banking transactions, talking cash registers, mail ordering, processing, and airline and hotel reservations, to name just a few. As a beginning point in an instructional session, the librarian can draw on these experiences as a means of illustrating the concept of a database as a collection of records in machine-readable format, accessible in a number of ways by a defined set of commands and protocols.

There is a growing number of people who communicate directly with databases from their armchairs using commercial access utilities such as CompuServe or The Source. On some level, they are already using the concept of the database to move between various systems to perform daily routines such as shopping, checking daily stock quotes, making airline and hotel reservations, and scanning news in electronic bulletin boards.

Many individuals have firsthand experience at building and maintaining databases on the job, such as organizing clipping files for a newspaper, indexing and abstracting documents for an advertising firm's in-house database, or searching LEXIS by case to retrieve a full-text listing. The examples are numerous. For each example, however, the concept is identical, whether the database is accessible through direct or remote means. Highlighting these examples and life experiences in the classroom is the first step in using the database model.

Just as the librarian searcher uses a set of guidelines when making the decision to search a particular file, those same guidelines can be used to direct the student. Building on this concept of the database, one can identify two dimensions of instruction: teaching a generalizable decision-making framework that can be applied when approaching any file of information; and teaching general structure of how the system operates.

The first dimension of instruction—organizing a framework for decision-making—includes: teaching the importance of knowing the scope and content of a particular database; determining how to match an information need with the scope and content of the database; alerting the student to the importance of identifying access points of the system (especially those that are most powerful or most useful for the student's information need); emphasizing that the student become well versed with the access protocols and search commands, which are not standardized across systems; explaining the importance of search efficiency, not only in terms of cost (when applicable) but also in processing time; knowing the types and formats of information in the system; distinguishing between controlled vocabulary searching and free text or key word searching; knowing how to interact with the system by interpreting its responses and output; and, finally, the importance of evaluating the output. This approach to instruction acknowledges the importance of procedural training, but emphasizes that knowledge about learning system specific features must be transferable.

However, this framework alone does not convey to students how information within the database is processed while he or she is searching. Although most people recognize that computer logic does not mirror human logic, the less one understands about this processing, the greater the tendency to accept output without questioning its accuracy. This second dimension—fostering an understanding of how the system operates—is integral because it supplies the environment in which the decision-making framework can be applied. This aspect of online catalog teaching is challenging because it demands that instructors go beyond teaching techniques to incorporating knowledge about how information is stored and processed. Fostering a mental model of this structure requires that we transcend search approaches and discuss file structure, how a search may be broadened or narrowed, index regeneration, database updates and maintenance, and sorting principles for records, especially with regard to filing rules. Some innovative visual approaches to conveying these principles have been developed by John Kupersmith.[31]

Finally, the culmination of the teaching session involves maintaining a balance between teaching the concepts that shape the decision-making framework for using a database and teaching the concepts that relate how information within the database is processed. In this context, we move beyond the earlier goal of maintaining a balance between teaching system-specific procedures and generalizable system concepts to advocating a different balance between components which are more compatible and more transferable. This approach places more of the responsibility for learning many of the details and minutiae about the specific system on the user. Experience has taught us that much of the detail that we teach is lost anyway, if not changed through technological developments by the time it is needed. Further, this teaching approach may enable students to maximize the usefulness of both online and printed instructions, which are designed specifically to address procedural matters. A broader approach may gain both better acceptance by students and better transferability to other systems.

Within an instructional setting, the database model provides librarians with a systematic approach to explaining online catalog structure. It goes beyond the inherent inadequacies of the card catalog analogy, where the exceptions overshadow what we initially identified as strong similarities. It also provides users with a basis for understanding the fundamental workings not only of the online catalog, but of other information-rich databases now accessible to them both within the library and in their own homes and workplaces. While we assume that older students may be more comfortable with the card catalog analogy, this work related experience with databases may provide them with not only a more recent, but a more relevant framework to draw upon when learning to use an online catalog.

In addition, the online catalog could serve as an example of a particular database, but not the only situation where general principles about using databases could be applied. Use of other examples, such as general database management programs available on microcomputers, would enrich the instruction. Such an approach would be challenging to students, because it can become a component in the realm of computers which has already influenced many of their lives in other settings.

Conclusion

While the focus of this chapter has been on online catalog instruction, we have drawn on recommendations from the literature of various fields to establish a perspective on teaching based on user behavior and user difficulties in searching online systems. Collectively, this body of research emphasizes and documents the importance of adopting a conceptual approach to teaching. Research on how users can perform complex searches using online systems suggests that step-by-step procedural instructions that emphasize the mechanics of searching are inadequate as a foundation for effective technology use.

While not enough has been confirmed in the area of psychological modeling to explain all the factors which affect human/machine relationships, we now know that cognitive knowledge about a system can enhance a user's searching ability. This research also suggests that library users need sound mental models in order to successfully negotiate complex interactive systems. If librarians do not provide conceptual models within which users can develop their mental understanding of the technology, users will construct their own mental models — models which may prove erroneous and incomplete. We have proposed using a database as an appropriate model for teaching online catalog use and have outlined several factors which make this a desirable model, most important of which is its structure and growing familiarity within society. However, small-scale experimentation with various analogies and models is needed if we are to come to a firm understanding of the users for whom specific methods prove most successful. Complex interactive systems require search strategies based on a solid understanding of how information is organized within a computer database. If we want users to be relatively self-sufficient, and also to know when and how to ask for assistance, then we must impart to them *sound* mental models for information seeking, regardless of whether the source is printed, human, or online.

As online catalog instruction has evolved, balancing the need to teach procedures and concepts has been a central concern. In this paper, we have identified yet another aspect of online system use that must be included in this balance — an overall understanding of the structure of the system with principles for determining the procedures used to search the system. This balance simply represents a further step toward a new stage in the evolution of online catalog instruction. It is important to remember that each stage in the evolution is indeed a transitory phase at best. And, at each phase we will continue to address evolving instructional needs.

Notes

[1]Harriet B. Gooch, "The New Catalog," *Bulletin of the American Library Association* 1 (July 1907): 284.

[2]Ray Lester, "User Education in the Online Age," *ASLIB Proceedings* 36, no. 2 (February 1984): 96-111; Sandra Ready, "Putting the Online Catalog in Its Place," *Research Strategies* 2, no. 3 (Summer 1984): 119-27.

[3]Brian Nielsen and Betsy Baker, "Educating the Online Catalog User: A Model Evaluation Study," *Library Trends* (forthcoming).

[4]Ibid.

[5]Charles Bunge was one of the first to identify and explore some of the key factors contributing to the stress librarians may encounter in assimilating technological change into their jobs. This issue was also examined in Beth Sandore and Betsy Baker's "Attitudes toward Automation: How They Affect the Services Libraries Provide," *Proceedings of the 49th Annual Meeting of the American Society for Information Science* 23, 28 September-2 October 1986, 291-99.

[6]At the 1985 LOEX workshop, which was devoted to the topic of educating online catalog users, many instruction coordinators reported overall low attendance rates at this method of instruction.

[7]Betsy Baker, "A New Direction for Online Catalog Instruction," *Information Technology and Libraries* 5, no. 1 (March 1986): 35-41.

[8]Reports focusing on users of online systems include Douglas Ferguson's *Public Online Catalogs and Research Libraries* (Stanford, Calif.: Research Libraries Group, 1982); Joseph R. Matthews Associates's *A Study of Six Online Public Access Catalogs: A Review of Findings* (Grass Valley, Calif.: Matthews Associates, 1982); the University of California Division of Library Automation's *Users Look at Online Catalogs: Results of a National Survey of Users and Non-users of Online Public Access Catalogs* (Berkeley, Calif.: Division of Library Automation, 1982); Marsha Hamilton McClintock's *Training Users of Online Public Access Catalogs* (Washington, D.C.: Council on Library Resources, 1983); and Brian Nielsen, Betsy Baker, and Beth Sandore's *Educating the Online Catalog User: A Model for Instructional Development and Evaluation* (Bethesda, Md.: Education Resource Information Center, 1985). ED 261 679.

[9]Carol Weiss Moore, "Reactions to Online Catalogs," *College and Research Libraries* 42 (July 1981): 295-302; University of California Division of Library Automation, *Users Look at Online Catalogs: Results of a National Survey of Users and Non-users of Online Public Access Catalogs* (Berkeley, Calif.: Division of Library Automation, 16 November 1982); Joseph R. Matthews Associates's *A Study of Six Online Public Access Catalogs: A Review of Findings* (Grass Valley, Calif.: Matthews Associates, November 1982); Research Libraries Group's *Public Online Catalogs and Research Libraries* (Stanford, Calif.: Research Libraries Group, September 1982); Nielsen and Baker, "Educating the Online User."

[10]Patricia Sullivan and Peggy Seiden, "Educating Online Catalog Users: The Protocol Assessment of Needs," *Library Hi Tech* 10, no. 3 (1985): 11; Christine L. Borgman, "Why Are Online Catalogs Hard to Use? Lessons Learned from Information-Retrieval Studies," *Journal of the American Society for Information Science* 37, no. 6 (1986): 387-400.

[11]Sullivan and Seiden, "Educating Users," 13.

[12]Christine L. Borgman, "The User's Mental Model of an Information Retrieval System: Effects on Performance" (Ph.D. diss., Stanford University, 1983; Christine Borgman, "Mental Models: Ways of Looking at a System," *ASIS Bulletin* 9 (December 1982): 38-39; Christine Borgman, "Psychological Research in Human-Computer Interaction," in *Annual Review of Information Science and Technology*, vol. 19 (New York: Knowledge Industry Publications, 1984), 33-64.

[13]Borgman, "Psychological Research," 34.

[14]Thomas H. Martin, et. al., *Feedback and Exploratory Mechanisms for Assisting Library Staff Improve On-Line Searching* (Washington, D.C.: Council on Library Resources, 1983). Cited in Borgman, "Psychological Research," 1984.

[15]See Borgman, "The User's"; John E. Tolle, *Current Utilization of Online Catalogs: Transaction Log Analysis* (Dublin, Ohio: OCLC, Inc., 1983); Jean Dickson, "An Analysis of User Errors in Searching an Online Catalog," *Cataloging and Classification Quarterly* 4 (Spring 1984): 19-38.

[16]Martin, et. al., *Feedback*.

[17]Nielsen, Baker, and Sandore, *Educating the Online Catalog User*.

[18]Ibid., 70-71.

[19]Frederick W. Lancaster, "Evaluation of On-Line Searching in MEDLARS (AIM-TWX) by Biomedical Practitioners," *University of Illinois Graduate School of Library Science, Occasional Papers*, 101 (Urbana-Champaign, Ill.: University of Illinois Graduate School of Library Science, 1972).

[20]Lancaster, "Evaluation of Online"; Borgman, "The User's"; Nielsen, Baker, and Sandore, *Educating the Online Catalog User*; Sullivan and Seiden, "Educating Online."

[21]Sherry Turkle, *The Second Self: Computers and the Human Spirit* (New York: Simon and Schuster, 1984), 32.

[22]H. Rudy Ramsey and Jack D. Grimes, "Human Factors in Interactive Computer Dialog," in *Annual Review of Information Science and Technology*, vol. 18 (White Plains, N.Y.: Knowledge Industry Publications, 1983), 29-59.

[23]Judith Wanger, "Education and Training for Online Systems," in *Annual Review of Information Science and Technology*, vol. 14 (White Plains, N.Y.: Knowledge Industry Publications, 1979), 219-45.

[24]Betsy Baker and Brian Nielsen, "Educating the Online Catalog User: Experiences and Plans at Northwestern University Library," *Research Strategies* 1, no. 4 (1983): 162.

[25]Alice Bright, Nancy Evans, and Peggy Seiden, "Assessing Instructional Needs for the Online Catalog" (Paper presented at the Second Bienniel LOEX Workshop, Eastern Michigan University, Ypsilanti, Mich., 10 May 1985).

[26]Betsy Baker, "A Conceptual Framework for Teaching Online Catalog Use," *The Journal of Academic Librarianship* 2 (May 1986): 90-96.

[27]Peter Drucker, "Evolution of the Knowledge Worker," in *The Future of Work*, ed. Fred Best (Englewood Cliffs, N.J.: Prentice-Hall, 1973); "Technology and Employment," *Editorial Research Reports* 2, no. 3 (22 July 1983): 542.

[28]James Ducker, "Futures Dossier: Electronic Information—Impact of the Database," *Futures* 17, no. 1 (April 1985): 164-69.

[29]Examples of such programs can be found in Linda J. Piele, Judith Pryor, and Harold W. Tuckett, "Teaching Microcomputer Literacy: New Roles for Academic Librarians," *College and Research Libraries* 47 (July 1986): 374-78; Hannelore B. Rader, "Teaching

Library Enters the Electronic Age," *College and Research Libraries News* 47 (1986): 402-4; Edward W. Tawyea and James Shedlock, "Teaching the User about Information Management Using Microcomputers," *Medical Reference Services Quarterly* 5, no. 2 (Summer 1986): 27-35; Betsy Baker, "Library Knowledge as a Component of Computer Literacy" (Paper presented at Small Computers in Libraries Software/Computer Conference and Exposition, Atlanta, Ga., 14 March 1986).

[30]The idea of using skills common to both public and technical services librarians in online system searching was expanded by Beth Sandore, "Maximizing Online Searching Skills between Public and Technical Services: The Concept of the Database," (Presentation at the Fall Conference of the Illinois Association of College and Research Libraries, Bloomington, Ill., 14-15 November 1986).

[31]John Kupersmith did a three-part series in *Research Strategies* that provides useful examples of linking online concepts with graphics. John Kupersmith, "The Graphic Approach," *Research Strategies* 4, nos. 2-4 (1986).

INDEX